◊♦◊ Life in Plastic ◊♦◊

Life in Plastic

ARTISTIC RESPONSES TO PETROMODERNITY

Caren Irr, Editor

University of Minnesota Press
Minneapolis
London

This project has benefited from support from the Theodore and Jane Norman Fund at Brandeis University.

Excerpts from Craig Santos Perez, "The Age of Plastics," *Big Energy Poets: Ecopoetry Thinks Climate Change,* ed. Heidi Lynn Staples and Amy King (Kenmore, N.Y.: BlazeVOX, 2017), reprinted with permission. Excerpts from Orchid Tierney, *ocean plastic* (Kenmore, N.Y.: BlazeVOX, 2019), reprinted with permission. Excerpts from Divya Victor, "Countertranslation," *The Margins: Asian American Writers' Workshop* (November 1, 2018), https://aaww.org/the-age-of-plastic/, reprinted with permission. Excerpts from Jennifer Cooke, "Second Hand," *The Other Room Anthology* 4, ed. James Davies, Tom Jenks, and Scott Thurston, reprinted with permission. Excerpts from *Styrofoam* by Evelyn Reilly (New York: Roof, 2009), reprinted with permission.

Published by the University of Minnesota Press
111 Third Avenue South, Suite 290
Minneapolis, MN 55401-2520
http://www.upress.umn.edu

ISBN 978-1-5179-0987-1 (hc)
ISBN 978-1-5179-0988-8 (pb)
Library of Congress record available at https://lccn.loc.gov/2021023173.

Printed in the United States of America on acid-free paper

UMP BmB 2021

Contents

Acknowledgments vii

Introduction: Concepts and Consequences of Plastic 1
Caren Irr and Nayoung Kim

I. The Plastic Sensorium

1 "Paper or Plastic?" and Other Conundrums of Environmental Change 11
W. Dana Phillips

2 Smelling *Polyester* 31
Paul Morrison

3 The Album Era 59
Loren Glass

4 The Plastic You: Plastination and the Postmortal Self 77
Jane Kuenz

II. The Plasticity of Genre

5 Plastic Man and Other Petrochemical Fantasies 97
Daniel Worden

6 Organic Form, Plastic Forms: The Nature of Plastic in Contemporary Ecopoetics 115
Margaret Ronda

7 On the Beach: Porous Plasticity, Migration Art, and the *Objet Trouvé* of the Wasteocene 137
Maurizia Boscagli

III. Plastic's Capitalism

8 "Refuge of Ignorance": A Prehistory of "Plastic" 165
Crystal Bartolovich

9 The Petrochemical Unconscious: Destructive Plasticities in Richard Powers's *Gain* 181
Christopher Breu

10 The Impossible Figure of Oceanic Plastic 199
Sean Grattan

IV. Postplastic Futures?

11 From Protoplastics to the Plastiglomerate: Science Fiction's Shifting Synthetic Sensibilities 217
Lisa Swanstrom

12 Futures in Plastic: Science Fiction, Climate Change, and the New North 239
Phillip E. Wegner

13 Plastic's "Untiring Solicitation": Geographies of Myth, Corporate Alibis, and the Plaesthetics of the Matacão 259
Jennifer A. Wagner-Lawlor

Contributors 281

Index 283

Acknowledgments

This collection would not have been possible without a great deal of camaraderie and assistance. I would especially like to thank Nayoung Kim, a skilled investigator and collaborator, for her invaluable research assistance. Support of a financial nature was provided by the office of the Dean of Arts and Sciences at Brandeis University. Editorial advice from Jason Weidemann, Danielle Kasprzak, Anne Carter, and Kristine Hunt has been essential to the success of the project. The comments of the external readers guided and encouraged our contributions in innumerable ways. The many usually anonymous acts of professional generosity involved in commenting on another person or group's work as it develops are essential to scholarly inquiry, and here, as so often, they have substantially improved our work.

I wish to dedicate this volume to my mother, Mickey Irr. For decades, her Styrofoam sculptures and cassette tape weavings, as well as her enormous stockpile of repurposed yogurt containers and her mysterious collections of plastic binding strips, have helped me envision alternative ways of engaging with the physical environment.

Introduction

Concepts and Consequences of Plastic

Caren Irr and Nayoung Kim

One of the many terrible ironies of the COVID-19 pandemic is the vast increase in plastic waste that it has triggered. Anxiety about vectors of transmission of the coronavirus led almost immediately to bans on reusable containers and shopping bags in favor of plastic items. Personal protective equipment (PPE) frequently consists of single-use gloves, gowns, and masks that are made from plastics, briefly employed, and immediately sent to the trash. From take-out containers and water bottles to body bags, plastic goods have proliferated thanks to the pandemic. As photographers around the world have documented, the resulting waste has rapidly accumulated in landfills and oceans, accelerating the process of environmental degradation and habitat loss that launched the virus into human populations in the first place.

Abundant use of disposable synthetic materials has taken place despite studies demonstrating that viruses survive on plastic surfaces far longer than they do on cardboard, cloth, or metal surfaces. Lobbying by the plastics industry certainly plays a role in the rapid resurgence of single-use polymers and suspicion of reusable materials, but the phenomenon also has deeper sources. Plastics are deeply integrated into the cultural imaginary of petromodernity. In a culture and economy defined by its dependence on the energy provided by finite fossil fuels, plastics promise a bright, cheap, and sterile perfection that obscures the broken, soggy waste on our shores. From the career opportunity recommended to Mike Nichols's hero in *The Graduate* (1967) to the celluloid on which the film narrative was captured, plastic is entwined with the cultural imaginary of advanced capitalist societies. It both preserves and menaces. With the dialectical ambivalence of any membrane, plastic both defines a protective barrier and introduces new contaminants. As synthetic materials produced by human beings reliant on petroleum products extracted from below the earth's crust, plastic surfaces simultaneously manifest a history of transforming the earth and an economy based on domination of the earth. Plastic is organized down to the molecular level by the contradictions of petromodernity.

Since the 1960s, aesthetic responses to the contradictions of plastic have increasingly often shifted from utopian exhilaration to environmental fears. Artists and authors in the global North have begun to pay sustained attention to the connections between plastic and petroleum and the dependence of plastic consumerism on the oil economy. They have also explored how fully cheap, lightweight, and convenient plastics are entwined with rapidly rising carbon dioxide levels and climate change. Reading plastic through the lens of planetary climate crisis in this manner complicates the stories of many contemporary commodities—from computer and medical technologies, to food and drink containers, numerous polyester textiles, essentials of the construction and building trades, and components of motor vehicles. In the twenty-first century, in other words, artists and activists addressing plastic have underlined the environmental risks on which contemporary petrocapitalism depends.

This attention to the entanglement of plastic utopianism with plastic waste opens up new sites, organisms, and materials to consideration. Contemporary aesthetic responses to plastic move from labs, operating rooms, and shopping centers to beaches contaminated by synthetic bottles, bags, and building materials in whole and fragmented forms. These artworks circulate in an environment in which fishermen have found plastic in the stomachs of creatures from the deepest seas, Arctic researchers have discovered microplastics in glacial ice, and the more than 90 percent of the plastic that goes unrecycled litters roadsides and seashores around the world. In widely reported data published in 2017, a research team of environmental scientists estimated that at least 8.3 billion metric tons of plastic have been created since 1950—more than 60 percent of which has accumulated in ocean gyres and landfills.[1] At current rates, more than twelve billion tons of plastic waste will contaminate the environment by 2050. At this point in the narrative, news stories commonly invoke something more familiar—noting, for example, that this much plastic would cover all of Argentina or outweigh the body mass of one billion elephants. Eight billion tons is so much plastic that each of Earth's seven billion human inhabitants is hypothetically responsible for more than one ton of plastic waste (although in reality, of course, plastic use and waste is concentrated in high-consumption nations of the global North and West). No matter how reporters struggle to make these mind-boggling figures comprehensible or which human populations are most responsible for its accumulation, the inescapable fact is that any amount of plastic takes hundreds, sometimes thousands, of years to degrade. This abundance of waste would be evident in the environment for eons even in the unlikely event that the production of new plastic stopped altogether immediately. Plastic production and waste will be with us for a long time to come, and dependence on plastic is now so advanced in many places that a radical culture change would be required to stop the addiction.

Change is exceedingly difficult, though, because the cultural norms that support the use of plastic are deeply embedded in the consumerist societies of the global North; the work, play, medicine, sanitation, and sensations of petromodernity are literally wrapped up in plastic. As Susan Freinkel establishes in *Plastic: A Toxic Love Story,* plastic responds to important needs—from a desire for cheap goods to escalating anxieties about health and contamination as well as excitement about the potential of nonorganic forms.[2] Plastic meets these needs during a pandemic as well as during so-called normal times, even though it also creates major new problems in both its production and consumption. It is formed in and by cultural conflict. For this reason, simple boycotts or calls for reusable goods are insufficient even though they may well be necessary. A transformation in plastic usage will also require a collective refusal to contain our imaginations within environmentally destructive visions of synthetic technologies and the massive waste they produce. Envisioning a sustainable modern life beyond plastic remains an essential task. This fundamentally aesthetic challenge prompts writers, filmmakers, visual artists, and more to tell the story of our manufactured environment and its relation to nonhuman nature in new ways. The resulting works place the cultural conflicts surrounding plastic in a speculative frame, revealing its essentially aesthetic and often genre-bending aspects.

The essays in this collection travel through this pressing set of problems. They explore the basic forms of modern polymers—touching on their origins in Greek and early modern notions of plasticity—and they evaluate the aesthetic effects of plastic's supposed sterility, hypermodernity, and convenience. They assess the multidimensional transformations to the human organism that plastics promise to produce. They explore the exhilarating potential for formal transformation embodied in plastic. They carefully and critically examine the interdependence of plastics and capitalist consumption practices, and they test the appeal of various utopian and dystopian scenarios for futures with too much, not enough, or unsettling alternatives to plastic. While focusing on the cultures of the global North—especially the United States and United Kingdom—these essays open up questions of the circulation of plastics in the oceans and organisms that connect the planet.

Together these essays also contribute to the ongoing project of conceptualizing plastic, plasticity, and its cognates. These essays use and refine key terms. To date, many discussions of plastic have focused on a single dominant trait: malleability. In the words of the Science History Institute, plastic is a polymer, "a substance made of many repeating units," that can be molded freely.[3] This moldable flexibility characterizes most philosophical formulations of plasticity. In G. W. F. Hegel's definition, for example, plasticity refers to the subject's receptivity to a given form and the ability to create or give form. It revolves around plastic's capacity to transform in response to the outward stimuli without changing its inherent property.[4] Such elasticity prompts Catherine Malabou to locate a progressive potential in plasticity in her neurological reinterpretation. The human brain is plastic, according to Malabou, in that it can respond to sociopolitical conditions affecting human subject by reworking synapses.[5] When a free subject faces systematic decimation, the brain destroys the synapses attuned to the subjugating conditions and replaces them with new ones that can be directed affirmatively.

In the beginning and middle of the twentieth century, assessments of the cultural effects of plastic were similarly preoccupied with its radical malleability. In his unfinished essay on Disney animation, for instance, Sergei Eisenstein refers to the dynamic stretchiness of the animated character's body as "plasmatic." The plasmatic body that humorously rejects an allotted form, contends Eisenstein, releases the viewers' imagination from social constrictions and incites a desire to joyously invent something original and unfettered.[6] In a similar vein, Roland Barthes expressed cautious awe for some plastic's democratic implications. Fascinated by plastic's formal capacities, Barthes understood plastic as disrupting conventional hierarchies between artificial-prosaic and natural-priceless materials.[7] These explorations of plastic utopianism associated the new material with prospects for social change.

For many twenty-first-century commentators, however, utopianism gives way to other moods. Plastic has become ubiquitous, and reflection on its marvels tend to be displaced by the ecological questions involved in inhabiting a plastic environment. Reflection responds to rather than envisions the future of plastics. As Timothy Morton reminds us, plastic is not a passive object; it can actively trigger a new range of actions and sensations. We cannot fully grasp this hyperobject's nearly unfathomable essence, nor what it entails, in isolation but must consider it in relations or assemblages.[8] A crucial assemblage for plastic is that of petromodernity. Literary critic Ursula K. Heise and art historian Amanda Boetzkes have shown that lightweight plastic, a byproduct of petroleum, symptomatically reproduces a dependence on global oil markets and the heaviness of large machinery. The transnational oil industry, these two critics suggest, becomes an intrinsic force in human subjectivity, saturating our imaginations with plastic forms.[9] The everyday life of petrocapitalism mingles apparently benign and chilling effects.

These ecological turns in reading plastic necessarily engage the question of waste. Contributions from waste studies have sharpened our understanding of waste as a contested site of cultural signification, one whose horizon continues to expand to a planetary scale. Mary Douglas's path-breaking work ensures recognition of the porosity of dichotomies such as filthy/clean and manufactured trash/natural organism.[10] Building on this constructivist insight, environmental critics such as the anthropologist Gay Hawkins have explored the specifics of plastic waste, exploring the relation between excess and absence as central to its ontology.[11] Crucial questions also arise about the environmental injustices associated with plastic, since it is clear that human and nonhuman bodies in the Global South receive waste and suffer from its effects more than those in the high-consumption centers. In this regard, plastic detritus serves as an essential synecdoche for the Wasteocene as a whole. The Wasteocene, Marco Armiero and Massimo De Angelis's adaptation of the concept of the Anthropocene, highlights the presence of planetary mass waste that scars and mutates human and nonhuman bodies.[12] Visual evidence of the Wasteocene appears in the garbage vortices in the Pacific, Atlantic, and Indian Oceans and agglutinated mixtures of rock and plastic in Kamilo Beach, Hawaii, for instance. Blurring the categories of living organism and anthropogenic detritus, the rock-plastic, or "plastiglomerate" as one research team has named it, embodies the new forms of toxicity for the Wasteocene.[13] With plastiglomerates, plastic not only imperils organic bodies; it also introduces a new form of matter into the planetary surround.

Exploring these plastic-affiliated concepts pulls the contributors to this volume toward a wide array of aesthetic concerns. W. Dana Philips and Paul Morrison explore the erotic and sensory potential of plastic in comics and film, respectively, while Loren Glass's essay on vinyl ponders the tactile as well as auditory worlds released by the recorded album. Jane Kuenz's consideration of the Body Worlds exhibits brings these discussions of the plastic sensorium to the full human corpus. The interplay between plastic objects and plasticity of form animates Margaret Ronda's essay on ecopoetics and Maurizia Boscagli's treatment of sculptural aesthetics, as well as Daniel Worden's investigation of Plastic Man comic books. Turning to historical and social questions, Crystal Bartolovich, Christopher Breu, and Sean Grattan open up consideration of the ways that narrative treatments of plastic transform our understanding of capitalism. Finally, Lisa Swanstrom, Philip Wegner, and Jennifer Wagner-Lawlor all investigate, from different points of entry, the transformative effect that an encounter with plastic has on the science fictional and utopian imagination.

Uniting all of these essays is their common effort to open up plastic—as a simultaneously aesthetic, ethical, and political problem—to careful consideration. Together, they consider both the playful and worrying sides of malleability, emphasizing both the disturbing extensions to duration and durability that plastic embodies as well as the various phases of its utopian potential. No single note of panic or exaltation sounds here, because when wrestling with plastic one inevitably comes to appreciate the fundamentally dialectical entanglement of waste and wonder.

NOTES

1. Ronald Geyer, Jenna R. Jambeck, and Kara Lavender Law, "Production, Use, and Fate of All Plastics Ever Made," *Science Advances*, July 19, 2017, http://advances.sciencemag.org/content/3/7/e1700782.full.
2. Susan Freinkel, *Plastic: A Toxic Love Story* (Boston: Houghton Mifflin Harcourt, 2011).
3. "Science of Plastics," Science History Institute, https://www.sciencehistory.org/science-of-plastics.
4. Georg Wilhelm Friedrich Hegel, *Phenomenology of Spirit*, trans. Adrian V. Miller (1807; Oxford: Clarendon, 1977).
5. Catherine Malabou, *The Future of Hegel: Plasticity, Temporality and Dialectic* (New York: Routledge, 2004); Catherine Malabou, *What Should We Do with Our Brain?* (New York: Fordham University Press, 2008).
6. Sergei Eisenstein, *On Disney*, ed. Jay Leyda, trans. Alan Upchurch (Kolkata: Seagull Books, 2017).
7. Roland Barthes, "Plastic," *Mythologies*, trans. Annette Lavers (New York: The Noonday, 1993), 97–99.
8. Timothy Morton, "Coexistence and Coexistents: Ecology without a World," In *Ecocritical Theory: New European Approaches*, ed. Axel Goodbody and Kate Rigby (Charlottesville: University of Virginia Press, 2011), 168–80; Timothy Morton, *Hyperobjects: Philosophy and Ecology after the End of the World* (Minneapolis: University of Minnesota Press, 2013).
9. Ursula K. Heise, "Local Rock and Global Plastic: World Ecology and the Experience of Place," *Comparative Literature Studies* 41, no. 1 (2004): 126–52; Amanda Boetzkes, *Plastic Capitalism: Contemporary Art and the Drive to*

Waste (Cambridge, Mass.: MIT Press, 2019); Amanda Boetzkes and Andrew Pendakis, "Visions of Eternity: Plastic and the Ontology of Oil," *E-flux* 47 (2013): 7–13.

10. Mary Douglas, *Purity and Danger: An Analysis of Concepts of Pollution and Taboo* (London: Routledge, 2013).
11. Gay Hawkins and Stephen Muecke, eds., *Culture and Waste: The Creation and Destruction of Value* (Lanham, Md.: Rowman & Littlefield, 2003); Gay Hawkins, *The Ethics of Waste: How We Relate to Rubbish* (Lanham, Md.: Rowman & Littlefield, 2006).
12. Marco Armiero and Massimo De Angelis, "Anthropocene: Victims, Narrators, and Revolutionaries," *South Atlantic Quarterly* 116, no. 2 (2017): 345–62.
13. Patricia L. Corcoran, Charles J. Moore, and Kelly Jazvac, "An Anthropogenic Marker Horizon in the Future Rock Record," *GSA Today* 24 (2014): 4–8.

◊♦◊ **PART I** ◊♦◊

The Plastic Sensorium

1

"Paper or Plastic?" and Other Conundrums of Environmental Change

W. Dana Phillips

Plastic is a 2017 graphic novel with a story by Doug Wagner, art by Daniel Hillyard, coloring by Laura Martin, and lettering by Ed Dukeshire. The two principals, Wagner and Hillyard, collaborated on installments of an earlier series, *ICE,* about an Immigration and Customs Enforcement agent who takes on terrorists. The pair has now produced *The Ride: Burning Desire,* which is about a female former police detective from Atlanta and ex-con who works as a bouncer at a club featuring male, female, and transgender dancers, and catering to a wide range of sexual tastes and fetishes.[1] Wagner has described *The Ride* as "fetish noir" on his publisher's website.[2] The storyline in *Plastic,* and its aesthetic, are in the same vein as the other work on which Wagner and Hillyard have collaborated. In a 2017 interview, Wagner called the comic "a cocktail of over-the-top action and gory, psychological horror intended to make the reader's skin crawl while activating their gag reflex."[3] The plot of *Plastic* concerns a kidnapping, multiple murders, reckless violence, and vengeance; the artwork features muscle-bound male and statuesque female characters; the coloring is lurid; and the lettering is often expressive. None of this—crime, indiscriminate violence, jacked-up bodies, grotesque sexuality, garish color palettes, and cartoonish scripts—is unusual in comix.[4] What is unusual is the role played in this particular comic by the peculiar material referenced in its title.

In the opening frame of *Plastic,* a road-killed possum litters the foreground; the ragged tree line of a swamp provides a backdrop for the action; a 1970s-model sedan occupies the middle ground.

Above the sedan's trunk, free-floating lettering reads "*SQEEK SQEEK SQEEK,*" and the vehicle, which must have a bad suspension, is rocking. A voice balloon reads, "Virginia. . . ." Apparently, a couple has parked in this less than idyllic spot in some Southern backwater (a bayou in Louisiana, as it happens), and they are having spirited intercourse. In the fourth frame, at the bottom of the first page, Virginia's lover, who has asked her to slow down, climaxes. A pair of clasped hands slides down the condensation on the window glass of the rear passenger-side door: "*SMEEEK.*" The man then suggests a postcoital run to fetch donuts—Virginia likes them crème-filled—and gets out of the car to urinate: "PLAASHH." He says they also are short on supplies, then opens the car's trunk and removes a plastic toy soldier from it. The soldier is olive green, female, and wears only a bra and panties. She is striking a 1940s pinup pose. The man stares at her with a wild intensity; his eyes appear in closeup, deep-set and with dilated pupils. He then takes a plastic scrub brush and a plastic bag out of the trunk. He says Virginia needs cleaning after lovemaking, and like so much else in this narrative, this extraordinary statement will not be explained until several pages later. As the scene ends, the man and Virginia have intercourse once again.[5]

The second scene of chapter 1, which is entitled "For Virginia . . . ," takes place at a convenience store. The male protagonist buys a dozen donuts, a sixer of beer, a plastic tub of petroleum jelly, a box of matches, and a new plastic scrub brush. While ringing up these purchases, the jaded clerk asks, "Paper or plastic?" American consumers must answer this question thousands of times a day. It seems innocuous, yet this customer is galvanized by it: his posture freezes, his pupils dilate, and he stares off into space, as if the clerk's question were somehow deeply personal. We begin to understand that the protagonist's sensorium is not like our own as, with evident relish, he chooses plastic. For him, his girlfriend Virginia, donuts, plastic female toy soldiers, and plastic bags are all objects of appetite and desire. They stimulate him, though the female toy soldiers and the bags do more than that. They trigger a response that seems uncanny.

While her boyfriend shops, Virginia waits in the car outside the convenience store, where she is harassed by a trio of muscular young men. When her lover returns, he overhears their insults and attacks the men savagely, using the plastic bag full of his purchases as a weapon. The violence is extreme, causing a lot of splatter. One man's ear is ripped off, his head covered with the plastic bag, and his mouth scrubbed with the plastic brush. Another suffers a broken leg, and calls his attacker a "balloon-fucking pervert." It now appears—to the reader, at least, if not to her lover, who never acknowledges this fact directly—that Virginia is an inflatable sex doll (hence the lover's need for petroleum jelly). In the last frame of this scene, the protagonist rejoins Virginia in the car and her face is depicted for the first time. Her eyes are frozen wide open and her lips form a nearly perfect circle. Seams are visible at her shoulders and neck, and she looks underinflated. Ladylike, she is wearing a sleeveless summer dress. Her lover pays no attention to these details.

The morning after the attack at the convenience store and another night of backseat sex, the protagonist and Virginia sit holding hands by the shore of a lake at dawn. As he proposes a trip to Rome, "the *new* city of love" (he seems not to have heard of Rome before), he wipes a gooey white substance from Virginia's lips and sucks it from his thumb. We know that Virginia likes crème-filled donuts best, but we are being teased with a coarser possibility. This tactic is often employed in *Plastic* with regard to erotic matters. Its creators take their cues from underground comix, where gross-out humor is standard. But this story offers a sidelong, less sophomoric perspective on the violation of taboos and on perversity, and dares us to raise an eyebrow. For instance, in chapter 2, entitled "Nothing a little plastic can't fix . . . ," the protagonist searches for Virginia after she is taken from him, and asks a couple in an open doorway for directions. The woman is dressed in a black vinyl catsuit and the man, who has ripped abs and a full beard, is wearing a wig, a crop top, and a mini-skirt held up by suspenders. He looks like a cross-dressing lumberjack. Only later do we learn that the anomalous pair are patrons of a sex club called Mixed Emotions.

Plastic is shaped, paradoxically, both by an aesthetic of excess and by an aesthetic of understatement regarding what it does and does not depict, and in the unruly manner of this depiction verbally (the cartoonish lettering often looks like graffiti; onomatopoetic words like "squeak" are misspelled) and visually (the images are realistic, yet they are also caricatures; this is particularly true of the more Hulk-like male characters). Arguably, a paradoxical manner is conventional in comix like this one. Yet recognizing a convention, especially one that encourages paradox, may not help one make sense of its employment in a given case, if sense is to be made. As with other narratives where affect takes precedence over (for instance) characterization and plotline, and surface is valued more than depth, *Plastic* is pervaded by ambiguous ambiguities—and mixed emotions. To seek clarification is to fail the hipster litmus test that comix like *Plastic* pose. A blurb on the cover (from the creator of *The Walking Dead*), gives fair warning: "This is the weirdest sh*t I've ever read." The cover art is a headshot of Virginia; her mouth is open and filled either with blood or with jelly from a donut. Her lantern-jawed lover, who looks like a drifter in a film noir, crouches in her overflowing mouth and gazes out with a smirk on his face. The reader has been forewarned.

As an entailment of its genre, in *Plastic* it remains unclear just what taboos a "balloon-fucking pervert" violates. His balloon fucking, if it is a crime, is victimless; and he does seem genuinely to care for Virginia. He is, in fact, a true and a sentimental lover. Otherwise, his transgressions of norms and statutes are many and surpassingly strange. For instance, the title page of chapter 3, "I must be doing this wrong . . . ," features an image of his hand picking up a donut. The donut is covered with rainbow sprinkles and fresh blood. The garish image suggests the pervasive oddity of this man's life. We learn about his life only piecemeal: many pages pass before we discover that Virginia is a sex doll and that the couple's diet is limited to donuts, which her lover feeds to Virginia by cramming them in her mouth. Not until the third chapter do we find out that the man's name is Edwyn, and that he is an erstwhile serial killer, the once-infamous Baggy Man.[6] This information makes sense, retrospectively, of a scene that occurs earlier, in chapter 2, when Edwyn murders a hit man with a handsaw, places the man's bloody decapitated head in a freezer bag, and labels it "Killer" with a marker pen. This is his signature, as an FBI profiler might say. Bagging and tagging the head shows that Edwyn is organized, like a homicidal, sociopathic, but still methodical Marie Kondo. He is prepared, too: wounded in his struggle with the hit man, Edwyn says, as he winds shrink-wrap film around his lower torso, "Nothing a little plastic can't fix." He then drives off in the hit man's car.

In a donut shop called Holes and More, Edwyn encounters a blonde who looks just like Virginia (who has been kidnapped earlier in the story). The blonde's name is Ginny, and she is wearing a tee shirt in the same shade of lavender as Virginia's dress. Ginny lets Edwyn have as many plastic sporks as he wants, which is all of them. After the corrupt local sheriff comes in to the shop and pressures Ginny to have sex with him, Edwyn leaves a female plastic toy soldier (she is stabbing downward with a bayoneted rifle) on the door of his police cruiser as a warning. Edwyn then hides in the trunk before the vehicle pulls away. A few pages later, he catches the sheriff attempting to rape a hitchhiker named Gwen (who has lavender-dyed hair). He suffocates the sheriff with a freezer bag, rips out his tongue, and stabs it with a spork. The lawman's head also goes into a freezer bag. Edwyn explains to Gwen, who is covered with the sheriff's blood and has been cowering in the passenger's seat, that he "met Virginia online," and that she has saved him from ". . . urges." The heavy use of ellipses in this comic is another way in which its creators tease meanings: what ". . . urges" has Virginia helped Edwyn to resist? It seems that she enables him to *indulge* his urges. And when he says he "met" her online, he is being euphemistic: online must be where he *bought* her.[7] Like Ginny in the donut shop, Gwen the hitchhiker is sympathetic. She joins Edwyn in his campaign to liberate Virginia, who is being held captive by a local crime boss, the father of one of the men Edwyn assaulted outside the convenience store. In chapter 4, "Then it's just the eyes . . . ," Edwyn finds a stash of Semtex, for him a novelty and a marvel ("Explosive . . . plastic?"), in the basement of a shack where the kidnapper's henchmen are holed up. When the gang confronts him, he removes the eyes of its leader with another spork. Later, as he sets Semtex charges in the ramshackle old bait shop where Virginia is held hostage, Edwyn says to himself, "Plastic makes everything better," a belief at the core of his personal creed.

Edwyn's genuine love for Virginia—he does not objectify her, which under the circumstances he might well do, and without offending—tempts us to credit him with having a "character" in the novelistic sense of the term, which implies personal depth, and to regard him as an antihero, albeit a much more ironic and morally challenged one than is usual. However, *Plastic* is not a graphic novel, but emphatically a comic. It is to be looked at as much as it is to be read, and its creators seem mostly concerned not with meanings but with effects, which is why they use comically misspelled words in all caps, like "SQEEK" and "SMEEEK" and "PLAASHH," to suggest sounds. So rather than trying to make sense of Edwyn's bizarre personal story (he also keeps his mother's head in a freezer bag stowed in his car's trunk), or of the uncanny doubling of Virginia and Ginny (and Gwen), or of the many other puzzles *Plastic* toys with, I want to turn now to the matter of plastic as it features in this comic, where it is instanced in various forms: an inflatable sex doll, cleaning brushes, female toy soldiers (some of them make a final appearance in the nude), shopping and freezer bags, a tub of petroleum jelly, a PVC catsuit, sporks, shrink wrap, and Semtex. Another set of questions must be raised in regard to these plastic items, questions I will attempt to answer.

Edwyn is a tetchy fellow, who is mightily aroused by the plastic items he encounters at almost every turn in the narrative. Yet for someone hypersensitive to plastic, Edwyn makes no distinction between the many forms of plastic he encounters, and like most consumers seems to see plastic in terms of convenience and as a commodity, the most fungible of materials. But a sex doll is a far different thing from a spork, which is, in turn, a far different thing from Semtex. Inflatable sex dolls are made from PVC (polyvinyl chloride) or TPE (thermoplastic elastomer). PVC is cheaper and is produced using several substances harmful to humans, including a variety of phthalate, while TPE is more expensive and safer to use.[8] Virginia appears to be a low-end, PVC model; this means that she and Edwyn are, unwittingly, in a toxic relationship. Plastic sporks are made from polypropylene or polystyrene, which are relatively less harmful plastics, at least insofar as their chemistry is concerned; sporks can be purchased in bulk online or at big box stores. Semtex is a proprietary material, popular with terrorists, in which the explosive agents are plasticized in order to stabilize or "phlegmatize" them; it is named after Semtin, a suburb of the Czechoslovakian city where it was first developed.[9] Unlike sex dolls and sporks, Semtex is clearly very dangerous and not widely available. Edwyn ignores such differences, and treats all forms of plastic in stereotyped ways. He is not a connoisseur.

That he is a typical consumer, with an indiscriminate taste for junk food and other cheap stuff, is somewhat at odds with the fact that Edwyn appears to be a plastic fetishist. According to the fifth edition of the *Diagnostic and Statistical Manual of Mental Disorders,* better known as the *DSM-V,* fetishistic disorder, which is one of a number of paraphilias, involves "using nonliving objects or having a highly specific focus on nongenital body parts" in the pursuit of sexual pleasure. For a behavior to qualify as paraphilic, which makes it clinically significant, it must be "intense and persistent."[10] Edwyn's relationship with his PVC companion seems to qualify as fetishistic, yet while it is certainly "intense and persistent," it may not amount to a full-blown disorder. It does no one any immediate harm, and seems to keep Edwyn at least somewhat anchored in reality. Virginia, after all, is as much a doll as she is a sex toy; just as dolls do for little girls, she helps Edwyn situate himself in some semblance of domesticity and heteronormativity.[11]

Fetishists do tend to devote themselves to particular materials, like leather or rubber, just as Edwyn is devoted to all things plastic. But his admiration for plastic things may have more to do with the technological wonders of the extended polymer (as when he marvels, as if he has never heard of Semtex, "Explosive . . . plastic?") than with the sensuous properties of plastics per se. The latter would be hard for anyone who is not a specialist in the engineering of plastics to describe in other than vague, impressionistic terms. No doubt such a specialist would focus more on the chemical properties of plastics than on their tactile properties, odor, or taste, which are negligible by design. Plastics therefore would seem to have only limited sensory appeal.[12] In fact, their relative lack of odor and taste is essential to their marketing: no one wants a meal to savor of *spork.* As the anthropologist Gay Hawkins has observed, plastics "discourage sensual attachments—their use in the making of transient objects signifies a finite value, a value waiting to be used up."[13] They are meant to be consumed without being savored. Part of the joke in *Plastic* is that Edwyn does not grasp this basic fact about his favorite substance. His apparent fetish for plastic is like a fetish for drywall or asphalt or concrete, or for any other industrial material that features prominently in our everyday experience of the built and manufactured world though we may never pay it any attention.

Part of the difficulty here is that plastic is omnipresent in Edwyn's world, as it is in ours, and yet its materiality is elusive. In this respect, plastic is rather like the donut shop Holes and More. The name of this business affords an apt philosophical description of donuts in general, in that it honors the principle of *ex nihilo nihil fit* (from nothing, nothing is made), but it does not specify what donuts actually are made of. Here, the Hole, the nothingness, is as essential as the "and More." But "and More" recalls primitive numbering systems (where counting may take the form of *one, two . . . many*), given its failure to supply the most vital information: how much "more," and how much "more" of what material? Standing before the door of Holes and More, a customer might have no idea what was for sale inside. It could be Swiss cheese. It could be sex dolls. That a woman who looks just like Virginia works at Holes and More has something to do with Edwyn's enjoyment of his visit to the shop, though plotwise Ginny proves to be a red herring. She serves Edwyn his donuts and gives him sporks, and then she promptly disappears from the narrative.

Plastic (as) MacGuffin

Plastic is full of red herrings, not the least of which may be the material referenced in its title.[14] That material may be the ultimate MacGuffin, both in the comic and in reality. That is, although it seems substantive, meaningful, and valuable, in the end it proves evanescent, overdetermined, and transforms into something worse than junk. At the end of *Citizen Kane,* the sled Rosebud gets incinerated after its owner's death. Unlike Kane's sled, however, little to no plastic is incinerated once we are done with it. Discarded plastic disappears from our lives (or so we like to believe), but we do not mourn its loss. Most people promptly forget all about it. Yet it endures elsewhere, as litter along highways and in bodies of water, in landfills, and as recyclable material waiting to be processed, usually in impoverished developing nations (where plastic may accumulate for years without ever getting melted down for reuse). In recent years, this paradoxical aspect of plastic, its superabundance and its evanescence in our lives, and its complicated materiality, has begun to get more and more attention. As Hawkins asks, "How did a material as durable as plastic become qualified as disposable, as a single-use, throwaway material? How did plastic become the archetypal expression of immediacy and ephemerality: barely there before it was gone?"[15]

Research is stranger than fiction, which is probably incapable of capturing the subtleties and complexities of the material world it gestures toward. This is the case even when fiction presents itself in the guise of environmental literature, especially the novel and other narrative forms.[16] It is hardly surprising, then, that plastic proves to be more diverse, and more perverse, than the gonzo creators of the story spun in *Plastic* realize. What we think of as "plastic" includes some ten thousand different varieties (and more). Susan Freinkel describes plastics as "a collection of loosely related clans." Most of the raw plastic used in commercial applications comprises long-chain polymers derived from ethylene gas, a byproduct of the refinement of petroleum. Polymerization occurs when a chemical catalyst—different kinds are in use; some, like the many varieties of phthalate, are toxic—turns an ethylene monomer into a long chain of linked molecules, or polymers. (Not quite a case of creation ex nihilo, then, but for the layman it comes uncomfortably close.) The result is polyethylene, which has the useful characteristic of being flexible enough to assume a variety of different shapes and finishes, so that a number of disparate items can be fashioned from this singular substance. Its plasticity obscures its complicated origins, and thus its materiality. "Although we talk about plastic as a thing, it doesn't have the thingness, the kind of grounded organic identity, found in natural substances," Freinkel writes; "a piece of plastic is essentially inscrutable, offering few clues as to its past or future." That is why no one has a feel for plastic of the sort a potter might have for clay or a carpenter for quarter-sawn oak.[17] To work in the production of plastic does not mean becoming an artisan. It means employment at a refinery and having some familiarity with the relevant principles of materials science. It may require a degree in chemical engineering. Plastic is esoteric, yet none of us are ever very far from this substance, since it defines what Freinkel calls "the synthetica that has come to constitute such a huge, and yet strangely invisible, part of modern life." If you are a contemporary human being, you are unlikely to kick the plastic habit: "It's nearly impossible to escape the plastic bubble."[18]

High-end durable goods like surfboards and boats are made from thermoset plastics, which cannot be recycled; shopping bags, and the bottles that water and soda come in, are made from thermoplastics, which can be recycled but mostly are not.[19] Plastic is in our homes and our workplaces: it is in our clothing, our toys and tools, our cars and trucks. Increasingly, it is in our bodies, too, since there is plastic in our food and water—even in the air we breathe. The catalysts in plastic are not essential to its substance, merely to its production, and can leach out or off-gas over time. Like the holes in donuts, plasticizers are apt to disappear once the plastic has been produced and consumed. This is why people tested for the presence in their systems of additives used in the production of plastic always test positive.[20]

In sum, and as Amanda Boetzkes puts it, "plastic is a paradigmatic material for our time."[21] For Boetzkes, "our time" refers to the current period of late capitalism and post–World War II industrial modernity. A more capacious view of the era of plastic is available: materially, plastic also belongs to earth history as charted by geologists in long timelines assuming a scale of roughly 4.5 billion years. The Anthropocene concept, proposed by earth scientists as the latest division of that time scale, has sparked a search for hard-rock benchmarks, so-called golden spikes, of its onset.[22] The radiation that was disseminated globally by the detonation of atomic weapons after World War II is one such golden spike; plastic has been suggested as another. Michiel Abbing writes, "At Kamilo Beach in Hawaii, geologists discovered a type of rock in 2014 that has been given the scientific name *plastiglomerate,* a combination of *plastic* and *conglomerate,* the geological term for sediments that have become glued together," like the puddingstone one finds along the New England coastline.[23] Plastiglomerate incorporates bits of plastic whatnots in a matrix of lava. This novelty satisfies the requirement that Anthropocene markers appear in the geological record. Plastic, then, is more than "paradigmatic." It contributes to a material condition—a condition of the material world, of Earth—in its own right and very directly.

The Penumbral Ecology of Plastic

The ecology of plastic, much like its geology, is only beginning to be understood, even though its environmental impacts were first noted in the 1960s. This ecology (like all ecologies) features the multiple, recursive causalities, the complexities, and the chaotic phenomena that began to trouble theoretical ecologists in the decades after World War II.[24] Equally troubling, in the case of the ecologies of plastics (here a shift to plurals is needed, because these ecologies differ according to scale and chemical composition), are the challenges they pose to the classic concept of environment as *everything outside an organism.* Plastics refute that simple logic, and further relativize and complicate an already relativistic and complex concept, one that resists popularization. The glut of plastic objects in the Northern Pacific Gyre, for instance, has become emblematic of plastic "pollution." Articles about this phenomenon are often accompanied by photographs of beaches covered in plastic waste a foot or more in depth all along the high-tide line. But in the Gyre, most of the plastic present is not flotsam and jetsam drifting on the surface. Instead, it is a particulate suspended in the water column, and eventually it will accumulate in thick deposits on the sea floor.

"What plastic does in the environment," Abbing writes, "is break down into smaller and smaller fragments" thanks to wave action, the chemical effects of salt water, and ultraviolet radiation, which renders plastic brittle. These fragments have a name, *microplastics,* which is becoming more and more current in news stories about plastic pollution and the "plastic soup" that is Abbing's subject matter. Abbing further corrects a popular misconception when he notes that microplastics are subject to ongoing fragmentation, which further reduces them in size. You can see microplastics on beaches all around the world, along with the plastic pellets or "nurdles" used in the production of commodities and shipped globally. These pellets are regularly swept away from production facilities by inland floods, and containers full of them often go overboard in storms. The pellets are among the plastics you may find and scoop up by the handful in the tidal wrack, along with dried seaweed, bits of shell, the feathers of shorebirds, and the pincers of dead crabs.

Nanoplastics are harder than microplastics to come to grips with literally, and imaginatively as well. They are smaller than one micron or 100 nanometers, which is to say, smaller than the ten thousandth part of 1/1000 meters (a nanometer is *one billionth* of a meter). Nanoplastics, since they offer a much greater surface area in the aggregate, bind more toxins than microplastics, "one hundred to one thousand times more." With nanoplastics in mind, Abbing suggests that "it is already better to speak of a plastic broth rather than a plastic soup."[25] If plastic pollution makes oceans (and large freshwater lakes) more broth-like than soup-like, then it can be said to have become an "environmental" factor in its own right, like sunlight or the nitrogen cycle. It is now inherent to the novel ecosystems in which many animals and plants live and are nourished.

Detecting the absorption of nanoplastics in the bodies of animals that have consumed them, either by swimming in the sea or after eating other creatures that already have incorporated nanoplastics into their flesh and organs, is extremely difficult.[26] Among the animals whose bodies have been compromised by plastics we must include ourselves, even if we avoid eating fish and shellfish (filter feeders like oysters are especially vulnerable to plastic contamination). "City dwellers," Abbing reports, "may inhale more microplastics than they ingest by eating seafood." In the sea, microplastics and nanoplastics are becoming so all-pervasive that they can be said to be in the process of redefining marine environments as significantly artificial, and as extensions of the synthetic world that prevails onshore. But in the sea, plastic pollution is compounded many times over by extreme fragmentation (think, for the sake of comparison, of the fineness of the sediments in glacial milk). Abbing describes microplastics on the ocean floor as resembling "a kind of permanent snowstorm," and notes that by 2050, "the seas will contain more plastic than fish."[27] This suggests that plastics will begin to perform in marine environments much like the calcium-rich exoskeletons of shellfish, corals, and foraminifera that contribute to the formation of limestone, but the result will have a very different chemical profile from that useful substance.

The many ways in which plastic not only defines the externalities of our lives, but also enters into the fabric of our being, suggest that some key concepts need redefinition. For example, we cannot understand plastic litter simply as "matter out of place" or MOOP, following Mary Douglas's classic definition of "dirt" and the Burning Man policy on postevent cleanup that Douglas inspired: "Everything that wasn't originally *on* or *of* the Black Rock Desert, no matter how small, is considered MOOP, and is to be removed as part of our Leave No Trace efforts."[28] If plastic is already everywhere, then deciding when it is "out of place" or "no trace" of it is left is impossible. Creating indices of the natural is a fundamental difficulty of both ecological assessment and environmental history, as the pristine world is a long time gone. Plastic is now part and parcel of the natural as well as the built environments, and cultures, we inhabit. This is not going to change: petroleum-based plastics do not biodegrade, they merely fragment. "The plastic that went into producing every plastic bag ever handed out and every water bottle made is still out there, somewhere."[29] Since that "somewhere" is also everywhere, our notions not only of pollution but also of "environment" and, more particularly, of "ecosystem" are due for an update.

Plastic is going to force us to revise our understanding of the environment, just as it confounds our attempts to contain and confine pollution. The difficulty here is ecological, economic, and geopolitical, as Peter Dauvergne explains in his book on the "shadows" of consumption, where he describes how "political and economic processes displace the costs of consumer goods onto distant ecosystems, communities, and times," which creates "shadows" obscuring those costs for consumers in the developed world. "Concentrating ecological impacts on the most vulnerable is not only unjust for billions of people; it is also far more likely to tip societies and ecosystems into uncontrollable decline and collapse."[30] By evoking "decline and collapse," Dauvergne activates memes central to environmental discourse and rhetoric, where they inform apocalyptic, doom-ridden prophecies.[31] This is unsurprising, and it may be unavoidable, as debates about climate change illustrate. Plastic is proving to be just as spooky as climate change, and poses a similar problem for policy makers, who "need to address consequences having no clean lines of causality and to take precautionary measures against effects flowing through complex systems with unpredictable outcomes."[32] In the case of plastics, "flowing" is not a metaphor. It is precisely what plastics do, especially in marine environments, where they can create ecosystemic complications of diverse kinds, thanks to the phenomena of "entanglement, ingestion, smothering, hangers-on, hitch-hiking and alien invasions" that they introduce there.[33] The last three of these phenomena (which suggest the plot of a 1950s horror film) qualify micro- and nanoplastics as habitats in their own right, since the "plastisphere," "a thin shell of microbes living on every piece of floating plastic," counts as "a new human-generated ecosystem." A plastisphere can be very diverse, "with more than a thousand different species of organisms present."[34] This is not the biodiversity environmentalists have been taught to celebrate.

The development of anthropogenic plastipheres, and the global dispersion of plastics in both terrestrial and aquatic environments (again, both marine and freshwater, like the Great Lakes), belies notions of particulate and point-source pollution (i.e., of "matter out of place"). Max Liboiron suggests we think instead in terms of miasmas, "because the miasma theory shares several characteristics with the behaviours of plastic chemicals. Miasmas may appear to be an unscientific and folksy concept, but they were the first and longest-running scientific theories of disease that did not attribute illness to spiritual causes." Miasmas were proposed as the origins of epidemic diseases like the cholera that decimated the Soho district of London in 1854. The cause of cholera was eventually found to be a bacterium, but thinking of the disease in terms of the "influence" of miasmas, "in contrast to the particle model of harm used today that describes the actions of discrete pollutants," had advantages. Arguably, it was more properly environmental. Liboiron writes:

> Miasmas were inextricable from the landscape, urban architecture and the human population. Their mechanism of harm was not direct, but additive and somewhat mysterious: weather, personal histories, architecture, diet, the alignment of stars, the location of cesspools, plumbing and employment conditions all had to be counted by politicians trying to cure the sick, and by sanitarians aiming to reduce the presence of miasmas in their locales.

Miasma theory emphasized what would be called the ecology of disease today. This meant that "illness and its causes were systematic rather than discrete, holistic rather than piecemeal," so that "countless variables, presupposing causes and unique contexts both within and outside of bodies join to produce a specific effect." While miasmas were seen as local, not global, and while plastics endure whereas miasmas do not, the theory does afford the proper perspective on the diffusion of plastics throughout the global environment and our bodies: "Since every body has multiple plasticizers in it at all times, they create what is called 'the cocktail effect.'"[35]

As is the case with climate change, feedback loops, knock-on effects, and causal cascades also compound the impacts of the soup or broth or "shadow" or "miasma" or "cocktail" of plastics, and on a global scale as well as locally, as anyone who has considered a dump thoughtfully comes to realize. A. R. Ammons, for instance, writes:

> belt buckles, do-funnies, files, disks, pads,
> pesticide residues, nonprosodic high tension
>
> lines, whimpering-wimp dolls, epichlorohydrin
> elastomotors, sulfur dioxide emissions, perfume
>
> sprays, radioactive williwaws: the people at
> Marine Shale are said "to be able to turn

> waste into safe products": but some say these
> "products are themselves hazardous wastes":[36]

Epichlorohydrin can be converted to bisphenol A (BPA); epichlorohydrin elastomer (not "elastomotor") is an elastic polymer, some forms of which can be used to make—among other things—nonedible sausage casings. Marine Shale operated a hazardous waste incinerator from the mid-1980s to the early 1990s in backwater Louisiana, the same miasma-suffused environs where *Plastic* is set. After a federal lawsuit, the Amelia incinerator became an EPA Superfund site.

Because of the many recursive effects produced by plastic once it is widely dispersed in all habitats, including bodies of water and bodies of flesh and blood, it is tempting to see it, through the lens of the new materialism, as having agency. (Gay Hawkins and others have begun to see plastic in just this way.) But attributing "agency" to plastic may be simplistic, especially in light of the great diversity of plastics produced over the last seventy-five years and the need for those plastics to be brought to life, though only in a manner of speaking, by means of the chemicals employed to polymerize a monomer. Chemical agency is not down on all fours with the agency central to new materialism, which relies on a model based on human agency. Even endocrine disruptors like BPA, which might seem to be agents or at least *actants* of the sort celebrated in the new materialism (which often makes it seem as if the agency of the material were good news, and something to be celebrated), are disruptive only because they are able to create effects on the endocrine system mechanically. Their "agency" is not willful, nor is it "emergent." Coincidentally, they have shapes similar to hormones and can plug into endocrine receptors, and their effects on individual endocrine systems vary widely.[37]

That Edwyn, the protagonist of *Plastic,* reacts to the material in its various forms as if it were indeed lively runs through the comic like an in-joke, so very *in* that it seems obscure, a conundrum the reader struggles to understand, and one that Edwyn himself seems not to recognize, happy consumer and devoted lover of a PVC sex doll that he is. For all his perversion, where plastics are concerned Edwyn is naïve, if not exactly innocent. Environmental plastics, like Edwyn, also pose a conundrum, but not one that needs to be interpreted. This conundrum marks a real dilemma, and an existential crisis to boot. The creators of *Plastic* are as blind to this crisis as their protagonist seems to be; that is, they also appear to think that "plastic makes everything better," or at least affords a cheap means of achieving closure, in the form of an apocalyptic ending. In chapter 5 of their comic, "Buckle up, Virginia . . . ," Edwyn and Virginia are struck by the same bullet during the comic's penultimate confrontation with the kidnapper and his men. Edwyn begins to bleed, while Virginia emits a high-pitch squeal as she deflates, another instance of the comic's sly humor: she *is* a balloon after all. Edwin swears further vengeance: "*Nobody* hurts Virginia." (Of course, nobody has hurt her: all Virginia needs is a patch, and that she lacks anything resembling human agency and feeling is precisely the joke being made as she deflates.) As he utters these defiant words, Edwyn is hunched over the open trunk of his car, with a fistful of sporks in one hand and a block of Semtex in the other. He buckles Virginia in the front passenger seat of his car, and in a final act of extreme violence, crashes the car through the window of his enemy's study. There is a massive explosion, and Virginia's severed head (it is melting and her mouth is now closed), a flaming spork, and other fiery *disjecta membra* fly through the air. In contemporary narrative, and even when the narrative plays up environmental angles, no ending is more commodified than the apocalyptic ending, which seems to be the only way the modern industrial world can imagine its future. In the Mad Max films, for instance, the solution to conflict driven by climate change and the grim realities of a post–Peak Oil world is burning still more petroleum and building an armored fleet of souped-up, turbo-charged cars, monster trucks, and motorcycles. Everything comes to an end, and yet everything reboots, as if the postapocalyptic world were merely a matter of accepting apocalypse as the new normal, and as if there were no ending to the end. In *Plastic,* the solution to conflict is a conflagration caused by plastic explosives and the dispersion of still more plastics throughout the already toxic Louisiana countryside. The serial killer Edwyn comes out of retirement and kills again and again. The plastic bubble bursts and is reconstituted on a much larger scale, and it happens all at once. Only Gwen the hitchhiker survives the conflagration, and she tells the driver who gives her a lift to New Orleans that her name is Virginia.

NOTES

1. The *ICE* series appeared in 2015 (before the Trump administration began to transform Immigration and Customs Enforcement), and *The Ride: Burning Desire* is part of a long-running series featuring various writers and artists. Wagner and Hillyard often collaborate with others; for examples of their jointly authored work, see volumes 2 and 3 of *ICE* (12-Gauge Comics, 2015); and Doug Wagner, Daniel Hillyard, et al., *The Ride: Burning Desire* (Portland, Ore.: Image Comics, 2019).
2. See promotional material for *The Ride* at 12gaugecomics.com, the home page for Wagner's production company.
3. See David Brothers, "A Love Story for the Modern Day: Plastic [Interview]" (March 22, 2017), imagecomics.com/features.
4. "Comix" is the generic term for comic books featuring "adult" content, originating in the work of artists like R. Crumb who were featured in underground publications like Zap Comix beginning in the late 1960s.
5. Doug Wagner, Daniel Hillyard, Laura Martin, and Ed Dukeshire, *Plastic* (Portland, Ore.: Image Comics, 2017), unpaginated.
6. Edwyn's last name, Stoffgruppen, is revealed on the comic's back cover. *Stoff* is stuff, material (usually fabric). *Stoffgruppen* is a term used by German chemists.
7. Ebay.com currently features sixteen pages of listings for female sex dolls.
8. For prices, and product descriptions written by enthusiasts, see the online guide at mySEXDOLL.net.
9. For basic facts about Semtex, see Wikipedia.com.
10. *Diagnostic and Statistical Manual of Mental Disorders, Fifth Edition; DSM-V* (Washington, D.C.: American Psychiatric Association, 2013), 685.
11. To suggest that Edwyn may not suffer from a full-blown fetishistic disorder is not to suggest that he does not have other severe mental disorders shaping his wayward urges, but the comic does not invite its readers to pursue a clinical diagnosis of its protagonist.
12. Apart from their bright colors, that is, but those derive from dyes. Raw plastics are colorless. While some contemporary artists and theorists have celebrated plastics for their ability to take on almost any shape (the plasticity that defines them) and hue, plastic artwork tends toward ironic commentary on consumer culture of the familiar postmodernist sort. And arguments that plastic helps to undermine rigid notions of the natural overlook the extent to which such notions have long been seen as problematic in fields like theoretical ecology. See the discussion of benchmarks and penumbral ecologies below.

13. Gay Hawkins, "Plastic Bags: Living with Rubbish," *International Journal of Cultural Studies* 4, no. 1 (2001): 9.
14. Here it is worth recalling that "plastic" was an adjective before it was pressed into service as a noun.
15. Gay Hawkins, "Plastic and Presentism: The Time of Disposability," *Journal of Contemporary Archaeology* 5, no. 1 (2018): 92.
16. Even the deftest forms of literary realism cannot capture the phenomena charted by scientific realism, which are orders of magnitude more complicated than, for instance, the daily habits and mores of the middle classes on which literary realism has tended to focus. See Dana Phillips, *The Truth of Ecology: Nature, Culture, and Literature in America* (New York: Oxford University Press, 2003).
17. This is not to say that plastic wholly lacks sensuous qualities, some of which may be relatively attractive: given a choice, even the most environmentally aware person would not pick a pine-wood sex doll over a plastic one.
18. Susan Freinkel, *Plastic: A Toxic Love Story* (Boston: Houghton Mifflin Harcourt, 2011), 4, 31, 3, 113.
19. See Michiel Roscam Abbing, *Plastic Soup: An Atlas of Ocean Pollution* (Washington, D.C.: Island Press, 2019), 9.
20. Bisphenol A, or BPA, is used in a number of plastic products and "undoubtedly enters the human body, with studies showing exposure of >95% of populations" (Tamara S. Galloway, "Micro- and Nano-plastics and Human Health," in Melanie Bergmann et al., eds., *Marine Anthropogenic Litter* [Heidelberg: Springer Open, 2015], 357). Max Liboiron notes that "every person tested in the United States and Canada, and many other countries, carries plastic chemicals in his or her body" ("Plasticizers: A Twenty-First-Century Miasma," in Jennifer Gabrys, Gay Hawkins, and Mike Michael, eds., *Accumulation: The Material Politics of Plastic* [London: Routledge, 2013], 134). Of course, modern medical technology itself is thoroughly reliant on plastic.
21. Amanda Boetzkes, *Plastic Capitalism: Contemporary Art and the Drive to Waste* (Cambridge, Mass.: MIT Press, 2019), 32.
22. See Erle C. Ellis, *Anthropocene: A Very Short Introduction* (Oxford: Oxford University Press, 2018).
23. Abbing, *Plastic Soup*, 54.
24. See chapter 2, "Ecology Then and Now," in Phillips, *The Truth of Ecology*, 42–82.
25. Abbing, *Plastic Soup: An Atlas of Ocean Pollution*, 51, 34.
26. See Galloway, "Micro- and Nano-plastics and Human Health," 351–54, where the technologies used in several laboratory studies of the use of plastic nanoparticles as drug delivery systems are described.
27. Abbing, *Plastic Soup: An Atlas of Ocean Pollution*, 57, 30.
28. "Matter Out of Place: MOOP," burningman.org/event/preparation; and see chapter 2, "Secular Defilement," in Mary Douglas, *Purity and Danger: An*

Analysis of Concepts of Pollution and Taboo (London: Routledge Classics, 2002), 36–50, especially 44–50.

29. Jennifer Clapp, "The Rising Tide against Plastic Waste: Unpacking Industry Attempts to Influence the Debate," in Stephanie Foote and Elizabeth Mazzolini, eds., *Histories of the Dustheap: Waste, Material Cultures, Social Justice* (Cambridge, Mass.: MIT Press, 2012), 201.
30. Peter Dauvergne, *The Shadows of Consumption: Consequences for the Global Environment* (Cambridge, Mass.: MIT Press, 2008), xi, 230–31.
31. See Dana Phillips, "Posthumanism, Environmental History, and Narratives of Collapse," *Interdisciplinary Studies in Literature and Environment (ISLE)* 22, no. 1 (Winter 2015): 63–79.
32. Dauvergne, *The Shadows of Consumption*, 30.
33. Murray R. Gregory, "Environmental Implications of Plastic Debris in Marine Settings—Entanglements, Ingestion, Smothering, Hangers-on, Hitch-Hiking and Alien Invasions," *Philosophical Transactions of the Royal Society B* 364 (2009): 2013–25.
34. Abbing, *Plastic Soup: An Atlas of Ocean Pollution*, 56.
35. Liboiron, "Plasticizers: A Twenty-First-Century Miasma," 134, 135, 136, 137, 142,
36. A. R. Ammons, *Garbage* (New York: W. W. Norton, 1993), 108.
37. See Liboiron, "Plasticizers: A Twenty-First-Century Miasma," 134–44, especially Figure 8.2 on page 141. On the strengths and weaknesses of the new materialism, see Dana Phillips, "Excremental Ecocriticism and the Global Sanitation Crisis," in Serenella Iovino and Serpil Opperman, eds., *Material Ecocriticism* (Bloomington: University of Indiana Press, 2014), 172–85.

2

Smelling *Polyester*

Paul Morrison

Christian saints smell to high heaven. "We are the aroma of Christ to God among those who are being saved," St. Paul told the Corinthians (II Cor. 2:15); "Some men are good smelling and some are stinking to God," John Wycliffe informed the faithful.[1] Greco-Roman divinities are suffused with the aroma of immortality. Homer houses Zeus in a fragrant cloud; "When Bacchus approached," Ovid notes, "the air was full of sweet scent of saffron and myrrh" (*Metamorphoses*, I. iv). But in a world in which cleanliness is considered next to godliness, the approach of divinity is heralded by the scent of Lysol and the rustle of polyester. Francine Fishpaw (Divine)—the domestic deity of John Waters's 1981 film *Polyester*—manifests her divinity by sniffing out the unclean, the unwholesome, the ungodly. "The filthiest woman alive," the dog-shit-eating-diva of *Pink Flamingos* (1972) now keeps the cleanest house on the block, and her preternaturally keen nostrils recoil in olfactory anguish from farts in the conjugal bed.

We first find Francine at her vanity, a conventional locale for both women and drag queens (Figure 2.1). John Berger notes that a man paints a picture of a naked woman because he enjoys looking at her. But because he lacks the courage of his scopophilia, he places a mirror in her hand and calls the painting *Vanity*. Francine's sojourn before the mirror serves to justify the most conventional of scopic economies—woman connotes "to-be-looked-at-ness," in Laura Mulvey's still influential formulation.[2] But what of Francine's nose? After having fixed her face, she smells her armpits and feet. Unhappy with what her nostrils discern, she attacks the offending body parts with an array of deodorants and aerosol cans. That Francine should

FIGURE 2.1. Francine at her Vanity. John Waters, *Polyester* (1981), New Line Cinema.

be self-regarding is only expected. That she is also self-smelling is less so. That her olfactory relation to her body figures our olfactory participation in a motion picture—*Polyester* is in "odorama"—is downright perverse.

Dr. Arnold Quackenshaw (Rick Breitenfeld), the crackpot professor who introduces *Polyester,* explains the operations of odorama: "scratch and sniff" cards keyed to numbers on the screen effectively transform the "viewer" into a "smeller." (For those unfamiliar with the plot: Francine's suburban dream begins to disintegrate under her nose. Her porn-king husband [David Samson] is having an affair with his skinny secretary [Mink Stole]; the two eventually hatch a plot to murder her. Dexter [Ken King], Francine's son, is arrested as the Baltimore foot stomper and Lu-Lu [Mary Garlington], her daughter, gets pregnant. Francine turns to booze before finding consolation in the arms of Todd Tomorrow [Tab Hunter], the owner of the Edmondson Drive-In Cinema. But even Todd proves feckless: her cocaine-snorting lover conspires with her mother [Joni Ruth White] to defraud her of her home and divorce settlement. Eventually all the evil characters come to grief, and a newly sober Francine and her rehabilitated children reconstitute a happy and properly hygienic family unit.) Waters termed "odorama" one of "the most ludicrous promotional gimmicks of all time," which, in a world as thoroughly deodorized as ours, it no doubt is. But life, as Walter Benjamin notes, was not always so antiseptic: "During long periods of history, the mode of human sense perception changes with humanity's entire mode of existence. The manner in which human sense perception is organized, the medium in which it is accomplished, is determined not only by nature but by historical circumstances as well."[3] Odorama is a homage to Hans Laube's "Smell-O-Vision," which announced itself as the full coming-into-being of the cinematic body: "First they moved (1895)! Then they talked (1927)! Now they smell!" Although the olfactory was a late and short-lived addition to the somatic repertoire of film—it was first used in the appropriately titled *Scent of Mystery* (1960)—smell is generally considered a primitive or archaic mode of sensory perception. Max Nordau argues that "smellers among degenerates represent an atavism going back, not only to the primaeval period of man, but infinitely more remote still, to an epoch anterior to man."[4] But what of the Divine nose? *Polyester* would seem to conjoin an allegedly archaic mode of sensory perception, the olfactory, with a distinctly modern and deodorized medium, the celluloid world of film. (Or, better, a "distinctly present futural" medium, as Amanda Boetkes terms plastic: "Because of plastic's robust and expansive topological reach, it appears in the present *from* the planet's future." Francine's love interest is, after all, named Todd Tomorrow.)[5] How, then, are we to position "smelling polyester" within developmental narratives of somatic organization and aesthetic production? By what logic does a smeller—a three-hundred-pound drag queen who is either blessed or cursed with preternaturally keen nostrils—turn to plastic?

Hegel follows Kant in arguing for an unodorant aesthetic life:

> The sensuous aspect of art refers to the two theoretical senses of sight and hearing, while smell, taste, sight, and feeling remain excluded from being sources of artistic enjoyment. For smell, taste, and feeling refer to matter as such, and with its immediate sensuous qualities. . . . On this account these senses cannot have to do with the objects of art, which are destined to maintain themselves in their actual independent existence and admit of no purely sensuous existence.[6]

Film is celebrated for its sensuous plenitude and immediacy, but it too is restricted to the "theoretical senses of sight and hearing." Theater stinks. The smell of greasepaint is proverbial, and Equity contracts apparently specify the frequency with which costumes are to be cleaned. In *The Beautiful and the Damned,* Gloria Patch, another high priestess of hygiene, visits a movie studio for the first time: "She liked it. There was no heavy closeness of greasepaint, no scent of soiled and tawdry costumes which years before had so revolted her behind the scenes of a musical comedy."[7] There are exceptions. The "feelies" of Aldous Huxley's *Brave New World,* to cite a fictional example, radically expand the sensuous resources of film, even if their popularity in our dystopic future is itself evidence of a deficient capacity for feeling. Horkheimer and Adorno argue that smell betrays "the archetypal longing for the lower orders of existence, for direct contact with circumambient nature, with the earth and mud."[8] But a movie that produces olfactory effects through the "ludicrous" promotional gimmick of "scratch and sniff" cards is utterly innocent of the body natural, which is not in fact the source of olfactory immediacy. There is no pretense that odors emanate from the diegetic content of the screen, and particularly naughty viewers are always free to scratch flatulence when the screen indicates roses or roses when the screen indicates flatulence. In painting, Kracauer argues, nature disappears (*nature morte,* as the French say); in film, it makes a triumphant return. Hence, the subtitle of his epochal study of the art (or non-art) of the motion picture, "the redemption of physical nature."[9] Bazin contends that film should—and, in the case of Orson Welles, does—provide "a realism that is in a certain sense ontological, restoring to the object and the décor their existential density."[10] But is "existential density" really such an impoverished thing? Under what somatic regime can an art of the two "theoretical" senses of sight and sound be said to constitute "the redemption of physical nature"? Roland Barthes considers plastic to be insufficiently of the earth: "It embodies none of the genuine produce of the mineral world: foam, fibres, strats." Amanda Boetzkes concurs:

> It is integrated into, or has even replaced, earthly substances: textiles, clothing, paper, lumber, cork, and rubber. More than

> this, plastic exists by voiding itself of its earthly basis, an inherent form, and an inherent value. It is a phenomenon above and beyond the matter of its objects.[11]

Plastic is rather more "of the earth" than is commonly supposed: early plastic was made from plant cellulose; Henry Ford used soybeans; in the 1920s, the Germans turned to cows' blood.[12] Boetzkes's point is, however, well taken. The cultural meaning of plastic inheres in the voiding of its "earthly basis," in its quasi-Platonic existence "above and beyond the matter of its object."

If all art is destined to maintain itself in its actual independent existence and admit of no purely sensuous existence, all art might be said to aspire to the condition of plastic. Even an art that is overtly hostile to it:

> Once out of nature I shall never take
> My bodily form from any natural thing,
> But such a form as Grecian goldsmiths make
> Of hammered gold and gold enameling[13]

An artist less ambivalent about his modernity—Yeats identified himself as one of "the last romantics"—might have settled on a less retrograde material: plastic, gold enamel, or Grecian marble reconfigured for a postnatural, posthuman age. Yeats's "artifice of eternity" is a golden bird that sings to keep a drowsy emperor awake; a thoroughly modern aesthetic might have championed a plastic pink flamingo. Gold is still very much "out of nature," but plastic is its metaphorical negation, a second, counternatural nature. Newer technologies—radio, television, telephone—turned to Bakelite in order to embody their modernity; modern artists turned to plastic, nylon, wire, Lucite, metal, and glass for much the same reason. The "cones" of Naum Gabo's 1927 *Construction in Space: Two Cones,* for example, are in fact "constructions," not representations of natural forms, and the materials from which they are forged, cellulose nitrate and cellulose acetate, are early plastics. The work is patently counternatural, yet it proved no less ephemeral for that. Gabo's homage to the "futural" logic of his age paradoxically had no future.

Construction in Space: Two Cones survived only a decade in the Philadelphia Museum of Art before it essentially self-destructed. Gabo blamed the museum, not his materials; as if to prove his point, he made an exact replica of his original work, which he donated to the Tate in London. It too, however, ended its days as a heap of atrophied brown cellulose, and it is now viewable only online in the Tate's digital Gallery of Lost Art. Claes Oldenburg's *False Food Selection* (1966), a wooden box filled with plastic food—eggs, bacon, a banana, an oatmeal cookie—suffered a similar fate. Plastic promised to banish "anxiety, concern, and worry from the American home—conquering germs, chores, food spoilage, cigarette burns, and dour blasts from the past."[14] Even when the food itself is plastic, however, spoilage ensues: Oldenburg's egg whites turned yellow and his banana deflated. Neil Armstrong's spacesuit, which was constructed from twenty-one layers of fabric and plastic—nylon, neoprene, Mylar, Dacron, Kapton, and Teflon—is now too fragile and brittle to be routinely displayed.[15] Cellulose nitrate has been a "distinctly present," if highly dangerous, "futural medium" since the 1830s. Billiard balls made of the plastic would occasionally explode on impact, and many a movie theater went up in flames due to the instability of the cellulose nitrate in early film.[16] (Recall the cinematic inferno in Tarantino's *Inglorious Basterds*.) By the 1930s, cellulose acetate began to replace cellulose nitrate for reasons of safety, but as the example of Gabo's *Constructions in Space* suggests, it too proved highly unstable. Plastic consists of a single molecule repeated over and over; to become fully "plastic" or malleable, however, it requires the addition of "plasticizers." But therein lies the problem: the chemical union is not a happy one. As if to reject the very element that constitutes it, plastic eventually squeezes the plasticizers out, which leaves it brittle and fragile. And therein lies the paradox: plastic is both the present "futural" form of an impending ecological apocalypse, the counternatural substance that will not die, and the all-too-natural material that, try as we might, cannot be preserved.

The material that figures global waste on a catastrophic scale was allegedly born of the desire to waste nothing. When surveying one of his oil refineries (or so the story goes), John D. Rockefeller asked about flames issuing from a smoke stack. He was told his company was burning off ethylene gas, a by-product of the refining process. "I don't believe in waste," Rockefeller replied; "Figure out something to do with it." That "something" turned out to be polyethylene.[17] Deteriorating plastics are said to "bleed" or "weep," a language that recalls medieval relics—fragments of the True Cross and the like—but that hardly seems appropriate to the postnatural, posthuman world of the synthetic. We are accustomed to thinking of the human body as plastic: "The whole world *can* be plasticized, and even life itself since, we are told, they are beginning to make plastic aortas."[18] We seldom acknowledge, however, that we think of plastic as human. "Bleeding" or "weeping" plastics smell to high heaven; one of the first signs that it is degrading is the odor emanating from it. Acetate gives off the scent of acetic acid, which is found in vinegar; PVC "weeps" chlorine, which makes it smell like a swimming pool; other decaying plastics are redolent of everything from burnt hair to new car smell. An olfactory take on the world may indeed be "an atavism" going back "to the primaeval period of man" or to an "epoch anterior to man," but the strange, synthetic perfumes wafting from decaying plastic are the products of advanced capitalism. Smell has no author function. Like a fart in a crowded elevator, that thing of darkness that no one acknowledges as his own, odor is not finally personal property. Dr. Quackenshaw speaks of the "untold millions" the producers of *Polyester* spent in order to develop odorama, yet smells, even under consumer capitalism, cannot be patented: there is no meaningful copyright protection for fragrance formulations. You can't rip off Calvin Klein underwear; you can, however, clone a Calvin Klein cologne, which is why fragrance recipes, like Colonel Sanders's eleven herbs and spices, tend to be carefully guarded secrets. Market research suggests that we experience smells as intrinsic to commodities. More often than not, however, they are mere olfactory flourishes. New car scent, unattached to any actual new car, can be bought at your local car wash. The olfactory may be the most "primitive" of all sensory modalities, but advanced capitalism is fully attuned to the market potential of artificial aromas. The question is not, then, how to position the smeller within developmental narratives of somatic organization and aesthetic production, my earlier formulation notwithstanding. The Divine nose demands something more radical: its olfactory acuity confounds the temporal (and hierarchical) logic of early and late, the spatial (and hierarchical) logic of above and below. The smeller is both what the counternatural march of civilization represses and what the counternatural march of civilization produces; plastic is both the all-too-natural material that cannot be preserved and the counternatural material that will not die.

Darwin associates the developmental with deodorization: in the process of evolving from the lower animals, humankind loses its acuity of smell. Freud as well: the devaluation of olfactory stimulation is one with the birth of the monogamous couple and "the founding of the family"; an unodorant sexual life brings us to "the threshold of civilization itself."[19] Francine's olfactory acuity is, however, second to none, and if she too is committed to the "civilized" eradication of smells, it is that very commitment, as Horkheimer and Adorno suggest, that provides virtually unlimited opportunities for indulging the nose:

> The sense of smell is considered a disgrace in civilization, the sign of lower social strata, lower races and base animals. The civilized individual may only indulge in such pleasure if the prohibition is suspended by rationalization in the service of real or apparent practical ends. The prohibited impulse may be tolerated if there is no doubt that the final aim is elimination. . . . Anyone who seeks out "bad" smells, in order to destroy them, may imitate sniffing to his heart's content, taking unrationalized pleasure in the experience.[20]

The bourgeois pursuit of domestic hygiene, the relentless ferreting out of "bad" smells, radically expands the reach of the nose. "The house has halitosis," as the 1960s TV commercial used to say, and never before in history have so many domestic crevices and orifices been so gleefully penetrated by so many noses. The Western political imagination tends to associate "osmologies," universes structured by the diacritics of smell, with "primitive" peoples and places; among the Dassanetch, for example, a farming and cattle-herding people of Ethiopia, time is structured as a succession of odors.[21] Rural Ethiopia has, however, nothing on suburban Baltimore. In *Pink*

Flamingos, Babs Johnson (Divine) and her son Crackers break into the home of their archrivals, the Marbles, usurpers to the title "The Filthiest People Alive." Before going down on her son, Babs slobbers all over the Marbles's furniture, in order, as she puts it, to make it "rise up and reject its owners." This is clearly not the high priestess of hygiene, but to be the filthiest woman alive and to keep the cleanest house on the block is not as antithetical as it might seem. There is little practical difference between a living room so defiled that no one will sit in it and a living room so clean that no one dares. Olfactory pervert and olfactory police are functionally indistinguishable.

Polyester was Waters's first relatively big budget production ($300,000 in 1981), the first to employ something resembling an established Hollywood star (Tab Hunter), the first to be shot entirely in 35 mm, the first to escape an "X" rating for the eminently more marketable "R," and the first and only to be in odorama. As if the dog shit Divine consumes in *Pink Flamingos* had been sublimated, in orthodox Freudian fashion, into gold, *Polyester* sets about transcending the place of excrement, which is where Waters's film career began. The film about the Fishpaw family is a film that Francine Fishpaw might take her family to see. Eve Sedgwick and Michael Moon argue that Francine's "flaring nostrils are a sign of, among other things, the now internalized censor, hysterically sniffing out embodiments and enactments of filthy flesh, the primary business of the earlier films."[22] Divine is, however, both censor and connoisseur, and if her flaring nostrils seek out "bad" smells in order to eradicate them, they also serve as technologies of pleasure happily released from the alibi of the biological. For Freud, an inverse relation obtains between civilization and the free expression of sexuality; for Waters, civilization extends, Pinocchio-like, the purview of the nose. "I got something I want to show you," Todd Tomorrow tells a giggling, coquettish Francine, "and it's long, and it's sleek, and it's powerful. It's my new vette." The joke here, of course, is that sometimes a vette is just a vette. The smell of the new car drives Francine into an olfactory frenzy, but it is only the smell, as it were, that she smells. (The lexicon of smell tends to be highly limited and largely tautological. Shit smells . . . well . . . like shit.) The obvious temptation is to view the vette as a phallic symbol, but the phallic, unlike the organ it strategically veils, emits

FIGURE 2.2. Olfactory Orgasms: Francine and New Car Scent. John Waters, *Polyester* (1981), New Line Cinema.

no odors. Freud argues that an inverse relation obtains between civilization and the free development of sexuality. In a world in which a new vette occasions olfactory orgasms, however, sexuality and civilization are like love and marriage: you can't have one without the other. Freud is credited with the "invention" of the vaginal orgasm.[23] Waters can lay claim to the olfactory (Figure 2.2).

In *The Interpretation of Dreams,* Freud notes that "comparisons between nose and penis are common," although as Magnus Hirschfeld cautions, the former sometimes promises more than the latter delivers: "Often there is connected with fetishistic prepossession for large noses a more or less unconscious phallic cult, or the old folk belief, which is in no way organically founded, that the size of the nose is indicative of the size of the male organ."[24] (Waters's 1994 *Serial Mom* features a character with the suggestive name of "Mr. Nazlerod.") But the Divine nose is not a displacement upward from the penis (or is it the phallus?), and an olfactory orgasm is not an imitation of the "genuine" thing. Patently counternatural materials—plastic, rubber, vinyl, and the like—figure in a normative sexual economy (if at all) only to the extent that they remain parasitic on the body natural. A dildo, to cite the obvious example, has a physiological prototype.[25] New car scent, however, bears no necessary relation to "filthy flesh" or "earth and mud." It is not, then, strictly true, as Foucault contends, that we are incapable of inventing any new pleasures. Divine advances an *ars erotica* of the nose.[26]

In *The Art of Poetry*, Horace cautions against any counternatural conjoining of body parts: "Suppose a painter wished to couple a horse's neck with a man's head, and to lay feathers of every hue on limbs gathered here and there, so that a woman, lovely above, foully ended in an ugly fish below; would you restrain your laughter, my friends, if admitted to a private view?"[27] The name "Mr. Nazlerod" suggests a "substitutive" relation between body parts; with the "Fishpaws," however, Waters chooses to place limbs on creatures that have none. Like the "nose candy" that Francine's mother and lover routinely snort, *Polyester* is given to an eroticism, including the synesthetic eroticism of "feeding the nose," that is liberated from the body's so-called naturally given imperatives. Charles Pierce once remarked that the perfect lover makes passionate love all night and then turns into a pizza (Figure 2.3). The priorities are clearly Freudian—sex is the prime mover—but they are not necessarily Francine's. In her dream of the jock-strap-clad pizza delivery boy, for example, it is difficult to know if the boy or the pizza enjoys pride of place.

The legitimacy of the Freudian hierarchy may strike us as self-evident, but only because Freud himself was largely instrumental in construing, or at least codifying, sex as "the explanation for everything." It was eating, however, that brought our first parents to grief, and as a strictly historical matter, eating and drinking "have been understood to lead more quickly to sex than sex to eating and drinking."[28] (Waters: the only reason to have sex is that cigarettes taste better afterwards.) The senses, particularly taste and smell, should be proof against the ingestion of dangerous or counternatural substances, but the abundance of addicts in *Polyester*—most of the major characters are hooked on one thing or another—suggests less the failure of the body natural than its utter absence. (The role of Francine is, after all, played by a man, and Divine delivers the most convincing performance in the movie.) Francine takes to drinking after learning of her husband's infidelities and her children's problems. "You're the most drinkenest gal I've ever met," as Cuddles rather engagingly puts it, and Francine ultimately finds herself at an AA meeting. She is reluctant to make the statement of identity

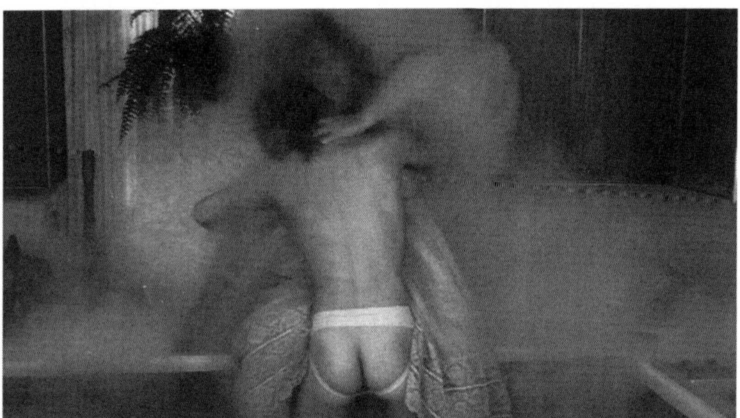

FIGURE 2.3. The Perfect Lover: Francine and the Pizza Delivery Boy. John Waters, *Polyester* (1981), New Line Cinema.

demanded of her—"Hello. My name is Francine Fishpaw and I'm an alcoholic"—and her hesitation is met with angry cries of "Say it! Say it!" Francine ultimately capitulates, but the force that interpellates her as an addict is manifestly not internal to her. Twelve-step programs characteristically insist that the subject give itself over to some "higher power," which remains strategically unspecified. *Polyester* forces that power—the social—to acknowledge itself as such. The hortatory violence of "Say it! Say it!" always precedes, implicitly or explicitly, any declaration of identity, including those that seem to arise from the body's own internal imperatives. Foucault argues that "the obligation to confess is now relayed through so many different points, is so deeply ingrained in us, that we no longer perceive it as the effect of a power that constrains us; on the contrary, it seems to us that truth, lodged in our most secret nature, 'demands' only to surface."[29] To us, certainly, but not to Francine. What emerges from within—"I am an alcoholic, a drug addict, a homosexual, a drag queen": name your vice(s)—is first imposed from without.

A "bird of hammered gold and gold enameling" is a unique objet d'art; pink flamingos are defined by abundance—they are native to the dollar store or shopping mall, not the museum or gallery. A bird of gold enameling is the aesthetic analogue of an understanding of subjectivity as "self-delighting, self-appeasing, self-affrighting"; pink flamingos suggest an imposition of identity from without. (Plastic has no "raw" state or intrinsic form; in the molding process for Bakelite, for example, the "raw" material and the finished object are produced simultaneously).[30] Susan Bordo condemns what she terms the "cultural plastic" of postmodern bodies and identities, the celebration of individual self-fashioning unencumbered by the determining weight of history, social location, biology, and biography.[31] What "cultural plastic" paradoxically does require, however, is the illusion of a soul. Consider, in this context, the gentle and not-so-gentle forms of violence that our culture routinely directs against the fat female body, a category that potentially includes every woman and no woman. Every woman, because in a misogynist culture, no woman, to rehearse Wallis Simpson's murderous logic, can ever be too thin; and no woman, because in a misogynist culture, there are no fat women, only skinny women imprisoned in fat bodies. Jenny Craig directs her normalizing energies toward the soul, in the certain knowledge that the body will follow suit. A promotional brochure for Bally Total Fitness, which features a buff young woman on its cover, reads: "A good body starts with what's *inside*" (emphasis in original). Cybertrim, a diet supplement, encourages its potential consumers (presumably biological females) "to reveal the woman you really are." Divine is not, however, a skinny woman imprisoned in a fat man's body; in all her work with Waters, she is never presented as anything other than what she herself purports to be. *Polyester* is unusual in Waters's canon in that it construes Divine's weight as erotically disqualifying. Todd Tomorrow seems to fall under her erotic sway, but we soon learn that he is a gold digger, and her husband and his skinny mistress body shame Francine relentlessly. Critiques of "plastic culture"—and they are legion—tend to function as implicit apologies for a metaphysics of depth: "Plastic has become the defining medium of our Synthetic Century precisely because it combines the ultimate twentieth-century characteristics—artificiality, disposability, and synthesis—all rolled into one. The ultimate triumph of plastic has been the victory of package over product, of style over substance, of surface over essence."[32] But the defining medium of our Synthetic Century "bleeds" and "weeps," and physiological "self-fashioning" privileges "essence." The policing of the body, the "packaging" of the flesh, "starts with what's *inside*."[33]

A metaphysics of depth also structures bourgeois aesthetics. It is the therapeutic properties of art, for example, that transform Francine's degenerate children, Dexter and Lu-Lu, into model citizens. Like Freud's Leonardo, Dexter sublimates perversion into painting, a foot fetish into fine art, and Lu-Lu translates libido into macramé. Sublimation is a developmental narrative in vertical form, and it is only once removed from repression or internalized censorship. Yet if all of this suggests that *Polyester* is indeed in the business of transcending filthy flesh, it is precisely through reverting to his foot stamping ways that Dexter saves his mother's life, and Lu-Lu kills her father's girlfriend, who is also after Francine, with her macramé. (Only John Waters could stage death by macramé.) The Fishpaw family attains bourgeois respectability through sublimation, the psychoanalytic analogue of upward mobility. It preserves itself, however, through something like desublimation, by reverting to its degenerate ways.

The Fishpaw residence, as the family-value protestors who ring it never tire of shouting, was bought from the profits of porn, and Francine is intent on transforming filthy lucre into bourgeois respectability. Hence, the French provincial furniture, the smart cocktail cart, and the obsessive cleanliness. That *Polyester* was the first of Waters's movies to escape an "X" rating is not accidental: the movie is very much about the relation of bourgeois respectability to the gutter. (An abortive ad campaign for a videocassette collection of Waters's films was to read: "Let's get trash back into the home where it belongs.") *Serial Mom* suggests just how rigorously middle-class culture polices the circulation of trash. Beverly Sutphin (Kathleen Turner) murders a neighbor for failing to recycle her domestic waste, and the family-value protestors who picket the Fishpaw house carry placards that read "We hate filth." Francine has both too much and too little cultural capital to traffic in trash: too much not to recognize that mass-produced garden ornaments are considered déclassé (as Cuddles, Francine's nouveau riche friend, might say); and too little to be able to transform trash into High Art. Pink flamingos originated in Leominster, Massachusetts, the self-styled "Plastic Capital of the World," in 1957; although designed by a sculptor, Don Featherstone, they were fabricated using injection mold technology. A bird of hammered gold bears the reassuring marks of the artist's craft, and its uniqueness, real or imagined, gestures toward the museum. Plastic flamingos are indistinguishable one from another; unlike wood or stone, which must be carved or "hammered," plastic can be molded and cast into an endless number of identical objects.[34] (Hegel considered the aristocratic art of sculpting superior to the plebian practice of casting.) Francine's French-provincial furniture is doubtless mass produced as well, but unlike injection mold technology, it labors to maintain the illusion of craftsmanship. When asked about his choice of pink flamingos for a title—the birds do not figure prominently in the movie—Waters noted that his childhood home in suburban Maryland was innocent of them. His mother, the president of a local gardening club, banished the ornaments, which flourished only in the working-class neighborhoods of Baltimore. *Pink Flamingos* introduces the birds—metaphorically if not literally—into newer, swankier habitats.

William Burroughs (who should know) termed Waters the "Pope of Trash"; he has been variously celebrated as the "Baron of Bad Taste" and the "Godfather of Gross." *Variety* characterized *Pink Flamingos* as "one of the most vile, stupid, and repulsive films ever made"; Richard Harrington credits Waters with setting "standards of poor taste that few filmmakers have ever managed to lower";

and Waters himself characterized *Pink Flamingos* as "an exercise in bad taste."[35] The latter is a boast: for those in possession of sufficient cultural capital, bad taste makes for High Art. *Pink Flamingos* was included in the Museum of Modern Art's Bicentennial Salute to American Film Comedy, and the original *Variety* notice now figures prominently on the twenty-fifth anniversary poster for the re-released film:

> Nothing is more distinctive, more distinguished, than the capacity to confer aesthetic status on objects that are banal or even "common" (because the common people make them their own, especially for aesthetic purposes), or the ability to apply the principles of a "pure" aesthetic to the most everyday choices of everyday life, e.g. in cooking, clothing, or decoration, completely reversing the popular disposition which annexes aesthetics to ethics.[36]

Waters distinguishes himself by conferring aesthetic value on a "disgraced" material, a common object that working people make "their own, especially for aesthetic purposes." (Gay men made pink flamingos their own, especially for camp purposes.)[37] The conspicuous display of bad taste is intended to shock the good bourgeoisie—those who come to *Pink Flamingos* from *Hairspray* tend to be particularly discombobulated—but it in no way challenges the class determinates of taste itself. Even the "Pope of Trash" has his standards:

> To me, bad taste is what entertainment is all about. If someone vomits watching one of my films, it's like getting a standing ovation. But one must remember that there is such a thing as good bad taste and bad bad taste.[38]

Good bad taste displays a plastic pink flamingo with the requisite irony and wit, with the immense cultural capital of a John Waters; bad bad taste does so straight. "To understand bad taste," Waters cautions, "one must have very good taste," which reduces good bad taste to a simple refinement on garden-variety good taste.[39] The argument seems to me uncharacteristically normalizing; happily, however, the "Pope of Trash" does not always practice what he preaches.

Francine's two love interests in *Polyester* are both associated with film: the husband who dumps her is a porn king, the owner of the Charles Art Theater; Todd Tomorrow, the false lover who temporarily comforts her, owns the Edmondson Drive-In Cinema, which shows only first-run, fine-art films. (A bewildered Francine reads *Cahiers du Cinéma* at intermission.) A plastic pink flamingo in a gay urban ghetto registers differently from the same bird in a trailer park in Idaho; a midnight showing of *Pink Flamingos* at the Roxy registers differently from a screening at the Museum of Modern Art. Aesthetic value is inextricably bound to the material conditions and context of aesthetic consumption, but both the cinematic venues in *Polyester* are wildly inappropriate. Porn in the palace of art; a Marguerite Duras retrospective in a drive-in: Waters plays havoc with the power of material context to negotiate between good and bad taste, to translate bad bad taste into good bad taste, to maintain the distinction between high culture and low. Waters defines his aesthetic in terms of the somatic responses it induces: "If someone vomits while watching one of my films, it's like getting a standing ovation." The proprietors of the Charles Art Theater and Edmondson Drive-In Cinema are equally invested in the production of perverse somatic affects.

Schopenhauer condemns the representation of food in Dutch painting as altogether too natural:

> Painted fruit is yet admissible for it exhibits itself as a further development of the flower, and as a beautiful product of nature through form and colour, without our positively being forced to think of its edibility, but unfortunately we often find, depicted with deceptive naturalness, prepared and served-up dishes, oysters, herrings, crabs . . . and so on, all of which is wholly objectionable.[40]

Schopenhauer fears that art will transform us all into what Joseph Litvak, following Proust, terms "strange gourmets," connoisseurs of counternatural natural delicacies.[41] As in Kant, painted flowers (and their logical extension, painted fruit) can be admitted to the realm of representation, for flowers are "free, independent beauties," unrelated to the faculty of desire. Aesthetic contemplation can thus remain "disinterested," readily distinguished from responses "pathologically conditioned." Serve up the beautiful products of nature as prepared dishes, however, and a taste for the aesthetic threatens to degenerate into the merely culinary. Waters cops to a perverse fondness for cinematic venues that prohibit food: "I like really snotty, elitist theaters in New York like Cinema III (my favorite because it's so comfortable and the ticket price is always expensive), or the Paris theater where if you ask for popcorn they look at you as if you're a leper asking for heroin and sneer, 'Really! We don't have refreshments!'"[42] For the snotty, there are rather rigid, if largely unspoken, rules that govern the proper relation between eating and art.[43] A tub of popcorn and a large soda will do at a drive-in; a Marguerite Dumas retrospective requires something on the order of a low-fat latte and a pistachio biscotto. But the question thus arises: what is the appropriate "refreshment" at a John Waters film?

Waters himself provides a possible answer:

> The one film that influenced me more than any other is the "Visit Our Concession Stand" ad that drive-ins invariably show between features. The production values on this standard short featuring the all-American family happily munching monstrous meat ball sandwiches, overpriced tubs of popcorn, and disgusting warmed-up hamburgers varies from city to city, but you can always count on a certain ridiculous cheapness in the look of the film, no matter where you are. All my life I've tried to capture this magnificent sleaziness in my own productions but always feel I've come up short when I compare my work with other "Eat Our Meatball Sub" ads.[44]

We eat what we behold, and what we behold, in all its magnificent sleaziness, is an all-American family happily munching on monstrous meatball sandwiches. Freud begins *Three Essays on the Theory of Sexuality* by insisting that sexuality is not a "response to a natural need whose paradigm is hunger"; the sexual drive (*Trieb*) is not in fact an instinct (*Instinkt*). Were the analogy compelling, sexual maturation would be "a behavioral sequence narrowly determined by its 'source,' with a fixed and quite precise 'object,' since sexuality would focus uniquely and in a manner predetermined for all time on the other sex."[45] Waters does Freud one better: eating under consumer capitalism hardly qualifies as instinctual, at least for the privileged few. Monstrous meatball sandwiches and disgusting warmed-up hamburgers answer to no "natural need." Eugenie Brinkema argues that "criticism errs in taking gastronomy's interest in good taste as self-evident; on the contrary, that which tastes good and is in good taste in both gastronomy and aesthetics is constituted around a negative in the form of a revolt against taste, a cultivated decay that appends a 'dis-' to the gustatory."[46] Waters concurs. Far from satisfying the body's naturally given imperatives—whatever they might be—a "Visit Our Concession Stand" aesthetic delights in violating, or inducing us to violate, the conventionality of the disgust barriers that police what goes in and out of the mouth.

Polyester gives us a version of this counternatural culinary aesthetic, albeit in the unlikely context of Todd Tomorrow's first-run, fine art, drive-in theater. Here the "Visit Our Concession Stand" film features oysters, beluga caviar, and vintage champagne. Both the Edmondson Drive-In, which screens only fine art films, and the Charles Art Theater, which shows only porn, produce perverse somatic effects: eating oysters and jerking off respectively. And the one, Waters insists, is every bit as perverse as the other. In *Ulysses*, Leopold Bloom speculates on how we first came to engage in the former:

> All the odd things people pick up for food. Out of shells, periwinkles with a pin, off trees, snails out of the ground the French eat. . . . Yes but what about oysters? Unsightly like a clot of phlegm. Filthy shells. Devil to open them too. Who found them out? Garbage, sewage they feed on.[47]

Waters's answer is simple: we found them out by first seeing them in "Visit Our Concession Stand" ads in first-run, fine art, drive-in theaters. Disgust is no guard against an acquired taste for counternatural

natural objects, an oxymoron that implicitly concedes the impossibility of ever distinguishing the Body Natural from the Body Plastic. The Divine of *Pink Flamingos* eats dog shit; the Divine of *Polyester* eats "unsightly clots of phlegm"; and for Waters, it is six of one, half a dozen of another. In Stanley Kubrick's *Spartacus* (1960), eating shellfish is both a prelude to, and an adumbration of, "authentic" sex (assuming, of course, that gay sex is ever acknowledged as "authentic"). In *Polyester,* eating oysters is a perversion sufficient unto itself.[48] Eating and drinking does not lead to (perverse) sex; (perverse) sex does not lead to eating and drinking; perversion is not a phase in a behavioral sequence narrowly defined by its source and with a fixed and quite precise telos.

Freud argues that we have come to think of ourselves as prosthetic gods:

> Long ago man formed an ideal conception of omnipotence and omniscience which he embodied in his gods. To these gods he attributed everything that seemed unattainable to his wishes, or that was forbidden to him. One may say, therefore, that these gods were cultural ideals. Today he has come very close to the attainment of this ideal, he has almost become a god himself. . . .
>
> Man has, as it were, become a kind of prosthetic God. When he puts on all his auxiliary organs he is truly magnificent; but those organs have not grown on to him and they still give him much trouble at times. . . . In the interests of our investigations, we will not forget that present-day man does not feel happy in his Godlike character.[49]

Divine's "female troubles" rival those of any heroine in a Douglas Sirk weepie, but she is, by movie's end, happy in her Divinity. Francine is, after all, a Fishpaw, and Fish-paws, unlike Freud's prosthetic god, do not labor to have auxiliary organs "grown on to" or organically fused with them. Plastic prosthetics are now marketed as "lighter, stronger, and more life-like than ever before," and relatively low-cost, lower limb prosthetics are being fabricated from plastic waste.

Yet as any number of cautionary tales remind us, what is "lifelike" easily morphs into life itself: "The whole world *can* be plasticized; and even life itself since, we are told, they are beginning to make plastic aortas." Žižek argues that the problem arises when "the prosthetic is no longer experienced as such," when it 'disappears' into or 'grows on to' the Body Natural, when it becomes part of "our immediate organic experience."[50] There is, however, no such moment, no possibility of such a moment, in *Polyester.* "Odorama" allows us to participate in the preternatural keenness of the Divine nostrils, but there is no danger that scratch-and-sniff cards will "grow on to" the viewer/smeller. "Smell-O-Vision" labors to replicate the "natural" conditions of olfactory perception. Odors are released through the theater's ventilation system, which mysteriously envelope the moviegoer; like 3-D glasses, the gimmick promotes illusionistic immersion in the sensuous immediacy and plenitude of the screen. In *Polyester,* however, the introduction of the overtly prosthetic merely exposes the body as "always already" prosthetic, both the Divine body up there on the silver screen and the body sitting down there in the darkened auditorium.

Laura Marks argues that *Polyester* privileges synthetic or "symbolic" smells:

> Smells can . . . defy their embodied nature and become symbolic. It's interesting that the smells that have been used successfully in movies, such as John Waters's *Polyester,* are synthetic smells—new car smell, air freshener. These smells may be understood as symbolic scents, the way certain sounds such as car alarms, are symbolic sounds. In perception they bypass Pierce's Firstness, the raw experience, and Secondness, the jolt of recognition, and leap to Thirdness, the symbolic. We experience them in conventional ways.[51]

This is not strictly accurate: odorama includes the synthetic, but it also features smells taken "out of nature"—roses, flatulence, skunk, and the like.[52] Pierce's "Firstness" presupposes an intensity and immediacy of sensory experience that purportedly eludes ideological determination. But as George Orwell insists, the ideological is never more efficacious than when it insinuates itself in and as "raw experience":

> [Smell is] the real secret of class distinction in the West . . . the real reason why a European of bourgeois upbringing, even when he calls himself a communist, cannot without a hard effort think of a working man as his equal. It is summed up by four frightful words, that people are now chary of uttering, but which were bandied about quite freely in my own childhood. Those words were: the lower classes smell.

Our culture looks down its nose at the nose—the olfactory is routinely demonized as the lowest sensory modality—but there is paradoxically (or consequently?) no appeal from its judgements:

> No feeling of like or dislike is quite so fundamental as a physical feeling. Race-hatred, religious-hatred, differences of education, of temperament, of intellect, even differences of moral code, can be got over; but physical repulsion cannot. You can have an affection for a murder or a sodomite, but you cannot have an affection for a man whose breath stinks—habitually stinks, I mean.[53]

A liberalism of affection that can embrace, willy-nilly, murderers and sodomites might seem infinitely capacious, but it balks at the prospect of habitual halitosis. Consciously held race hatred and the like are at least theoretically amenable to rational correction. Insinuate that hatred as "prereflective" somatic experience, however, and its authority is unimpeachable.

Nietzsche locates his genius in his nose: "I perceive physiologically—*smell*—the proximity or—what am I saying?—the innermost parts, the entrails, of every soul."[54] The contention that smell is somehow revelatory of the internal essence of persons and things has any number of classical precedents, but a hermeneutics of the nose is rare in the modern world. Nordau insists that this is as it should be. The "underdeveloped or insufficiently developed senses help the brain little or not at all to know and understand the world," and the few olfactory metaphors for cognition that we do possess—"I smell a rat"; "She came out of it smelling like a rose"—tend to imply a failure of scopic intelligibility.[55] Freud's prosthetic god seeks "omnipotence and omniscience," and Divine does in fact sniff out a number of suburban secrets and scandals. But power-knowledge was never her ambition. A psychoanalytically inflected criticism necessarily "views" smell as symptomatic, diagnostic. Havelock Ellis argues that "the perfume exhaled by many holy men and women . . . was doubtless due . . . to abnormal nervous conditions, for it is well known that such conditions affect the odor, and in insanity, for instance, the presence is noted of bodily odors which have sometimes been considered of diagnostic importance."[56] Ellis reduces the somatic to the symptomatic, but even if smell were helpful in understanding the world, Waters has no investment in promoting a hermeneutics of the nose. A psychoanalytic reading would prove relevant to *Polyester* only if it were to follow Lacan in abandoning the notion of the "symptomatic" altogether: *sinthome,* the archaic term that Lacan substitutes for classical Freudian symptomology, transforms a decipherable message that is "structured like a language" into an experience beyond analysis, a kernel of enjoyment that is immune to the efficacy of the Symbolic. An olfactory orgasm occasioned by new car smell is nothing more—or nothing less—than the smelling of a smell, a charmingly kinky organization of the subject's jouissance. And as *sinthome* is also synth-homme, artificial or plastic man, and saint-homme, holy man, the Lacanian term for an eroticism beyond biology or "Firstness," beyond repression or sublimation, means, in effect, Divine in *Polyester.*

NOTES

1. John Wycliffe, *Select Works of John Wycliffe,* ed. T. Arnold, Vol. 1 (Oxford: Clarendon, 1869), 107–8.
2. John Berger, *Ways of Seeing* (London: Penguin, 1977), 51; Laura Mulvey, "Visual Pleasure and Narrative Cinema," in *The Sexual Subject: A Screen Reader in Sexuality* (New York: Routledge, 1992), 27. The scene alludes to "the boudoirs, bedside tables, and ornate mirrored vanities of Sirk's *All that Heaven Allows* and *Written on the Wind,*" as well as "the languorous wandering" of a

negligee-clad Elizabeth Taylor in the opening moments of *Butterfield 8*. See Elana Gorfinkel, "*Polyester:* The Perils of Francine," https://www.criterion.com/current/posts/6590-polyester-the-perils-of-francine (September 17, 2019).

3. Walter Benjamin, "The Work of Art in the Age of Mechanical Reproduction," in *Illuminations*, ed. Hannah Arendt, trans. Harry Zohn (New York: Schoken, 1969), 222. Benjamin was profoundly influenced by Marx's insistence on the historicity of sensory perception.
4. Max Nordau, *Degeneration* (New York: D. Appleton, 1898), 503.
5. Amanda Boetzkes, *Plastic Capitalism: Contemporary Art and the Drive to Waste* (Cambridge: MIT Press, 2019), 201.
6. Georg Wilhelm Friedrich Hegel, *Introductory Lectures on Aesthetics*, trans. Bernard Bosanquet (Harmondsworth, UK: Penguin, 1993), 23. Kant distinguishes between the three "objective" senses, which contribute to cognition, and the two "subjective" senses, which do not.
7. F. Scott Fitzgerald, *The Beautiful and the Damned* (New York: Macmillan, 1922), 398.
8. Max Horkheimer and Theodor W. Adorno, *Dialectic of Enlightenment*, trans. John Cumming (New York: Continuum, 1993), 184.
9. Siegfried Kracauer, *Theory of Film: The Redemption of Physical Reality* (New York: Oxford University Press, 1965).
10. Andre Bazin, *Orson Welles* (New York: Harper & Row, 1978), 80.
11. Roland Barthes, "Plastic," in *Mythologies*, trans. Annette Lavers (New York: Noonday Press, 1992), 98. Boetzkes, *Plastic Capitalism*,185.
12. Stephen Fenichell, *Plastic: The Making of a Synthetic Century* (New York: Harper, 1966), 9.
13. William Butler Yeats, "Sailing to Byzantium," in *The Collected Poems of William Butler Yeats* (London: Macmillan, 1981), 218.
14. Fenichell, *Plastic*, 259.
15. The suit was brought out in honor of the fiftieth anniversary of the moon landing.
16. As the *Times* quite sensibly noted, "No man can play billiards with any real satisfaction if he knows that his billiard balls may explode." As quoted in Fenichell, *Plastic*, 47.
17. See Boetzkes's reading of the advertisement for the multinational banking conglomerate HSBC: "In the future, there will be no difference between waste and energy." Boetzkes, *Plastic Capitalism*, 202–3.
18. Barthes, "Plastic," 99.
19. Charles Darwin, *The Descent of Man, and Selection in Relation to Sex* (New York: D. Appleton, 1898), 17–18. Freud argues that it is man's world historical erection that facilitates the transition from smell to sight: "The diminution of olfactory stimuli seems itself to be a consequence of man's raising himself from the ground, of his assumption of an upright gait; this made his geni-

tals, which were previously concealed, visible and in need of protection, and so provoked feelings of shame in him." Sigmund Freud, *Civilization and Its Discontents,* in *The Standard Edition of the Complete Psychological Works of Sigmund Freud,* trans. James Strachey (London: Hogarth, 1953–1974), 21: 99–100, 1n.

20. Horkheimer and Adorno, *Dialectic of Enlightenment,* 184.
21. Constant Classen, David Howes, and Anthony Synnott, *Aroma: The Cultural History of Smell* (New York: Routledge, 1994), 96.
22. Michael Moon and Eve Sedgwick, "Divinity: A Dossier," in Eve Kosofsky Sedgwick, *Tendencies* (Durham, N.C.: Duke University Press, 1993), 245.
23. On Freud and the invention of the vaginal orgasm, see Thomas Lacquer, *Making Sex: Body and Gender from the Greeks to Freud* (Cambridge, Mass.: Harvard University Press, 1990), 236–37.
24. Freud, *The Interpretation of Dreams,* 5:387. Magnus Hirschfeld, *Sexual Pathology: A Study of the Derangement of the Sexual Instinct,* rev. ed., trans. J. Gibbs (New York: Emerson, 1940), 73.
25. The "lesbian dildo debates" hinge on this very issue: if dildos are in fact ersatz penises, are they compatible with a "woman-identified" sexuality? See Heather Findlay, "Freud's 'Fetishism' and the Lesbian Dildo Debates," *Feminist Studies* 18, no. 3 (Autumn 1992): 563–79.
26. Michel Foucault, *The History of Sexuality: An Introduction,* trans. Robert Hurley (New York: Vintage, 1990), 71.
27. Horace, *Horace on the Art of Poetry,* ed. Edward Henry Blakeney (London: Scholartis, 1928), 41.
28. William Ian Miller, *The Anatomy of Disgust* (Cambridge, Mass.: Harvard University Press, 1997), 95.
29. Foucault, *History of Sexuality,* 60.
30. Jeffrey L. Meikle, *American Plastic: A Cultural History* (New Brunswick, N.J.: Rutgers University Press, 1995), 115.
31. Susan Bordo, *Unbearable Weight: Feminism, Western Culture, and the Body* (Berkeley: University of California Press, 1993), 277–300.
32. Fenichell, *Plastic,* 5.
33. On Waters and the "unruly" female body, see Dana Heller, *Hairspray* (Chichester, UK: Wiley-Blackwell, 2011), 49–79.
34. Fenichell, *Plastic,* 33.
35. John Waters, *Shock Value: A Tasteful Book about Bad Taste* (New York: Delta, 1981), viii; Richard Harrington, "Revenge of the Gross-Out King! John Waters's *Pink Flamingos* Enjoys a 25th Year Revival," *Washington Post* (Sunday, April 6, 1997).
36. See Pierre Bourdieu, *Distinction: A Social Critique of the Judgement of Taste,* trans. Richard Nice (Cambridge, Mass.: Harvard University Press, 1984), 260–67.
37. Barthes terms plastic a "disgraced" material: "In the hierarchy of the major

poetic substances, it [plastic] figures as a disgraced material"; Barthes, "Plastic," 98. The issue of gay cultural capital is obviously central to Waters's aesthetic.

38. Waters, *Shock Value,* 2.
39. Waters, *Shock Value,* 2.
40. Arthur Schopenhauer, *The World as Will and Representation,* Vol. 1, trans. E. F. J. Payne (New York: Dover, 1966), 208.
41. Joseph Litvak, *Strange Gourmets: Sophistication, Theory, and the Novel* (Durham, N.C.: Duke University Press, 1997).
42. John Waters, *Crackpot: The Obsessions of John Waters* (New York: Vintage, 1987), 108.
43. Scott Eyman notes that concession stands became commonplace in movie theaters during the Great Depression: "With the Depression came the realization that a simple stand manned by a high school student could produce hundreds of dollars of pure profit even in a bad week. Even if the viewer was distracted by noisy foods like popcorn or the rustling of candy wrappers, a movie's sound track would keep the viewer from getting lost. By 1936, sales of food in movie theaters would top $10 million." Scott Eyman, *The Speed of Sound: Hollywood and the Talkie Revolution, 1926–30* (Baltimore, Md.: Johns Hopkins University Press, 1997), 368–69.
44. Waters, *Shock Value,* 192.
45. Freud, *Three Essays on the Theory of Sexuality,* 1; see also Jean Laplanche, *Life and Death in Psychoanalysis,* trans. Jeffrey Mehlman (Baltimore, Md.: Johns Hopkins University Press, 1976), 14.
46. Eugenie Brinkema, *The Forms of the Affects* (Durham, N.C.: Duke University Press, 2014), 154–55.
47. James Joyce, *Ulysses,* ed. Hans Walter Gabler (New York: Vintage, 1986), 143.
48. The famous "Do you eat oysters?" scene in Stanley Kubrick's *Spartacus* (1960) initially fell victim to the censors. It has been restored, but with Anthony Hopkins, rather than Laurence Olivier, voicing the role of Crassus:

    CRASSUS: Do you eat oysters?

    ANTONIUS: When I have them, master.

    CRASSUS: Do you eat snails?

    ANTONIUS: No, master.

    CRASSUS: Do you consider the eating of oysters to be moral, and the eating of snails to be immoral?

    ANTONIUS: No, Master.

    CRASSUS: Of course not. It is all a matter of taste, isn't it?

    ANTONIUS: Yes, master.

    CRASSUS: And taste is not the same as appetite. . . .

    Were Crassus not trying to seduce Antonius (Tony Curtis), he might almost be taken for a Kantian: "Taste is not the same as appetite." The censors suggested substituting "artichokes and truffles" for "oysters and snails."

49. Sigmund Freud, *Civilization and Its Discontents* (New York: Norton, 1961), 39.
50. Slavoj Žižek, *Absolute Recoil: Towards a New Formulation of Dialectical Materialism* (New York: Verso, 2014), 279.
51. Laura U. Marks, *Touch: Sensory Theory and Multisensory Media* (Minneapolis: University of Minnesota Press, 2002), 124.
52. The smells, which correspond to numbers on the odorama card, are as follows: roses, flatulence, model-building glue, pizza, gasoline, skunk, natural gas, new car smell, smelly shoes, and air freshener.
53. George Orwell, *The Road to Wigan Pier* (London: Secker & Warburg, 1959), 115–16.
54. Friedrich Nietzsche, *Ecce Homo,* trans. R. J. Hollingdale (New York: Penguin, 1979), 126.
55. Max Nordau, *Degeneration* (New York: D. Appleton, 1898), 503.
56. Havelock Ellis, *Studies in the Psychology of Sex,* Vol. 1 (New York: Random House, 1942), 62.

3

The Album Era

Loren Glass

In the early aughts I took all my CDs out of their jewel boxes, downloaded their contents onto an external hard drive, and slipped them into a series of binders, in which they continue to sit idle. The entire time-consuming enterprise ended up being a wash, since the byzantine complexities of intellectual property law in the digital age prevented me from playing much of the music on iTunes. For the next few years I subscribed to start-up streaming services, relying on their opaque algorithms to help me make selections from their seemingly infinite field of musical choices. But I began to sense an absence in my listening life. Not only did I miss the material object, the compact disc that I now see as an ersatz echo of the long-playing albums I grew up with, but also, and more distressingly, my entire listening repertoire had been disrupted. I began to have trouble deciding when to listen to music and for how long; indeed, I no longer knew what to listen to nor how music fit into the larger media ecology of my cultural interests.

In other words, I became aware of the historical significance of the long-playing album through its absence, through a belated realization that the era of its cultural dominance was over. But when did it end? And when did it begin? How should one go about periodizing an era based on the prominence of a particular plastic format for storing and listening to music? The long-playing record (LP) simultaneously marks a period in time and an experience of time. It habituates us to certain forms of temporally delimited multisensory experience that in turn determine our retrospective relationship to the period in which the material it stores was produced. A theory of the Album Era cannot just demarcate a period in history but must engage the very nature of history itself as a way of organizing our experience of time.

We can begin with the point, so to speak, on which these questions converge: the point where the needle hits the groove, that microscopic material link across time and space that transmits the sound on the record to the ear of the listener. This link, wherein the contours of the groove re-present in the semipermanence of plastic the otherwise ephemeral shape of the sounds we hear, embodies the idea of analog media. Vinyl, the synthetic plastic polymer of which records have been made since the 1940s, retrospectively has come to determine what we mean when we distinguish analog from digital technologies of sound reproduction, and therefore how we conceptualize the historical shift from the analog to the digital age. As a storage medium, vinyl combines analog continuity with indexical contiguity, thereby creating an overdetermined material connection between past and present. In its transference of sound to signal to groove to needle to signal to sound, vinyl enables an emotionally charged and epistemologically fetishized relationship between moments of production and reception. It enables, in other words, a particularly personal relationship to a specific past, an intimate entanglement between private memory and public history.

The circuit only seems seamless. The transmission of sound to and from the groove on the disk has been interrupted by other more attenuated and editable media since the 1920s, when electronic means of amplification and transduction were introduced into the process of sound recording and transmission. Then in the thirties magnetic tape revolutionized the recording process, and it was only after the final product was approved that it would be pressed onto vinyl. Finally, after World War II, AM and then FM radio were crucial to disseminating and popularizing the music that listeners would purchase on records. But vinyl differs from all of these surrounding media in its material fixity and durability. Unlike magnetic tape, which can be edited, altered, and erased, vinyl is durably fixed in the form we receive it, emphatically cementing it to the time in which it was made. The most stable and permanent storage medium for recorded sound, vinyl has come to epitomize a fixed analog form in the frantically fluid media ecology of the digital era.

Its cultural and economic dominance of the music industry was relatively brief. As Dominick Bartmanksi and Ian Woodward affirm in their analysis of vinyl's persistent appeal in the digital age, "Vinyl rose spectacularly in the mid-1950s only to quite abruptly exit the mainstream in the mid-1980s." And, in further refining this periodization they add, "The productive reciprocal feedbacks between new music now widely accessible on records and the collective social effervescence of the 1960s gradually made vinyl a kind of 'charismatic' cultural object that spliced new aesthetic sensibilities with a nearly revolutionary political awakening."[1] The Album Era, in other words, coincides with one of the great cultural and political watersheds in modern world history, compelling us to think of it in terms of larger issues of social change, historical transformation, and collective memory. I propose that we visualize it in the form of a long-playing record, a sort of spiraling vortex of history whose center hole sits circa 1970 and whose grooves circle outward into the past and the future (Figure 3.1).

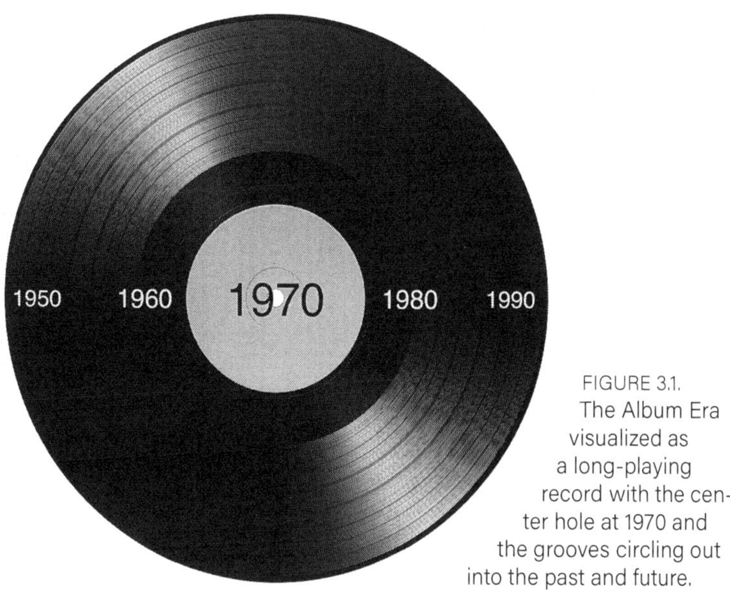

FIGURE 3.1. The Album Era visualized as a long-playing record with the center hole at 1970 and the grooves circling out into the past and future.

As this figure indicates, the period can be broken down into more discrete increments and, in the spirit of the chronological specificity so highly valued by record collectors, we can pinpoint its inception: June 21, 1948, when Columbia Records held a press conference at New York's Waldorf Astoria Hotel to announce its new 12" 33⅓ rpm long-playing microgroove record made of Vinylite, a lightweight synthetic polymer that promised long-lasting, high-fidelity sound reproduction.[2] The format was designed for classical music, particularly symphonies and operas whose length far exceeded the capacity of the prewar platters made of brittle shellac. But it rapidly became popular for Broadway musicals and movie soundtracks as well, since the length of time delimited by the format accommodated the length of these genres in their original presentations. These genres, unlike rock and roll, were natural fits for the long-playing record. Such bestselling albums enabled listeners to experience the live shows they couldn't afford to attend in person, a vicarious pleasure that would become central to the marketing of albums more generally.

Columbia also innovated their packaging for this new format, under the transformational leadership of Alex Steinweiss, unanimously heralded as the inventor of the modern album cover. Before he arrived at Columbia as art director in 1939, the term *album* referred to sets of 78s packaged like thick pages in a book; cover art was an informational afterthought. When he returned to Columbia as a freelancer after the war, he established the basic design of the new covers for Columbia's LPs: a cardboard sleeve with pasted-on artwork on the front and liner notes on the back. It quickly became the industry standard. Trained by the revolutionary poster designer Joseph Binder at Parsons, Steinweiss brought a modernist sensibility of innovation and experimentation to record cover design that would become integral to the multifarious idea of the "concept" album.

The LP rapidly diversified in genre over the course of the 1950s, as jazz musicians and vocalists began to adopt it for the temporal latitude it enabled over and against the two- to three-minute radio-friendly single associated with rock and roll. Trailblazers such as Frank Sinatra and Miles Davis began to work with their producers to conceptually coordinate album tracks in terms of both sequence and sound, and their labels began to commission visual artists to design aesthetically appealing covers that contributed to this conceptual coordination. It is at this formative moment that the crucial cultural and economic distinction between the single and the long-playing record comes into being, as an index of the difference between adolescence and adulthood. As Richard Osborne affirms, the album format enabled jazz "to adopt the long-playing characteristics of seriousness, adulthood, and non-commerciality."[3] This contrast, between the 7" 45 rpm single as a cheap commercialized product marketed to adolescents and the 12" 33⅓ rpm album as an expensive and mature work of art for adults, provides one of the primary markers of the inception of the Album Era, as well as our individual experience and recollection of it. As we will see, it is a marker that maps the individual lives of the era's pioneers onto the larger transformations in the industry.

This thumbnail history establishes the general "when" of the Album Era, but how do we answer the specific "what"? Which albums should we discuss and why? While such choices will inevitably (and symptomatically) be subjective, there is nonetheless a critical consensus establishing a canon from which we are compelled to choose. Tens of thousands of LPs were produced during this period, but the vast majority of them consisted simply of songs thrown together, frequently in haste by record labels to capitalize on hit singles. The contingent requirements of the format relative to the standard length of the popular song meant that only a relatively small number of LPs were successfully conceived and produced *as such* and only a handful of these in turn achieved any lasting critical consecration. And, conveniently, a magazine was launched at the height of the era that was instrumental in appraising and affirming the historical significance of these LPs, both contemporaneously and in retrospect. Since popular and critical acclaim are the logical criteria here, it seems reasonable to use the *Rolling Stone* 500 Greatest Albums of All Time (2005) as the archive with which to work. Not surprisingly, the list maps pretty comfortably onto the historical coordinates I've been developing here.

Figure 3.2 organizes the *Rolling Stone* list by album release date, broken down into ten-year increments. Visualized in this way, the

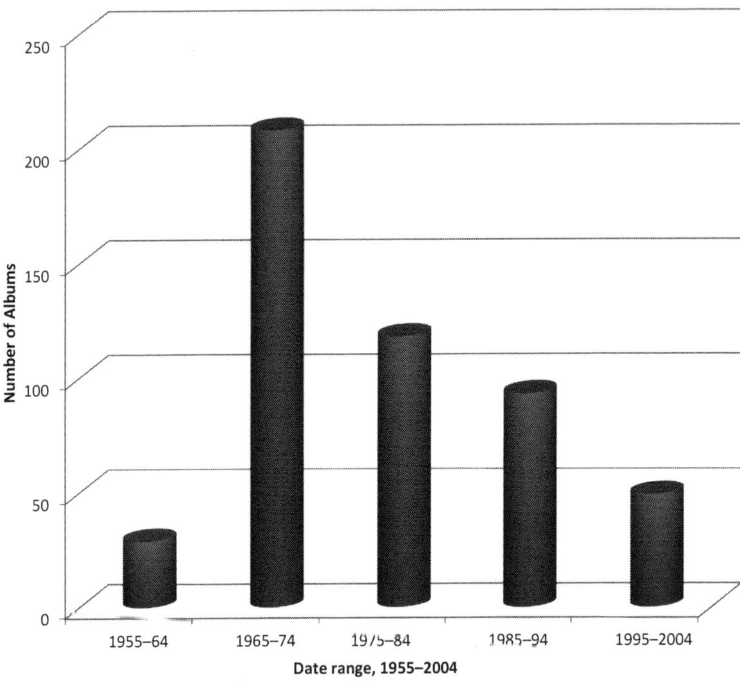

FIGURE 3.2. *Rolling Stone* 500 Greatest Albums of All Time by release date, with the peak album era represented by the second bar.

era begins in the mid-fifties (with Frank Sinatra's *In the Wee Small Hours,* an early concept album with a classic cover picture designed by Alex Steinweiss), peaks between 1965 and 1974, and then tapers off into the eighties and nineties. Not only does the era find its vortex in the late sixties and early seventies, but also the albums in the earlier period anticipate this vortex while those that follow hearken back to it. A good number of the albums on the list issued after 1975 are actually collections of classic jazz, blues, R&B, and folk artists whose music informed the styles of the albums produced during the peak period, which sparked renewed interest in them, further confirming the "vortex" structure that I am proposing here. Thus #22 is Chess Records' *The Great Twenty Eight* (1982) by Chuck Berry and #38 is Chess Records' *Muddy Waters Anthology* (2001).

The artists with the most albums on the *Rolling Stone* list—the Beatles, Bob Dylan, and the Rolling Stones—grew up listening to

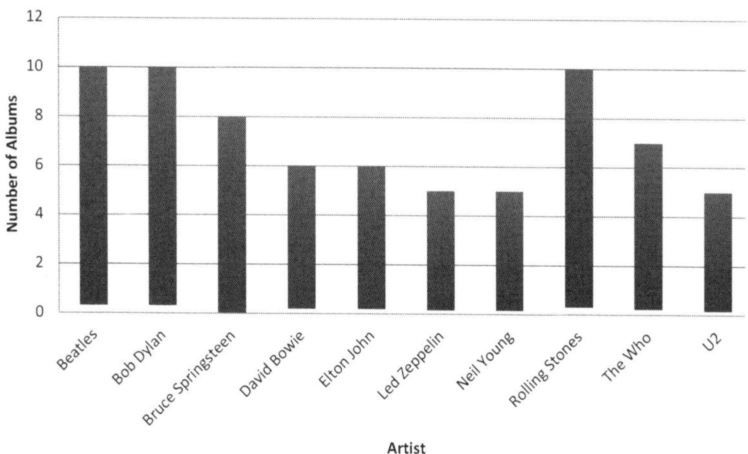

FIGURE 3.3. Artists with over five albums on the *Rolling Stone* 500 Greatest Albums of All Time list. Other than U2, their albums are concentrated in the period between 1965 and 1974.

and imitating these foundational figures, and their listed albums are concentrated around the peak period between 1965 and 1974. Of all the artists with five albums or more on the list, only U2 represents a later period (Figure 3.3). The Beatles, whose albums occupy four of the top ten positions, are a special case. They essentially established the album as the prominent format for popular music, revolutionizing the music industry. *Sgt. Pepper's Lonely Hearts Club Band* (number one on the list) stands as an inflection point in the history of recorded music. As historian Roland Gelatt avers, "After *Sgt. Pepper,* the pop record business was essentially an album business."[4] And Osborne confirms, "*Sgt. Pepper* is the record that established the pop LP as a medium in its own right. . . . The LP was now an end in itself" (109). The Beatles insisted that this album, unlike all their prior ones, be issued identically around the world, ensuring that its historical significance be experienced as a simultaneous event. It was also the first album to include printed lyrics in the liner notes, inaugurating the experience of reading (and struggling to interpret) lyrics while listening to the songs. It wasn't the first "concept" album, but it established the concept of the concept album (frequently based on the classical model of the symphony or opera) as a kind of aspirational aesthetic horizon for popular musicians, and became the benchmark to which all future concept albums, from *Dark Side of the Moon* to *It Takes a Nation of Millions,* would inevitably be compared.

Since the Beatles broke up in 1970 their discography coincides with the peak of the Album Era. And since their greatest albums were strictly studio affairs, they exist exclusively as historical artifacts. The albums they made after *Sgt. Pepper* did not function as promotion for tours, and no one has or ever will see any of them performed live by the original band. They are securely, and charismatically, situated in the era during which they were produced and released. And the Beatles themselves came of age as the era unfolded, modeling the development of a mature aesthetic sensibility in tune with the times. Indeed, most of the prominently represented artists on the *Rolling Stone* list came of age during the Album Era, and their albums document their aesthetic (and psychological) maturation in ways that deeply inform our experience of their music, regardless of whether or not our own coming-of-age coincided with theirs. The Beatles, Dylan, and the Stones (as well as The Who, Neil Young, Led Zeppelin, Elton John, and David Bowie) entered the era as "boys" and left it as "men," in the process remodeling what it meant to "grow up." The LPs they produced during this time can be understood in part as multimodal *kunstleralbums,* mapping their passages to artistic adulthood onto the larger social transformations happening around them.

And they were predominantly Anglo-American men. Rock music has been a notoriously white and male-dominated genre, and the *Rolling Stone* list amply reflects this demographic hegemony. Nevertheless, the LP format, though initially dominated by white men, also enabled artists (and critics) of difference to emerge and be acknowledged as aesthetically respected and politically empowered adult voices, stitching the Album Era into the contemporaneous rise of identity politics and the new social movements. From Aretha Franklin to Joni Mitchell to Carole King, a generation of female musicians, mostly though not exclusively vocalists, in multiple genres came of age during the Album Era, and their albums, such as *Blue* (#30), *Tapestry* (#36), and *Lady Soul* (#83) are high on the list. And from Marvin Gaye to Stevie Wonder, the same arc is evident when it comes to race, indicated by the landmark albums *What's Going On* (#6) and *Innervisions* (#24). Finally, innovative artists such as David Bowie and Elton John incorporated an aggressively (if ambiguously) queer aesthetic into their albums of the early seventies such as *The Rise and Fall of Ziggy Stardust* (#35) and *Goodbye Yellow Brick Road* (#91). Like the Beatles, these artists grew up with the times, and their albums chronicle the simultaneity of biographical and historical experience.

The sense of this simultaneity is reinforced by the uniquely multimodal nature of the LP, which comes to us not just as a piece of plastic inscribed with sound but as a multimedia package designed for the sale, consumption, and storage of this sound. The LP thus appeals to us on a variety of sensory and conceptual registers. Obviously, its aural dimensions are key, and the fantasy of indexicality enabled by the format undergirds our sense of emotional and empirical attachment to the era in which these albums were made (and the musicians who made them); but the visual and verbal elements of the label, jacket, and sleeve are of equal importance and provide crucial complements to the listening experience, both in its immediacy and in its recollection. Frequently the packaging design reinforces the aura of indexicality associated with vinyl, deploying photographs (often of band and family members, thereby invoking another meaning of the term "album") and handwritten lyrics and liner notes. The visual design of the jacket and sleeve and the verbal strategies of the liner notes frame the temporal experience of the long-playing album as well as the ways in which it gets inserted into history.

Or instead of "frame" we might say "encircle," since the shape of the record is referenced in a variety of ways by the packaging that contains it. Such references range across literal and metaphorical registers, enabling the shape to accrue a variety of significations. Robert Brownjohn's clever circular sculpture on the cover of the Rolling Stones' *Let It Bleed* (1969) literally pancakes the possibilities, from a pizza to a bicycle tire to a clock face to a film canister, all stacked up as records on a turntable; R. Crumb's famous cover for *Cheap Thrills* (1968) spirals the album credits in comic sequence around a circular center featuring a cartoon Janis Joplin dragging a ball and chain; and Daniel Kramer's edge-softened cover photo for

Bob Dylan's *Bringing It All Back Home* (1965) overlays the circular shape of the camera lens that took the photo onto the LP within. Many album covers feature headshots that metaphorically situate the contents of the album in the brain of the artist, a conceptual relationship reinforced by the indexical aura of both photo and record. Afros and Jewfros had a particular aesthetic and cultural ap-

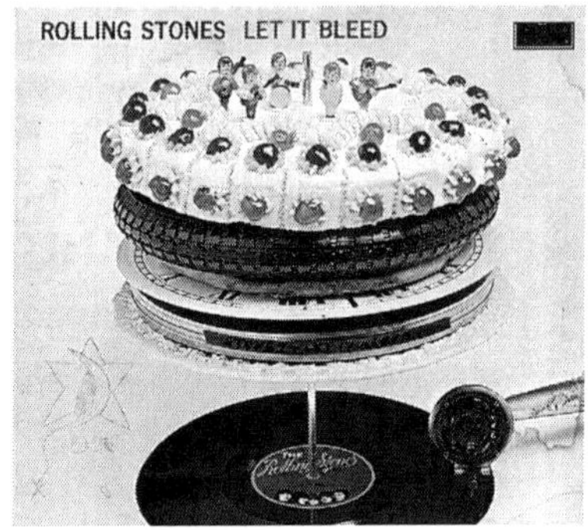

FIGURE 3.4. Rolling Stones, *Let It Bleed* (1969). Cover Design by Robert Brownjohn.

FIGURE 3.5. Big Brother and the Holding Company, *Cheap Thrills* (1968). Cover Design by Robert Crumb.

FIGURE 3.6. Bob Dylan, *Bringing It All Back Home* (1965). Photo by Daniel Kramer.

peal in this prominent genre of album cover, kicked off by Rowland Scherman's instantly iconic cover photo for *Bob Dylan's Greatest Hits* (1967) and then artfully recapitulated in Ira Friedlander's cover design for Roberta Flack's *Quiet Fire* (1971) and Esther Anderson's revolutionary cover photo for the 1974 reissue of Bob Marley's *Catch a Fire*.

FIGURE 3.7. Bob Dylan, *Bob Dylan's Greatest Hits* (1967). Photo by Rowland Scherman.

FIGURE 3.8. Robert Flack, *Quiet Fire* (1971). Cover Design by Ira Friedlander.

FIGURE 3.9. Bob Marley and the Wailers, *Catch a Fire* (1974). Photo by Esther Anderson.

Not only do album covers emphatically and repeatedly reference and trope on the circular shape of the object within, but the object within also gradually makes its presence and persistence known by the ring wear that appears on the jacket over time (Figure 3.10). Vinyl ages, and the cracks and pops we hear on used records mark the expanding temporal gap between production and reception, which is also a period of individuation, insofar as what began as a mass-produced commodity over time becomes the uniquely auratic object that we own. The LP is multiply marked by time, registering not only the date of its issue but also the passage of time since.

Many of the label trademarks reference the circular form of the album as well, increasing its ubiquity. Indeed, the labels, both major and minor, were themselves agents in establishing the relationship between time and the record, providing multiple guarantees of and instructions for the quality and preservation of the object over time. In this capacity, the labels worked to enhance the "charismatic" nature of the album as both a scientific invention and a cultural icon. The technical instructions and assurances they provide are as significant as the liner notes and the lyrics in shaping how we listen and how we remember what we heard. For example, Columbia guaranteed that its records were "scientifically designed to play with the highest quality of reproduction on the phonograph of your choice, new or old" and affirmed that you could purchase one with "no fear of its becoming obsolete in the future." Records age, but they don't die.

We can understand the label, jacket, and sleeve as examples of what Gerard Genette calls *paratexts,* "thresholds of interpretation" that condition our reception of the "text" that is the music on the record.[5] Holding the jacket in our hands as we listen, gazing at the cover art, looking at the photographs, reading the liner notes and lyrics, the meanings of what we hear are shaped by what we (frequently simultaneously) see and read. And this meaning-making process itself occurs over time, indeed over lifetimes, which is to say not only that we continue to return to and revise our understanding and appreciation of the LPs that we discovered in our adolescence, but also that we hand these down to our children, so many of whom go through a "stage" of listening to our music (usually The Beatles) before moving on to their own contemporaneous tastes.

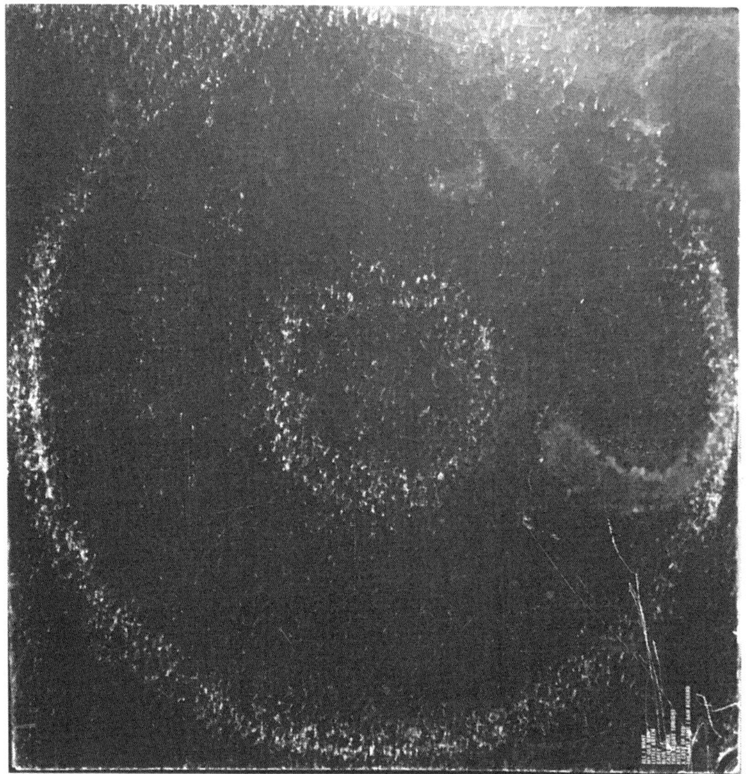

FIGURE 3.10. Ring wear on the record jacket marks the passage of time.

The meaning we make of the albums we hear is also conditioned by the critics we read. To continue with Genette's useful terminology, if the jacket, sleeve, and label are the "peritexts" that are materially linked to the music, rock criticism is the "epitext" that circulates autonomously in the wider public sphere, further shaping our personal and historical interpretation of the albums we cherish. As Devon Powers affirms in her important study *Writing the Record,* the pioneering rock critics of the sixties "made it possible to take popular music seriously and to mine it as a repository of ideas."[6] Groundbreaking critics such as Ellen Willis, Richard Goldstein, and Robert Christgau not only established that popular music could be taken seriously as art, they also innovated the literary language that would be used to evaluate and understand that music aesthetically and culturally. And LPs were the primary object of their critical discourse. This first generation of rock critics came of age alongside the musicians whose records they reviewed, further reinforcing the overlay of (auto)biographical and historical experience that informs my theory of the Album Era.

"It was twenty years ago today." It is fitting that the album everyone agrees epitomizes the era should anticipate in the opening lines of the opening song the nostalgia that would be mobilized to remember it. Innovative as it was, *Sgt. Pepper* is also a mashup of older musical styles and modes, and as the Album Era recedes into the past nostalgia emerges as the dominant affect in recollecting, both literally and figuratively, the records produced during it. This affective circuit is amply illustrated by Bloomsbury's popular 33⅓ series, each volume of which features a single critic writing about a single album of their choosing. Not surprisingly, they frequently begin with nostalgic anecdotes. Erik Davis's volume on *Led Zeppelin IV* (2005) opens with a "nostalgic lark on a dull journey" as he sticks the cassette into his car stereo and melts "into a profound and adolescent reverie" (2–3). Jonathan Lethem chooses to begin his volume on *Fear of Music* (2012) by invoking his fifteen-year-old self hearing the famous ad for the album on the radio in his bedroom (viii–xiv). Kevin Dettmar directly references Lethem's introduction in his study of Gang of Four's *Entertainment* (2014), claiming that in his case "it was the boy in his studio apartment, and he'd just turned 21" (2). Joe Bonomo's volume on *Highway to Hell* (2010) begins with a group of thirteen-year-old boys on a playground listening in rapt attention to a schoolmate who'd just met Bon Scott (1–2). The title of the introduction to John Dougan's volume on *The Who Sell Out* (2006) is "I'm a Boy" (3). And Sean Nelson's study of *Court and Spark* (2007) opens with the memory of when he first heard Joni Mitchell's voice as his mother sang along to "Help Me" on the car radio (1–4).[7]

Until I read Nelson's book, I thought I had a unique hook for my own volume on Carole King's *Tapestry* (1971), but I now realize that my anecdote of first hearing my mother's copy is something of a cliché. Nevertheless, in its felicitous collision of personal and social history, it conveniently illustrates my thesis. My mother left my father, came out as a lesbian, and joined the Women's Liberation movement in the year *Tapestry* was released; I was seven years old.

Like so many women of her generation, my mom listened to *Tapestry* often, and it comprises a key component of the soundtrack to my childhood. I still have her ring-worn copy: it is one of my earliest autobiographical insertion points into the Album Era.

And *Tapestry* conveniently encapsulates the transition from adolescent rock and roll to adult-oriented rock. It was a declaration of independence for Carole King, marking her break from the lucrative and already legendary collaboration she had with her ex-husband Gerry Goffin and the Brill Building assembly-line songwriting system in which they worked in the early sixties; but it also includes two songs that were products of that collaboration—"Will You Love Me Tomorrow" and "(You Make Me Feel Like) A Natural Woman"—hearkening back to her earlier career as one half of a successful songwriting team for Aldon music where she and Goffin wrote a string of hits for other artists, all of which were singles geared toward AM radio and the lucrative teen market.

Tapestry was released on February 10, 1971, at the height of the Album Era. Its iconic gatefold cover, with Jim McCrary's classic photo of the calmly confident and casually barefoot singer-songwriter comfortably seated with her tapestry in her lap and her cat on a pillow in the window seat of her Laurel Canyon home, provides a perfect visual and verbal complement to the songs, whose lyrics are featured on the back. Countless fans—of all genders and ages and ethnicities—have read these lyrics as they listened to this album, etching them into our collective memory. And the inner sleeve is ostentatiously dominated by an enlarged image of Lou Adler's Ode records trademark, an enormous "O" spiraling into a smaller "D," which in turn encircles a lower case "e." The trademark is designed to look like a spindle adaptor, felicitously if obliquely referencing King's career move from singles in the sixties to albums in the seventies (indeed the symbol frequently figured as the "o" in the number 70).

Tapestry was the first album to outsell *Sgt. Pepper*; it swept the Grammys in 1972 and would go on to become one of the bestselling albums of all time. It is a true popular music perennial, getting a sales bump with each introduction of a new listening format. Its durability can be illustrated by contrast to the more ephemeral apotheosis of Helen Reddy's "I Am Woman," which was explicitly written as a feminist anthem. Appearing first on her debut album with Capitol

Records, *I Don't Know How to Love Him* in 1971, it wouldn't achieve iconic status until she rerecorded it for the eponymous 1972 album that features its lyrics on the back cover. The single hit number one in December of that year and won Reddy a Grammy for Best Female Vocalist in 1973. If, on the one hand, this song marks a moment of mainstream acceptance for liberal feminism, it also marks the beginning of the end of the Album Era. Unlike *Tapestry,* which is an organic ensemble of songs best listened to as a whole, *I Am Woman* is an album of mostly covers thrown together as a vehicle for the single from which it takes its name. And it inaugurates the singles-heavy radio format that would come to be called, felicitously for my argument, Adult Contemporary.

The Album Era gradually ended with the introduction of the compact disc, the format whose sales began to exceed vinyl in the eighties. But the LP didn't disappear; rather, it was remediated and revitalized by rap. As Jeff Chang confirms in his canonical history, in the seventies in the Bronx "the man with the records . . . replaced the man with the colors" as the embodiment of cool.[8] And the men with the records were pioneering DJ's such as Kool Herc, Grandmaster Flash, and Afrika Bambaataa, who built their careers on the recorded ruins of rock. In the stagflationary seventies in New York City, records were cheap and easy to find. As Kembrew McLeod and Peter DiCola detail in their essential study, *Creative License,* used record stores like Manhattan's Downtown Records had "records in the bins, racks, stacks, shelves, counters, walls, ceiling, and in boxes and crates." And many of these records were what would soon be called classic rock. Grandmaster Flash recalls Afrika Bambaataa getting "the crowd moving to the Rolling Stones, Aerosmith, the Beatles, Grand Funk Railroad, Led Zeppelin, and even the Monkees."[9]

And rap sonically foregrounded the materiality of vinyl through scratching, the technique DJs developed to create a percussive beat by rapidly moving the record back and forth on the turntable. This remediation of vinyl as an instrument in and of itself and a crucial component of the rhythm section quickly became a signature sound of the hip-hop era, ensuring that the LP would persist as a charismatic object, now accruing new connotations as a signifier of skill and sonic sophistication.

Rap repurposed classic vinyl, plundering the immediate musical past to shape an emergent musical future. And if, on the one hand, DJing and sampling involved breaking down the analog continuity of classic albums into looping fragments and scratching beats, rap also maintained the model of the carefully sequenced LP as the marker of musical maturity. Chuck D remembers that when Public Enemy "made *It Takes a Nation of Millions to Hold Us Back* we were shooting to make *What's Going On* by Marvin Gaye and when we made *Fear of a Black Planet* I was shooting for *Sgt. Pepper's*."[10] Then as now musical coming-of-age is heralded by the creation of a conceptually packaged long-playing album that must be listened to in sequence and in its entirety in order to be fully appreciated and understood.

Rap and its intergeneric variants brought the analog-based *kunstleralbum* into the digital age. Whatever the actual material format, albums such as Jay-Z's *In My Lifetime, Vol. 1* (1997), Eminem's *Slim Shady LP* (1998), or Lauryn Hill's *The Miseducation of Lauryn Hill* (1998) and innumerable others invoke vinyl repeatedly with every percussive scratch and insist on being listened to in sequence in their entirety as autobiographical statements of artistic and political development. Indeed, the *kunstleralbum* as a chronicle of growing up (usually in and out of the ghetto into musical celebrity and maturity) is central to the rise of rap more generally, reflecting the genre's deep material and conceptual roots in the Album Era.

By now you can surely guess how I solved my listening dilemma: I started collecting LPs. By circling back to the aesthetic antecedents and afterlives of my own adolescent listening environment, I began to (re-)construct a version of the Album Era inflected by my own idiosyncratic investments but still based in the core canon as established by the inaugural curators of its archive. Collecting records became a process of excavating my own (sentimental) musical education while expanding and integrating it into the larger archive of the era, a relationship embodied by the collection itself, which of course continues to "grow." Indeed, every record collection embodies an idiosyncratic intersection between personal taste and popular culture, between the auratic properties of the unique object you own and the generic properties of the mass-produced commodity you (or someone else) originally purchased. This affectively charged intersection generates the charisma of the album as a material embodiment of the past.

It is a past made of plastic, one which we can access at will through the point of a needle, as if dipping a finger into history. And, as history itself gets digitized into zillions of disaggregated, discontinuous, and decontextualized bits of information, vinyl maintains a structure of analog continuity and indexical contiguity that strengthens our affective investment in the age of its popular hegemony and attests to the format's continuing appeal. Compared to digital formats it is cumbersome and inconvenient, requiring expensive equipment, extensive storage space, and meticulous curatorial care; but this is precisely what gives it weight, both literally and metaphorically. Our albums are anchors in a receding historical vortex. Without them we risk spinning out into a digital ocean with no reference points to assist in navigation.

NOTES

1. Dominick Bartmanski and Ian Woodward, *Vinyl: The Analogue Record in the Digital Age* (New York: Bloomsbury Academic, 2015), 8, 13.
2. This press conference and its aftermath figure prominently in most histories of recorded music in America. Two recent and authoritative versions can be found in Sean Wilentz's lavishly illustrated *360 Sound: The Columbia Records Story* (San Francisco: Chronicle, 2012), 127–69; and Gary Marmerstein's *The Label: The Story of Columbia Records* (New York: Thunder's Mouth, 2007), 153–74.
3. Richard Osborne, *Vinyl: A History of the Analogue Record* (Burlington, Vt.: Ashgate, 2012), 103.
4. Roland Gelatt, *The Fabulous Phonograph: 1877–1977* (New York: Collier, 1977), 331.
5. Gerard Genette, *Paratexts: Thresholds of Interpretation,* trans. Jane Lewin (New York: Cambridge University Press, 1997).
6. Devon Powers, *Writing the Record: The Village Voice and the Birth of Rock Criticism* (Boston: University of Massachusetts Press, 2013), 2.
7. All titles published by Bloomsbury Books, New York.
8. Jeff Chang, *Can't Stop Won't Stop: A History of the Hip-Hop Generation* (New York: Picador, 2005), 82.
9. Kembrew McLeod and Peter DiCola, *Creative License: The Law and Culture of Digital Sampling* (Durham, N.C.: Duke University Press, 2011), 55.
10. Quoted in McLeod and DiCola, *Creative License,* 23.

4

The Plastic You

Plastination and the Postmortal Self

Jane Kuenz

In October 2018, scientists at the Medical University of Vienna found microplastics in fecal samples from eight human subjects in Europe, Russia, and Japan. Since that pilot study, researchers have estimated that the average person consumes up to 52,000 microplastic particles each year, mainly from synthetic fabrics in carpets, clothing, rubber products, and the like, much of it finding its way into our food during normal meal preparation. We inhale another 74,000 particles, and anyone drinking bottled water can add 90,000 on top of that. These are likely underestimates.[1] In the evolutionary history of the body's "inner socionatural system"—what Armiero and De Angelis call the "organosphere"—this is apparently a signal moment. If one lesson of the wasteocene is that the nature of capitalism is to contaminate, this corruption now includes the "strata of toxins [that] have sedimented into the human body" in an "accumulation of externalities" now threatening to kill us.[2]

The news that we are part plastic, at once shocking and predictable, comes at a time when great numbers of us are lining up to see plastinated human corpses parceled out and posed in one or another of the exhibits running worldwide to varying degrees of wonder, revulsion, attack, and acclaim. Since Gunther von Hagens's first BODY WORLDS exhibit opened in Japan in 1995, fifty million people have seen one of his shows in 140 cities in thirty-four countries across six continents. These numbers do not include attendance at the various copycat body shows, especially Premiere Exhibitions' "Bodies . . . The Exhibition," where another fifteen million people have marveled at "real human bodies" at Premiere's two permanent installations inside a mall in Atlanta and a Las Vegas casino.[3] These human *écorchés* are produced through the "groundbreaking method" von Hagens developed for halting physical decomposition after death by extracting and replacing all bodily fluids and soluble fat, first with ice-cold acetone and then synthetic materials. What's left is then cured with light, heat, or gases until it's rigid and permanent. Silicone injections work best for whole-body "gestalt" plastinates, epoxy resins for thin, while polyester is good to distinguish gray matter from white in brain slices.[4] By the end of the plastination process, 70 percent of the original body mass has been replaced with some kind of polymer.

In other words, plastination produces plastic bodies. Dry, odorless, shiny, and clean, plastinates are the perfect nonperishable: nonhazardous and noninfectious, with no leaky fluids or fumes, they store easily in simple plastic bags and require little maintenance.[5] Once processed, they can be parceled out in pieces, displayed for viewing, or sold as is. Until he pulled his online store offline in the wake of international criticism, von Hagens ran "a supermarket of body parts," selling bodies, heads, and torsos, whole and in slices, to the general public. According to the *Irish Times,* transparent body slices were available from €115 each, with an entire plastinated body going for €70,000, a torso for €55,644, and a loose head for €22,000.[6] Now, human products are available to "qualified users" only—institutions or individuals who agree to use specimens exclusively for research, education, or medical purposes. Even then, the Institute for Plastination reassures potential donors that "purchases of specimens are invoiced for 'preservation work' or 'plastination work,' but not for the specimens themselves."[7] Having figured out that attaching price tags to body parts does not play well to the general public, even when sold only to "qualified users," von Hagens Plastination now requires prospective clients interested in silicone plastinates, sheet plastinates, and "blood vessel configurations" to request quotes privately. Anyone else can purchase reproductions of body slices on Premiere's souvenirs or, until recently, BODY WORLD's jewelry, puzzles, and decorative items crafted from organic and nonhuman animal plastinates, such as slices of fruit or a giraffe's tail. When I was there in 2012, the small store that closed the tour in von Hagens's Plastinarium in Guben, Germany, displayed framed slices of pig snouts and a large plastinate coffee table top set over a bearskin rug.

Though he initially claimed to be "democratizing anatomy" by bringing it to the general public as a form of education and entertainment, von Hagens downplayed the "entertainment" part when he moved his BODY WORLDS shows from European fairgrounds (Vienna), event halls (Naxos), and night clubs (Berlin's Postbahnhof) to science museums of the kind that come with educational mission statements and in-house ethics and advisory boards.[8] Befitting this shift in venues are new modes of monetizing bodies emphasizing expertise and credentialing, specifically anatomy courses at the Guben Plastinarium with "conference and class rooms of different sizes, self-learning-stations with computers serving software, . . . and a wide selection of plastinates for all regions and types of theoretical anatomy classes." "More experienced professionals" can purchase "customized lessons" in "preventing shrinkage, coloring, special injection methods and many more."[9] There are now about 400 plastination labs in forty countries, most attached to medical centers at universities, but the main sites are von Hagens's in Heidelberg, Germany, and Dalian, China.

The legal and black-market traffic in organs and human tissue is not new, but plastination literalizes in a new way the instrumentalization of bodies as raw material. In turning corpses slated for burial or traditional dissection into plastinates for public display, von Hagens has been explicit about the conversion of physical waste into useful product, saying his patented process transforms a "useless corpse" to a "specimen" that is "useful, aesthetically instructive, and produced by nature."[10] Figuring the body as an item of use foregrounds the ethical issues implicit in this project once the body is removed from those uses sanctioned in law, such as medical research or organ donation, where the rhetoric of consent and the gift governs. Now, "consent" aligns with the human rights mantra of "dignity and respect" under the banner of consumer choice. On the BODY WORLDS extensive donor consent form, potential donors are asked to check off a number of options for their plastinated selves. They must confirm whether their "plastinated body can be used for the medical enlightenment of laypeople and, to this end, exhibited in public (e.g. in a museum)." They must agree or not to let their body be used as "an anatomical work of art," to be touched by lay people, to be the subject of a public autopsy. They must acknowledge that plastinates are like anatomy skeletons and, thus, do not need to be buried,[11] Over 60 percent of them have agreed to let their body be displayed "in unusual places," such as "on a reproduction of a ghost ship," specifically in a multiplastinate tableau of a scene reminiscent of *Pirates of the Caribbean*. They split by gender on the question of "the use of my body for the aesthetic-educational representation of sex acts."[12] In fact, donors go beyond these required choices, stating their own individual preferences ("I would like to be a whole-body specimen"), suggesting specific poses ("I would prefer the position of the Lymphatic Man of Palo Mascagni"), or making special requests ("If possible, I would like to preserve my tattoos"). Others highlight their best features ("My jaws could be especially interesting") as though auditioning for a role.[13] But there's no provision anywhere for agreeing or not to the use of reproductions of their plastinated bodies on posters and websites, much less, as is the case in the Premiere shows, on souvenir T shirts, postcards, mouse pads, and key chains. And there's no sign that the donors or their heirs ever profit from their donations—not from the body itself, nor from the ticket sales or T shirts.

In describing the plastinate as "produced by nature," practically a renewable resource, von Hagens flirts with a discourse of environmentalism and corporate sustainability that coexists with and elides the plastinated human body's status as an ontological anomaly: neither "the real" nor "the not real," whole body plastinates are an entirely "new body entity."[14] They collapse categories, striking viewers as simultaneously alive and dead, authentic and fake, made and ready-made, real human bodies and plastic anatomical models. When contacted by *Science* in 2003 about the work going on in Dalian's "Plastination City," ground zero for the growing industry in plastinated people and parts, officials at the Chinese Ministry of Health in Beijing identified the compound of buildings overlooking Xinghai Bay as a "manikin company."[15] Manikins are models simulating the human body, especially for use in medical, surgical, or clinical training. By beginning with human flesh and then retaining 30 percent of its organic material, the plastinate is not purely a manikin but simultaneously a body and a model. It is the copy *and* the original. If anything, as Hirschauer says, "a plastinated body is a model of itself."[16]

As von Hagens admits, "All models look alike." Although made from what was once an individual person, each body becomes something else through plastination: a universal "human" body, but not any particular person. At the same time, the success of body shows depends on an illusion of authenticity grounded in realness, where "realness" is linked to specific raced and gendered bodies of particular people. Plastinates, however, are, by design, no longer specific, historically contextualized persons with a race or national origin, much less a name or preferences of their own. Much of this deracination is accomplished simply by removing the skin and other external features like hair. Once abstracted from their own past, these postnational plastinates can be placed in any context that then immediately becomes the primary signifier of who and what they are. That acrobatic couple posed forever in a raised lift may have never even known each other much less performed acrobatic stunts while alive. Although, as Heinrich argues, the "open secret" of some of the exhibits is that the bodies are specifically Chinese, a fact that lends a certain "titillation 'value' to the overall spectacle," the stated goal of plastination is to create anonymity by removing external markers of identity.[17] Von Hagens argues that anonymity is consistent with a tradition within anatomy that "distinguishes plastinates [to be posed] from corpses to be mourned." Without anonymity, the plastinate could become, like the corpse, "an object of reverence." In shifting from art to science venues, however, von Hagens did not also remove his own signature from the plastinates or his name on the metal wall plaques identifying them to viewers. If, as Maurizia Boscagli writes, the attempt to caption the different artifacts in Kelly Jazvac's *Plastiglomerate* reconstructs history "at the individual level . . . as a history of consumption," here the plastinates are identified like sculptures, but not by the names or personal effects of the people they once were, much less the historical and ideological forces that brought them to this place, but by the title von Hagens has given them. Rather than "romanticizing and personalizing" the plastinates, these captions signal their disappearance from history and transformation into totems of contemporary lifestyle and leisure consumption: *The Runner, The Yoga Lady.*

Instead of providing specific information that identifies the donor, von Hagens focuses on "bringing life to a body" already dead and plastinated. In this, he follows Renaissance anatomists, who saw the body as an intricately designed machine and represented it in motion specifically to illustrate how the muscles work. Personhood itself, however, was understood as prior to movement and the cause of it. Though they illustrated dead bodies, Renaissance anatomists assumed a conscious agent making choices that the muscles execute. The earlier plastinated body shows went well beyond this illustration of the dead's agency by adorning the plastinates with accessories, clothes, and tools and by arranging them in spaces viewers will recognize and know, like workplaces or outdoor patios and gardens. In U.S. museums, where the discourse of "science" replaces the garden, the plastinates are still often posed with props that suggest a life and culture in which actual people might have actually lived. Some fence, ride horses, or shoot basketball; a "walking elder" stoops over a cane; while others are frozen in seemingly active scenes almost like *tableau vivant,* except dead, such as the two hockey players caught in mid-fall over the ice or the three poker-playing plastinates who performed as themselves in the 2006 James Bond film, *Casino Royale.*

As their appearance with Bond indicates, the European installations, especially the earlier ones, were racier and more playful. At the Guben Plastinarium, for example, where plastic-wrapped legs hang on racks like dry cleaning awaiting pick-up, a skeleton imitates John Travolta's trademark dance move from *Saturday Night Fever,* while in the "Wogen der Lust" (Waves of Lust) display, gestalt plastinates assume various sexual poses, all heterosexual.[18] In one, a woman wears high-heeled black boots, earrings, a lace bra, and von Hagens's trademark fedora hat. Her partner has a Mohawk and a tie. Both could have been swapped out for storefront mannequins at Saks. Since facial expressions are harder to read without the skin, feeling or pleasure are suggested by the postures of idealized romantic love familiar from the movies: he looks in her face; she wraps a leg around him, eyes closed. That last detail betrays von Hagens's willingness to take liberties with his own method when he wants, such as by leaving some external markers when they contribute to the narrative. Even though all of the skin has been removed, the eyelid is left on specifically so it can be closed to represent her pleasure. While some of von Hagens's efforts are comic, others are just macabre. At one point, he had planned a scene with married donors: she had died of cancer, and he killed himself soon thereafter by driving into a tree. The planned exhibit would include a wrecked Volkswagen, sawed in half and draped in an American flag, in which would sit his headless corpse, looking, somehow, for his wife's plastinated body off in the distance.[19]

Presenting plastinates as bodies in action encourages us to imagine their subjectivity. When that isn't enough, the plastinate's interiority—its self-awareness and consciousness—are explicitly thematized or represented, such as when two longitudinal halves of the same body high five each other or when a skeleton seems to shadow and observe its own flesh walking ahead. The metaphysical questioning implicit in splitting yourself apart in order to study yourself is reproduced in the "brain" room of Premiere Exhibit's "Bodies Revealed," where a seated plastinate sketches his own posed skeleton. Elsewhere, in a nod to the contemporary fixation on the brain as the site of "life" or personhood, such that one is only dead when finally pronounced "brain dead," plastinates appear with their brains exposed specifically to represent thought (*The Chess Player*) or positioned outside the body, such as when the archer's brain is positioned atop her skull in a topknot or the rider on his rearing horse, who holds out his brain in one hand for passersby to witness and confirm his continued existence.

In spite of attempts to grant them "life," mixing plastinates with other objects or arranging them in tableau undercuts claims to realness or authenticity by reducing everything to representation. We respond positively to many of the gestalt plastinates because they appear in poses already familiar to us from popular culture (John Travolta or the rearing horse) or art history, which means we already know what we're supposed to think of them. If anything, von Hagens often seems at pains to demonstrate his love of art and literature for anyone with sufficient cultural capital to appreciate it. *Muscle Man* copies a page out of Andreas Vesalius's *De humani corporis fabrica* (1543). The *Skin Man,* with his skin draped over one arm, references multiple representations of St. Bartholomew, including Michelangelo's version on the Sistine Chapel. The *Drawer Man* nods to Dali's *City of Drawers* (1939): in both, the body's trunk is imagined as a chest of drawers with parts that "[swing] open like doors."[20] Depending on the direction of the expansion, the exploded plastinates suggest either Giacometti statues (vertical) or Calder mobiles (horizontal). A reclining woman does double duty, citing both the traditional nude in the Western visual art tradition and the history of popular anatomy shows in the nineteenth century, especially their major draw, the anatomical Venus.

Some of these works appear on the walls of the Guben Plastinarium, along with oversized reproductions of Rembrandt's *The Anatomy Lesson of Dr. Nicolaes Tulp* (1631), de Lairesse's anatomical drawing of the hand and arm (1685), and Jacques Fabien Gautier d'Agoty's *Anatomical Angel* (1745), in which the muscles of a woman's flayed backside are pulled back and arranged like wings. As is typical in anatomy illustrations, she looks away demurely as though conscious of being exposed and, more to the point, as though conscious. These images from the history of anatomy are interspersed with posters for public anatomy lessons from ancient Rome to nineteenth-century England, and finally to England's first modern public autopsy in 170 years performed in 2002 by von Hagens himself. None of it is identified. Together and minus that identifying information, they encourage intertextual readings in which the history and traditions of art, anatomy, and plastination are interchangeable with each other at the level of representation. If 1950s film is the most obvious frame of reference for understanding the meaning of a plastinate's raised foot in a romantic kiss, classical Greek sculpture is the perspective from which to see a headless, plastinated male torso and call it beautiful. Rembrandt's portrait of Dr. Tulp's explaining the musculature of the arm to his colleagues is understood to be an iteration of von Hagens's autopsy of a 73-year-old man performed in an East London art gallery before a randomly selected but paying audience and later aired as a documentary on Britain's Channel 4.[21]

A similar elision is on display in the "Anatomische Safari," where plastinates of actually existing animals intermingle with plastinated unicorns, winged pigs, and other mythical creatures, while a flayed giraffe performing stunts now familiar from bad CGI competes with von Hagens memorabilia, including a wall of his honorary degrees and awards, the motorbike he used as a student in the mid-1960s, and the original door to the prison cell in Cottbus where he was held after his arrest in 1969 for trying to escape Eastern Europe. Besides a skeleton, the reproduction of the cell itself includes a bunk bed, toilet, desk, bowl, and spoon. But a different problem emerges when plastinated animals are mixed with other kinds of animal representations. A carved wooden elephant placed next to its plastinated double turns them both into crafted things. While that plastinate-topped coffee table arranged on the bearskin rug normalizes one animal product in relation to another, it also converts everything else in the Plastinarium, including the human bodies, into potential items of interior décor.

In his analysis of oil painting in the European tradition between 1500 and 1900, John Berger explains how oil's ability "to render the tangibility, the texture, the lustre, the solidity of what it depicts . . . reduced everything to the equality of objects." Oil itself and the method and aesthetic developed for it turn whatever is depicted into something "you can put your hands on." Thus, skulls or other forms of memento mori intended to remind everyone that life is fleeting become instead no different in appearance, much less metaphysical implication, than the bowl of fruit on the table in the still life. In an attempt to avoid this problem and retain the skull's symbolic meaning, some artists resorted to obvious ploys. In *The Ambassadors* (1533), for example, Hans Holbein has painted the skull as a distorted, slanted oval in the foreground, so that it appears in a "(literally) quite different optic from everything else in the picture." Had he not done this, the skull would be reduced to "an object like everything else, a mere part of a mere skeleton of a man who happened to be dead."[22]

Something similar happens in the plastinate displays, where the props and poses intended to signal authenticity located in "real human bodies" instead threaten the distinction between seemingly animated plastinate and mere inanimate thing, the plastic leavings of a person who happens to be dead. Instead of indicating "life," the juxtaposition of plastinates with their props produces the opposite effect or calls into question the logic of the initial gesture. What, for example, does it mean to plastinate an ostrich—remove the skin and expose the muscles—but then add back some of the feathers? The feathers should have as much or more claim to being the "real" ostrich, yet reattaching them turns them into something fabricated, almost an item of dress, like a feather boa. Elsewhere, human plastinates are similarly posed with other parts of human bodies that, like the feathers, are used to heighten the plastinate's prior or more authentic humanity or life. This is the lesson of the standing vascular gestalt plastinate (a full-body plastinate highlighting the circulatory system) holding and apparently contemplating a human skull.[23] As with the feathered ostrich, this scene only works if we assume that the skull is somehow more dead than the plastinate holding it.[24] Like Hamlet holding Yorick's skull aloft, the plastinate contemplating the skull references the entire history of memento mori in Western art, but it begs the question of what actually is the memento mori in the plastinated body museum.

If posing a vascular plastinate with a skull confers more "life" onto the plastic veins, including a plastinated slice alongside larger plastinates showing the same bodily interior similarly confuses categories. Because the images offered by the slices are already familiar to us from MRIs, we are tempted to see the slices as more organic and "real" than the complete organs even though both are plastinates. As van Dijck writes, "Since most viewers accept the implied relationship between slices and real bodies, the claimed unmediated naturalness of plastinated body slices seems merely an extension of the MRI induced gaze."[25] It's easy to forget that the slices aren't actually MRI scans but human flesh subsequently plasticized and then presented to look like an image we've already learned to identify as original or as a sign of the real. The various metal prosthetics featured on *The Orthopedic Body* (artificial knees, hip replacements, metal jaws—twelve orthopedic or surgical operations in all) similarly suggest the plastinated body is somehow more organic than the foreign objects introduced into it. It's true that the metal plates, clamps, joints, and screws highlight to the extent to which living bodies are already compromised and transformed by medical interventions, except that adding prosthetics and fixtures to a plastinate doesn't actually suggest a cyborg so much as a metal-on-plastic, mixed-media sculpture.

Categories matter, but they can be hard to pin down. Legal consent transforms a person into a donor and a corpse into a donation. Once sold for research and education, these donations become specimens. A specimen can be presented as slices, large or small. Put a plastinated slice on the wall, and people will study it as art. Put it on the table, however, and they'll use it as a coaster. Von Hagens seems to be aware of some of the general problems with his work, though the typical defensive move is to a joke. There's an entire room early in the Guben Plastinarium tour devoted to cultural representations or displays of dead bodies, beginning with mummies and continuing through Tibetan monks and the Sedlec Ossuary, and ending at Goth kids. Elsewhere, he's run red and blue toy train tracks like the veins and arteries of the body through a horizontal skeleton splayed out on a table. It's clever, but whimsically intermixing cultural forms or inserting objects external to the body, even toys, into the body itself risks exposing the want of ethical self-awareness his critics decry.[26] Seeing the body as a thing to move around in is explicit in von Hagens's comparison of anatomy preparation to walking through an apartment: "I wend my way through organs, bones and muscles and slide down nerves, as if I were moving around in a basement storeroom crammed with sacks of potatoes and peas and the electric wiring in between."[27] It is not difficult for a person who sees bodily organs as sacks of potatoes to reduce the body to an apparatus composed of moveable parts, as he does in *Act without Actors,* which features a disconnected penis inside a similarly disinterested vagina. Small wonder, then, that someone also failed to see a part as necessarily connected to its whole when they stole the fetus right out of the plastinate's pregnant body at the California Science Center as though taking a baby Jesus out of the outdoor Christmas manger scene.

"The human body should be turned into a statue," writes Von Hagens, but "without the detour through marble, plaster or bronze."[28] It will be a short step from this to finding the "real," natural body inadequate or inferior to the aesthetically beautiful and athletically fit model on display at the plastinated body museum. All of the shows hold out the promise of bodily enhancement and perfectibility through constant tweaking of the self to achieve maximum usefulness. Plastinates are figured as the latest advances in biotechnological reengineering that let the body "live on" in plastinated form.[29] In the Premiere's exhibits, for example, posters in the muscle room offer "Tips on Stress" ("Take a warm bath"), while the rooms devoted to respiration and digestion warn against cigarettes and too much soda, instructing us to chew each small bite 25 times. In a parody of neoliberal discourse about personal responsibility and choice, visitors are advised to "Take charge of your health at the Resource Center."

Plastination stops decomposition and decay; essentially, it kills death.[30] This is a major appeal to the people lining up to be plastinated—so many that BODY WORLDS can claim now to use only donated bodies.[31] Horrified at "the thought of being buried in the earth" and "completely disgusted by worms," they look forward to the durability and permanence of plastic. At the same time, they are drawn to the ideal of consciousness in death suggested by the plastinates themselves, to a kind of postmortal self-awareness, as though plastination will allow them to continue to have a personality and identity after death, someone with preferences and experiences. Specifically, they look forward to travel: "Now I can relax about the issue [decay], . . . since I can stay above ground after my death and may even have a chance to 'experience' trips to many places." One imagines "traveling around as a plastinate . . . from exhibition to exhibition. From city to city. From country to country. From continent to continent! Or finding a new home in a museum. Or a university!"[32]

The BODY WORLDS literature addresses and thanks donors

as members of a community that continues after plastination, as though they've joined a tour group and will meet up every April in a new country. Choosing to plastinate is figured in the language of informed consumer choice, like selecting a retirement community for optimizing one's postmortal life. Finally, death itself is just another stage of life that requires professional intervention. Rather than mark an end, plastination offers a new chance to make yourself useful: "My greatest hope with Plastination," writes a potential donor, "is that in the event I contribute nothing in life, I may do so in death." They thank von Hagens for giving "those of us who might serve as nothing great in life" the "opportunity" to do so in death. They look forward to serving the world and then standing back to admire their work: "When I've breathed my last, my body will perform an important function for mankind. Mind and spirit will gaze upon it with envy. . . . I even dreamed that I had been cut into fine slices and was admiring myself. It was a lovely dream."[33]

NOTES

1. "In First Microplastics Found in Poop," *National Geographic,* October 22, 2018, https://www.nationalgeographic.com/environment/2018/10/news-plastics-microplastics-human-feces/; "The Average Person Eats Thousands of Plastic Particles Every Year," *National Geographic,* June 5, 2019, https://www.nationalgeographic.com/environment/2019/06/you-eat-thousands-of-bits-of-plastic-every-year/; Ana L. Catarino, Valeria Macchia, William G. Sanderson, Richard C. Thompson, and Theodore B. Henry, "Low Levels of Microplastics (MP) in Wild Mussels Indicate that MP Ingestion by Humans Is Minimal Compared to Exposure via Household Fibres Fallout During a Meal," *Environmental Pollution* 237 (2018): 675–84.
2. Marco Armiero and Massimo De Angelis, "Anthropocene: Victims, Narrators, and Revolutionaries," *South Atlantic Quarterly* 116, no. 2 (2017): 359n3, 352, 348.
3. In *Strip Cultures: Finding America in Las Vegas,* I discuss the Luxor casino's "Bodies . . . The Exhibition" show in relation to a model of identity and community envisioned by the rise of social media and the networked and augmented spaces and global movement of capital and labor necessary for it. Jane Kuenz, "The Shipping Container Capital of the World," in *Strip Cultures: Finding America in Las Vegas,* ed. Stacy M. Jameson, Karen Klugman, Jane Kuenz, and Susan Willis (Durham, N.C.: Duke University Press, 2017), 243–89.
4. An explanation of the process is available on the BODY WORLDS website,

Frequently Asked Questions. https://bodyworlds.com/about/faq/ and Gunther von Hagens, "On Gruesome Corpses, Gestalt Plastinates and Mandatory Interment," in Gunther von Hagens and Angelina Whalley, *BODY WORLDS: The Anatomical Exhibition of Real Human Bodies* (Heidelberg: Arts and Sciences, 2006), 260; "About Plastination," Plastination Laboratory, University of Toledo, https://www.utoledo.edu/med/depts/medical-education/plastination.

5. "Dry," "odorless," and "clean" are von Hagens's terms in "On Gruesome Corpses," 260. See also Arvinder Pal Singh Batra and Jeewandeep Kaur, "The Art of Plastinated Cadavers," in *Journey from Primitive Anatomy to Plastination- A Bird's Eye View*, ed. Zora Singh and Parveen Bansal (New Delhi: Gulab, 2015), 143–65.
6. "Anatomist Sells Body Parts Online," *Irish Times*, October 22, 2010, https://www.irishtimes.com/news/anatomist-sells-body-parts-online-1.866088; "Human Cross Sections to Go on Sale in Germany," *Spiegel Online*, May 27, 2010, https://www.spiegel.de/international/zeitgeist/supermarket-for-body-parts-human-cross-sections-to-go-on-sale-in-germany-a-697086.html; "Dr. Death: Body Parts for Sale on Internet by Controversial Anatomist Gunther von Hagens," *The Telegraph*, October 2010, https://www.telegraph.co.uk/news/worldnews/europe/germany/8079609/Dr-Death-body-parts-for-sale-on-internet-by-controversial-anatomist-Gunther-von-Hagens.html
7. Each specimen includes an insert thanking the donor who made the plastinate possible: "The specimen provided is only available because it was donated for plastination to the Institute for Plastination. We thank the donor for this. There is no charge for the specimen itself, only the preparation costs." von Hagens and Whalley, *Donating Your Body, 8th ed.* (Heidelberg: Institute for Plastination, 2007), 18.
8. Linda Schulte-Sasse, "Advise and Consent: On the Americanization of Body Worlds," *BioSocieties* 1 (2006): 372. Sometimes, the sites of corpse shows are too jarring: the "Amazing Human Body" exhibit was held in what had once been the "Meat and Dairy Pavilion" of Sydney's Royal Agricultural Society's annual Easter showgrounds.
9. Plastination courses are also offered in Heidelberg and Munich where the pedagogy is experiential: "Rather than teaching with books we are using plastinates and more practical approaches to learn anatomy." "Courses," von Hagens Plastination: Real Anatomy for Teaching, http://www.vonhagens-plastination.com/anatomy-courses-11.
10. Gunther von Hagens, "Anatomy and Plastination," in von Hagens and Angelina Whalley, *Prof. Gunther von Hagens' Anatomy Art Fascination Beneath the Surface.(* Heidelberg: Institute for Plastination, 2000), 37.
11. This legal distinction converts a body governed by laws about handling the dead to an object for trade governed by an entirely different set of laws. Common law has upheld consistently the "no property" principle in relation to

human bodies, specifically that the dead body of a human being does not have an owner, although clearly some do: mummies, "bog men," or the remains of indigenous people are not just housed but are also owned by the museums reluctant to return them precisely because they have become property. Ellen Stroud, "Law and the Dead Body: Is a Corpse a Person or a Thing?" *Annual Review of Law and Social Science* 14 (2018): 115–25.

12. 59% of male respondents agreed to "the use of my body for the aesthetic-education representation of sex acts" compared to 42% of women. All of these donor questions and responses were recorded by the writer from materials at the Guben Plastinarium.
13. "When I went to the exhibit and saw the bodies kicking a soccer ball and throwing a baseball I just thought, volleyball, that's me." Anna Schecter, "Body Donors Pick Their Poses for Plastination Exhibit," *ABC News*, February 26, 2008, https://abcnews.go.com/Blotter/story?id=4345007&page=1. Other examples qtd. in Stefan Hirschauer, "Animated Corpses: Communicating with Post Mortals in an Anatomical Exhibition," *Body & Soul*, 12, no. 4 (2006): 34.
14. von Hagens quoted in "Inventing the 'Real' Body," *Taipei Times*, April 29, 2004.
15. John Bohannon, Ding Yimin, and Xiong Lei, "Anatomy's Full Monty," *Science* 301, no. 5637 (August 29, 2003): 1172-75. The other major plastination company is Dalian Hoffen Bio-technique, associated with Dalian Medical University, both linked to the use of executed prisoners, especially people associated with Falun Gong, without their consent.
16. Hirschauer, "Animated Corpses," 38. Compare this with readings citing Borges of plastinates as three-dimensional maps, so extensive they negate the difference between the territory and its representations or are "more like maps than like the self." Petra Kuppers, "Visions of Anatomy: Exhibitions and Dense Bodies," *Differences: A Journal of Feminist Cultural Studies* 15, no. 3 (2004): 130. See also Joseph Starr, "The Plastinate's Narrative," and T. Christine Jespersen and Alicita Rodriguez, "Forced Impregnation and Masculinist Utopia," in *The Anatomy of Body Worlds: Critical Essays on the Plastinated Cadavers of Gunther von Hagens*, ed. T. Christine Jespersen, Alicita Rodríguez, and Joseph Starr (Jefferson, N.C.: McFarland, 2009), 11.
17. Ari Larissa Heinrich, *Chinese Surplus: Biopolitical Aesthetics and the Medically Commodified Body* (Durham, N.C.: Duke University Press, 2018), 21. BODY WORLDS now uses donated bodies exclusively but acknowledges that it cannot account for the origins of some of its earliest exhibits. Under a settlement reached with the State of New York in 2008, Premiere Exhibitions must provide documentation for the origin and cause of death of each of the cadavers on display and to post a warning to future visitors that the body parts they will see "may have come from Chinese prisoners who were tortured and executed." Premiere has never denied that the corpses were poor,

unclaimed, or unidentified dead in China (Sewell Chan, "'Bodies' Show Must Put Up Warnings," *New York Times,* May 29, 2008, http://cityroom.blogs.nytimes.com/2008/05/29). Premiere's disclaimer is posted on its website and at the exhibits: "This exhibit displays human remains of Chinese citizens or residents which were originally received by the Chinese Bureau of Police. The Chinese Bureau of Police may receive bodies from Chinese prisons. Premiere cannot independently verify that the human remains you are viewing are not those of persons who were incarcerated in Chinese prisons." "This exhibit displays full body cadavers as well as human body parts, organs, fetuses and embryos that come from cadavers of Chinese citizens or residents. With respect to the human parts, organs, fetuses and embryos you are viewing, Premier relies solely on the representations of its Chinese partners and cannot independently verify that they do not belong to persons executed while incarcerated in Chinese prisons." Premiere Exhibitions, Bodies . . . The Exhibition Disclaimer, http://www.premierexhibitions.com/exhibitions/4/4/bodies-exhibition/bodies-exhibition-disclaimer.

18. All of the von Hagens plastinates are relentlessly cis-gendered, with intact and visible external genitalia and, for women, secondary sex characteristics, such as breast tissue. This is true regardless of what organ system or feature the plastinate is supposed to be highlighting.
19. This project is described by Daniel Engber in "The Plastinarium of Dr. von Hagens," *Wired,* February 12, 2013, https://www.wired.com/2013/02/ff-the-plastinarium-of-dr-von-hagens/. I've found no evidence that von Hagens ever actually completed it.
20. von Hagens and Whalley, *Donating Your Body,* 181.
21. Andy Miah, "The Public Autopsy: Somewhere Between Art, Education, and Entertainment," *Journal of Medical Ethics* 30 (2004): 576–79.
22. John Berger, *Ways of Seeing* (London: Penguin, 1990), 87–91.
23. The version of the *Thinker* on display in Guben featured a standing plastinate holding and looking at the bare skull on the table in front of him. Other versions of this work have the same plastinate looking at a head that consists only of arteries.
24. For Natalia Lizama, a melancholic longing characterizes all of the gestalt plastinates, "but is heighted in the . . . plastinates whose poses suggest self-awareness" and stems from the fact that they seem (to us) to know they will hold that pose forever. What does the plastinate want? Like the sibyl, it wants to die. "Afterlife, but Not as We Know It: Melancholy, Postbiological Ontology, and Plastinated Bodies," in *The Anatomy of Body Worlds: Critical Essays on the Plastinated Cadavers of Gunther von Hagens,* ed. T. Christine Jespersen, Alicita Rodríguez, and Joseph Starr (Jefferson, N.C.: McFarland, 2009), 16, 22.
25. Jos van Dijck, "Body Worlds: The Art of Plastinated Cadavers," *Configurations* 9, no. 1 (2001): 118.

26. Pastor Ernst Pulsfort, interviewed on National Public Radio, says von Hagens "[plays] with corpses like they are dolls," using "dead human meat" instead of "Play-Doh." "Body Art," *All Things Considered*, no. 8, April 30, 2001, https://www.npr.org/templates/story/story.php?storyId=1122244.
27. von Hagens, "On Gruesome Corpses," 263.
28. von Hagens and Whalley, *Donating Your Body*, 15.
29. On biopolitics and neoliberalism in the body museum, see Megan Stern, "Shiny, Happy People: 'Body Worlds' and the Commodification of Health," *Radical Philosophy* 118 (2003): 2–6; Hsuan L. Hsu and Martha Lincoln, "Biopower, Bodies . . . the Exhibition, and the Spectacle of Public Health," *Discourse* 29, no. 1 (2007): 15–34; Elisabeth Rondinelli, "Body Worlds and the Social Life of the Plastinated Body: Considerations on the Biotechnology of Plastination," in *Interrogating the Social: A Critical Sociology for the 21st Century*, ed. Fuyuki Kurasawa (London: Palgrave Macmillan, 2017), 247–68; and Céline Lafontaine, "The Postmortal Condition: From the Biomedical Deconstruction of Death to the Extension of Longevity," *Science as Culture* 18, no. 3 (2009): 297–312.
30. Ursula Streckeisen, *Die Medizin und der Tod: über Berufliche Strategien Zwischen Klinik und Pathologie* (Opladen: Leske and Budrich, 2001), qtd. in Hirschauer, "Animated Corpses," 28.
31. After being hounded by protests and suspicions about the source of the bodies on display, he advertises loudly on the "Body Donor" page of the website for the Institute of Plastination that all of his bodies (meaning whole bodies, not the miscellaneous parts) are volunteers. As of June 2019, 18,833 people had registered as donors, the great majority of those (16,754) from Germany. In fact, the Institute now has so many donors they have "indefinitely stopp[ed] the acceptance of new donor applications" and advised would-be donors to contact a local medical school instead. BODY WORLDS, Frequently Asked Questions, https://bodyworlds.com/about/faq/.
32. Qtd. in von Hagens and Whalley, *Donating Your Body*, 27, 26. After his 2008 diagnosis of Parkinson's, von Hagens announced he too would be plastinated, stating he envisioned being "sliced up" so he could be in different parts of the world at the same time. Esther Han, "Why Angelina Will Plastinate and Display Her Husband after He Dies," *Sydney Morning Herald*, December 4, 2018, https://www.smh.com.au/national/nsw/why-angelina-wants-to-plastinate-and-display-her-husband-s-dead-body-20181203-p50jvm.html.
33. Von Hagens, "Anatomy and Plastination," 31.

◊♦◊ **PART II** ◊♦◊

The Plasticity of Genre

5

Plastic Man and Other Petrochemical Fantasies

Daniel Worden

Plastic bodies abound in comics. The rendering of impossible bodily actions, contortions, and expansions is a hallmark of the medium, from early newspaper comic strips such as Winsor McCay's dream states in *Little Nemo in Slumberland* to the trope of "magical transformation" in manga series like Naoko Takeuchi's *Sailor Moon*. Animated film, closely related to comics in historical origins and content, has been described by film director and theorist Sergei Eisenstein as "plasmatic," a term that conjoins the colorful play associated with plastics to the neither-matter-nor-liquid viscosity of plasma.[1] For Eisenstein, Disney's plasmatic cartoons from the 1930s and 1940s offer "a complete return to a world of complete freedom," a vision that emerges "at the very summit of a society that had completely enslaved nature—namely, in America."[2] While plasmatic cartoons provide relief, in Eisenstein's view, from the exploited lives viewers lead under capitalism, they draw on a set of animistic, primal ideas about nature. As such, for Eisenstein, the political capacity of the plasmatic is limited, as it lacks a dialectical opposite and thus provokes merely a pleasant nostalgia for a more natural condition. Yet from our contemporary vantage point, the plasmatic and its expressive fluidity seems less of an expression of primal nature than an expression of the midcentury emergence of plastics as consumer goods. If plasmatic animations ask us to reconsider our relation to the natural world, they may indeed present a series of political ideologies that Eisenstein did not identify in his classification of the plasmatic as primitivist and animist. Christophe Bonneuil and Jean-Baptiste Fressoz have argued that one of the ways we can survive the Anthropocene and its attendant economic, environmental, and social crises is to find relations to each other and the environment "that liberate human and non-human alterities."[3] Emerging from the plastics revolution and thematizing its ideologies, the form-breaking mode of the plasmatic cartoon represents our instrumentalization of plastic and reworks our relations to plastics and the world we inhabit through them.

As Ursula K. Heise has argued, plasmatic animation's ability to morph and reshape subjects, objects, and settings gives it a unique ability to imagine the environment: "Speaking and acting animals, plants, and objects invite the viewer to see humans as only one of many manifestations of liveliness, intentionality, and agency in the fictional worlds of animation."[4] Along with this expanded view of life, "plasmatic bodies, both human and nonhuman . . . playfully explore ecological adaptation, resilience, and the synthetic, human-made ecologies that define the future of nature in the Anthropocene, the age in which humans transform even the most basic structures of their planet."[5] Plastics are one of the major ways that humans have transformed the environment, and the concept of the "plasmatic" names the quality of colorful, even infinite flexibility that plastics introduced into our cultural and material imaginaries. Indeed, as I will argue in this essay, the emergence and ubiquity of plastics by the mid-twentieth century in the United States is thematized in comic books, as a site of expansive possibility and as a force that fundamentally reshapes the human and the environment.

In Scott Bukatman's adoption of the term, plasmatic arts like comics and animation present an unbounded field of representation: "Forms were dynamic and mutable; all things were possible."[6] The infinite flexibility of an illustrated world is a central component of the inherently modern media of comic books. While plasmatic intensity and play has been tracked in animation and linked historically with the advent of modernism and technological innovations in film, photography, and printing, the aesthetics of plastic figure the world of the comic book and the comic book superhero as well, especially through the conceptual link from plastic flexibility to the speed and power of petroculture. As Bart Beaty notes, "comics—and superhero comics in particular—have placed a greater premium on the visualization of energy than other forms."[7] If plastics are, in Amanda Boetzkes and Andrew Pendakis's analysis, "valueless, infinitely transposable, and therefore seemingly voided of ontological stability," then superhero comics articulate a worldview that blends the energy of petroculture with the ephemerality of plastics, a world of superhuman possibility that strives to transcend material limits.[8] Yet, plastic's often zany possibilities also make clear the limitations of not only aesthetic forms—only so much stretching of the world can occur on a piece of paper with finite dimensions—but also narrative. Plastic heroes in comic books remain relatively singular, existing as anomalies within a less fluid world. Plastics promise an infinite fluidity that they cannot deliver.

Plastics are a part of superhero comics just as they are a part of our everyday environment, and plastics were becoming newly meaningful in American culture at the time of the superhero's emergence on the newsstand. As Jeffrey L. Meikle posits in his history of plastics, there were two conceptions of plastics by the 1940s, one stemming from early plastics like Celluloid and Bakelite, and the other from newer thermoplastics. While early plastics were represented and even designed as "an extension of natural materials" such as wood or metal, the new conception of plastics envisioned an "expansive culture of impermanence," in which Americans enjoyed "an irrational phantasmagoria of ungrounded images, all in brilliant synthetic colors, a carnival of material desire."[9] This tension between an enhanced natural world and an explosive synthetic one is articulated in the superhero narrative, which often features a hero who strives to preserve order with unprecedented power. Plastic in the superhero narrative, then, is the occasion of both immense freedom and profound stasis. Like plastics themselves, superhero stories about plastic heroes create the appearance of limitless freedom with the ironic effect of preserving habits of life, such as the casual consumption and disposal of plastics, that have become so natural as to seem neutral.

Plastic Man's Duality

Widely regarded to be the first superhero character in comics, Superman appears in 1938 in direct relation to modern energy sources, and especially the fossil fuels that are instrumental in the manufacturing of plastics. On the cover of *Action Comics* #1, Superman's first appearance, he lifts a car and smashes its front end, while three male figures cower and run away. On the interior page, Superman is introduced, and his powers include the ability to "run faster than an express train."[10] This triumph of superhero physiognomy over fossil-fueled industry is only one way that superhero bodies relate to the petrochemical age entrenching itself in the United States in the midcentury. Indeed, while Superman is a solar-powered superhero, and thus represents something like an organic contrast to fossil fuel-powered machinery, other superheroes like Plastic Man would more closely intertwine the imaginary of petrochemical plastics with the superhero. Indeed, during the golden and silver ages of comic books in the United States, from the 1930s to the 1970s, plastics would proliferate: "Global plastic production exploded at midcentury. World production rose from less than 50,000 tons in 1930 to 2 million tons in 1950 and 6 million tons a decade later. New types of plastics flooded the marketplace. Plastics substituted for materials such as glass, wood, and paper in existing goods or became the key substance in a huge array of new consumer goods."[11] This growth in plastics occurs alongside the emergence and proliferation of the superhero in U.S. comic books, resulting in a conception of both infinitely flexible and invincible bodies that replicate the qualities of midcentury plastic materials.

One of the many superheroes to appear on U.S. newsstands in the wake of Superman in 1938, Plastic Man is a minor figure if judged by the number of comic books published since the 1940s that bear the character's name. But, Plastic Man's superpowers and zaniness resonate across the superhero genre. While the contorting and stretched body figures in earlier texts like Charlie Chaplin's 1936 film *Modern Times* as evidence of industrialization's cruelty, Plastic Man embraces superhuman elasticity. As Scott Bukatman argues, "Plastic Man, with his morphing morphology . . . serves to demonstrate the plasmatic fantasy that underlies the entire superhero genre, with its transformative bodies, split identities, and infinite adaptabilities."[12] Moreover, Plastic Man works in the intricate and imaginary connection between superhero bodies and petroculture, forging a link between the imaginary possibilities of the plasmatic and the material reality of plastics as a material. In his essay about Plastic Man's creator Jack Cole, Art Spiegelman describes not just the character Plastic Man in terms of energy and force, but also the comics pages themselves on which he appears:

> Each panel seems to swallow several separate instants of time whole, as if the page were made up of small screens with different, though related, films whizzing by at forty-eight frames a second. Jack Cole's is an amphetamine-riddled art: Tex Avery on speed! And it's not just Plastic Man who bounces and twists; any one of Cole's incidental figures would seem as kinetic as Plas if it were transplanted into someone else's comic book. Each page is intuitively visualized to form a coherent whole even though the individual panels form a narrative flood of run-on sentences that breathlessly jump from one page to the next. The art ricochets like a racquet ball slammed full force in a closet. Your eye, however, is guided as if it were a skillfully controlled pinball, often by Plastic Man himself acting as a compositional device. His distended body is an arrow pointing out the sights as it hurtles through time.[13]

Spiegelman's metaphors for Plastic Man are mixed, and he avoids reference to nonhuman energy sources. This is because, perhaps, of Spiegelman's interest in projecting Jack Cole's work as art, and therefore organic rather than the industrial product that comics have been thought to be for most of their history in the United States. Interestingly, though, Spiegelman's emphasis on the unity of form and content in Plastic Man comics—the way in which Plastic Man's kinetic speed and flexibility is captured not just in narrative but in the composition of the comics page itself as a "coherent whole"—echoes the vision of abstract art articulated by painter Barnett Newman in his influential 1945 essay "The Plasmic Image." In that essay, Newman makes a distinction between the "plastic" qualities of a painting—its use of color and compositional structure—and the "plasmic image," which incorporates these plastic elements not just as surface features but as expressive content: "The plastic elements of the art have been converted into mental plasma."[14] While Newman envisioned and advocated for a mode of abstract painting that sought to convey abstract truths, the inherently narrative art of the comic book page in Plastic Man conveys not an abstract, transhistorical truth but an expression of the condition of the petrochemical age, moving at unprecedented speeds and reshaping bodies. In Plastic Man and his related stretchy superheroes, the speculative ideologies of plastics project safely consumerist yet pleasantly flexible utopias.

As mentioned above, Plastic Man was created by the artist Jack Cole, and the character first appeared in *Police Comics* #1 in 1941. As Art Spiegelman notes, Plastic Man's original name was "India Rubber Man," yet Cole's editor felt that the term *plastic* captured the excitement associated with the new wave of plastics emerging in the 1940s.[15] Among these new plastics, synthetic rubbers were manufactured with the use of petrochemicals, and they touted better elasticity and durability than natural rubber, while also being less prone to the economic volatility and price spikes of the natural commodity. Plastic Man's polymorphic body, which can stretch in seemingly infinite directions, is routinely likened to "rubber" in his 1940s comics, and in *Police Comics* #1, the United States Rubber Company even placed an ad touting the superior qualities of the U.S. Royal Rider bicycle tire, which contains material also used in the manufacture of Navy "torpedo planes."[16] The ad's juxtaposition of fighter planes with bicycle riding domesticates Plastic Man's superheroic fantasy, grounding speed in a mundane activity that nonetheless connotes high-speed adventure.

Police Comics #1 tells the character's origin story. A criminal gang robs the "Crawford Criminal Works," and one of the gang's members, Eel O'Brian, is shot by a security guard and doused in a "vat of acid."[17] Left for dead by his fellow criminals, Eel stumbles through a swamp and up a mountain before passing out. He wakes up in a mysterious mountain retreat, Resthaven, where he is nursed to health by a monk. While at Resthaven, Eel realizes that his body is "stretchin' like a rubber band!!"[18] In a three-panel sequence, he stretches his arms, cheeks, and head, reaching outside of the first panel border, becoming an abstract triangle in the second, and rounding out in the third panel through a peephole frame. This sequence emphasizes the new stretchy possibilities realized in the comic, a world where, as will become evident in later Plastic Man stories, plasticity becomes a feature not just of one unique individual but the world itself. Eel goes on to fight crime with his newfound abilities as Plastic Man. The dual identity offers a glimpse into what makes Plastic Man emblematic, as he is bound to the very criminal world he fights against. While he embodies the posthuman possibilities of new plastics in the midcentury, Plastic Man also seeks to contain and curtail the spread of plasticity, which the comic often figures as monstrous and villainous.

Plastic Man's adventures often pit him against other energy sources. In *Plastic Man* #7 (the character got his own series in 1943, two years after his introduction in *Police Comics*), Plastic Man confronts Dr. Volt, who has invented a box that shoots lightning bolts. Plastic Man foils Dr. Volt's attempt to break into a bank safe by stretching out in front of a lightning bolt, which Plastic Man is "insulated against" because of his chemically enhanced body.[19] Dr. Volt eventually blows up his own lair, and he is crushed while fleeing the scene when a bolt of lightning topples a tree. This moment of "poetic justice," as Plastic Man's sidekick Woozy Winks describes it, positions Plastic Man alongside natural forces.[20] He is a crime-fighter, enforcing the social order, and for Dr. Volt, the natural order also enforces itself, punishing him for manipulating lightning with, in Plastic Man's words, "genuine lightning."[21] As the cover of the issue makes clear, Plastic Man is figured as lightning itself (Figure 5.1), a naturally occurring phenomenon, even though he is also not lightning at all but an impossibly stretched human body.

This ambivalence between figuring Plastic Man as artificial and synthetic or as natural and organic is even more evident in *Plastic Man* #3.[22] In a convoluted story, Plastic Man is asked by the FBI to investigate the Strumby gang, which is smuggling precious materials into the United States. Simultaneously, Woozy Winks is convinced

FIGURE 5.1. On the cover of *Plastic Man* #7 (1947), the superhero takes the shape of a lightning bolt. Art by Jack Cole; from the Digital Comics Museum.

that Plastic Man is ignoring him because he smells bad. Woozy goes to a perfume store to buy a bottle of "Correcto," and finds the owner on the verge of committing suicide because he can no longer buy ambergris, due to the Strumby gang's monopoly on the precious material. Woozy then gets in a rowboat to hunt a whale, and is swallowed by a whale that is actually a submarine in disguise. Plastic Man flies overhead and sees this strange whale, which, it turns out, is the Strumby gang's secret hideout. A confrontation ensues, resulting in the capture of the gang and the release of their stockpile of ambergris. Both Plastic Man and Woozy get what they were after. Like in the Dr. Volt story, Plastic Man is cast as both as genuine as another energy source, in this case a whale and its oil, and as strangely other to the more natural entity. Plastic Man takes the form of a red whale in the comic, and then hugs the criminals' whale submarine. Taking the form of a whale to infiltrate a submarine that is designed to look like a whale, Plastic Man is both more natural and disturbingly alien, morphing from a whale to something that "looks more like an octopus" in the next panel.

As an embodiment of the possibilities of plastics, Plastic Man stands in for both the promise of this material—it will transform what is possible in everyday life—and its threat to human autonomy—Plastic Man's body becomes estranged from natural limits, a product of petrochemicals that ultimately undoes social stability. In *Plastic Man* #22, an entire city gets his stretchy powers, after a criminal accidentally dumps a chemical agent into the water supply.[23] Titled "Plague of Plastic People," the story presents plasticity as a threat to the social order. Plastic Man and his FBI boss strive to stop the menace of plastic people, even though the plastic people we see in action are not criminals but do-gooders. A prison guard uses his stretchy powers to prevent a jailbreak, and citizens offer to help Plastic Man fight crime. Yet, when the plastic powers wear off as the chemical works its way out of people's systems, Plastic Man is relieved that everyone "will go back to normal."[24] In keeping with the discourse around plastic in midcentury America, these new plastic objects were, on the one hand, positioned as extensions of natural products, meant to bring order to domestic and industrial space, and on the other, presented as radically new materials that would remake everyday life. Plastic Man embodies these tensions, and holds widespread radical transformation at bay through his own polymorphous flexibility.

Jack Cole's dynamic Plastic Man illustrations push the boundaries of the comics page, and his stories often involve madcap action and waste. As in Plastic Man's origin story and "Plague of Plastic People," chemical spills and wild energetic explosions are a mainstay of these early comics. Coupled with the frenetic pace of action and motion associated with Plastic Man, there is something of what Sianne Ngai has described as the "zany" in these stories. The frenetic energy expenditures of Plastic Man offers a striking example of "zany performance," which "involves a certain deformation of the forms of activity, a certain indifference to their qualitative differentiation."[25] Plastic Man's continual shifting—he routinely transforms into rugs, boats, fire hydrants, even other people—undoes the very stability of personhood. Ngai associates this aesthetic mode with gendered and racialized modes of labor that blur the distinction between play and work, in which performance becomes expected or demanded as labor. In Plastic Man comics, this erosion of stable character for the sake of performance as labor is clear. In early issues of *Police Comics,* Plastic Man routinely appears as the small-time criminal Eel O'Brian, an identity that allows him to infiltrate criminal gangs. This ruse quickly disappears in the comics, and Plastic Man jettisons his "real" identity. Indeed, in a 2004 *Plastic Man* miniseries by Kyle Baker, the character's origin as Eel O'Brian is described as an "exhausting backstory," something that haunts the superhero Plastic Man, better to be forgotten.[26]

Plastic Man, then, aspires to be a character without a history or personality, defined only by an ability to stretch, flex, and reshape. He is both a symbol of the ephemerality and substance-less-ness of plastics, and a zany embodiment of labor as joyous play. As Amanda Boetzkes has argued about contemporary art that uses plastics, the very foregrounding of plastics as a material produces a kind of stasis: "Plastic is amoral, atemporal, sensorially rich, and yet a profoundly anxious substance. The ubiquity of plastic is evidence of the state of paralysis in the face of the ecological condition. It airs a negative dialectic: what art reveals is precisely the inefficacy of acts of revealing."[27] The spectacle of Plastic Man's plastic body, in this regard, both enforces the "normal" operations of society, as Plastic Man fights crime, and naturalizes the ways in which plastics reshape our bodies, economies, and ecosystems. This curious duality is transplanted onto the stretchy superheroes that follow Plastic Man, all of whom represent both a strange future and a status quo.

Plastic Man's followers in superhero comics include the Elongated Man, Mister Fantastic, and Ms. Marvel. In each of these characters, one finds resonances of bodily flexibility, along with triumphalist imaginaries of a world remade. What plasticity in comics ultimately demonstrates is how plastics became not just a metaphor for thinking about bodies and actions, but also a framework for positing the remaking of bodies and actions themselves in the petrochemical era. Moreover, in these later comics, plastic becomes expressive not just of midcentury consumerist ideology, but also of material limits to consumption and economic growth.

After Plastic Man

Plastic Man's original publisher, Quality Comics, went out of business in 1956, and while DC Comics acquired Plastic Man and other Quality Comics properties, the character would not appear in comics again until 1966. In the meantime, DC Comics created another stretchy character, the Elongated Man (Ralph Dibny). While DC Comics' Elongated Man has similar powers to Plastic Man, the origin of his powers lies not in a mysterious chemical process but in the consumption of the fictional "gingo" fruit.[28] Originally appearing in the *Flash* comic book in the 1960s, Dibny serves, like Plastic Man, as a clearly goofy figure. In *Flash* #115, Dibny is performing as a circus act, stretching to catch a woman launched out of a cannon. He takes a vacation, though, to the "Mexican wilderness" to find the gingo plant: "The fruit of the gingo is the basis of the chemical which I isolated and gave me my extraordinary ability to stretch myself almost without limit!"[29] When Dibny finds a gingo tree, though, he is immediately distracted by a bright red light. The light turns out to be a shrink ray brought to Earth by aliens. The aliens plot to take over the planet once they have shrunk the world's inhabitants. While Plastic Man engages in adventures that pit him against energy inventors and chemical polluters, struggles that allegorize Plastic Man's imbrication in petrochemical plastics and pollution, Elongated Man's encounter thematizes the colonial extraction of rubber. Dibny's gingo fruit gives him flexible powers, figuring both the role natural rubber played in the growth of consumer capitalism and the persistence of materials like natural rubber even within the petrochemical plastics regime of the mid-twentieth century.[30] In the *Flash* story, the aliens' shrink ray ultimately fails once Elongated Man and the Flash team up, combining Dibny's flexibility with the Flash's super speed. Dibny and the Flash's reworked bodies give them heroic powers, while the alien's reworking of bodies poses an existential threat to humanity. In this sense, as in Plastic Man, Elongated Man poses a dichotomy between the flexible and pleasurable use of plastics, and the monstrous, villainous use of technology to reshape the world.

A year after the appearance of Elongated Man in DC Comics, Marvel Comics would introduce a plastic hero, too. The patriarch of the Fantastic Four, Reed Richards, aka Mister Fantastic, is also stretchy and flexible.[31] While Plastic Man is doused by acid and Elongated Man consumes an exotic fruit to become plastic, Reed Richards is, like many of Marvel's nuclear age heroes, exposed to cosmic rays that endow him with powers. While Elongated Man's origin relies on a fictional fruit to give him powers, Reed Richards' powers themselves are presented as quasi-scientific. In a "Fantastic Four Feature Page" from *Fantastic Four* #16, Richards explains:

> The shapes which I can mold my pliable body into are virtually limitless! I can shape myself into anything from a spare auto tire to a delicate, life-saving parachute! These shapes can be assumed with the speed of thought, but only because I have spent long hours practicing and developing my agility! Due to the extreme flexibility and elasticity of my molecular structure, I can absorb the impact of any type of shell (except an atomic missile) without suffering any physical harm! Naturally however, this can be extremely exhausting and leave me in a weakened condition for hours![32]

Reed Richards's theoretically limited powers—he cannot withstand an atomic bomb—express the fragility of an organic body, even from within the fantasy of plastic powers. Human weakness is a recurring trope in the Fantastic Four comics, as the heroes struggle with their newfound powers and responsibilities. Richards, especially, becomes absorbed with science and technology, isolating himself from his family and friends. The comics here register not just the zany heroism of plastic but also the ways in which it creates new limitations and hurdles.

Most recently, Marvel Comics' Kamala Khan, aka Ms. Marvel, has the plastic power set as well.[33] Khan is an "inhuman" in the Marvel universe, a kind of superhero who receives power from fictional "Terrigen mists." After getting her powers, Kamala Khan fights particularly resonant forms of crime and villainy in her native Jersey City. Ms. Marvel's first villain is the Inventor, a bird-headed figure who seeks to create sustainable energy by using disenfranchised millennials as batteries. Fighting against the Inventor, Ms. Marvel uses his technology against him. After shrinking herself, she enters a large robot, and tries to reprogram it. In a page reminiscent of an iconic scene in Charlie Chaplin's film *Modern Times,* Khan works her way through the machine's gears, while thinking about how her approach to superheroism, "working small," requires "thinking smart, not hard."[34] This twenty-first-century comic pits an inhuman superhero against forces of exploitation and gentrification that masquerade as progressive. As Sarah Gibbons has argued, Ms. Marvel's plastic powers thematize the "figurative flexibility to crises" expected of subjects in our moment of privatization and increasing climate instability.[35] With Kamala Khan, the plastic hero's narrative both figures the human as inherently synthetic and posits villainy in the entrepreneurial rhetoric of economic and sustainable development. In this series, Ms. Marvel fights to protect Jersey City, a notably smaller scale than in other superhero narratives. New York City adjacent, Ms. Marvel's Jersey City is represented as a close-knit community of modest citizens. Plastic powers do not remake the world here, and indeed, Ms. Marvel's plasticity thwarts economic development. Plastic here is a way of thinking about preserving community and stopping new modes of consumption and exploitation.

In all of these stories, plastic heroes thematize anxieties about technology, the environment, and the economy, yet the plastic heroes themselves present the inevitability and even zany heroism of a synthetic body, suffused with plastics. Both a celebration and a warning, the plastic hero stretches from heroic to monstrous and envisions both technological advancement and a halt to economic development. As Amanda Boetzkes notes, the challenge we face today is not knowing that plastics are harmful—this is well documented—but instead understanding "how we know in and through plastic as a condition, as an aesthetic predisposition, and as a possible ethical disposition."[36] In plastic superhero comics, the imbrication of plastics in our bodies and our imaginaries is evident, and the "ethical disposition" of plastic superheroes directs us toward an unflinching acceptance of plastics as a part of our perpetual present.

Loss and Persistence

There is one key example of a plastic superhero coming undone, in a way that further gestures to a more complex relationship to plasticity. In DC Comics' 2004 *Identity Crisis* series, Elongated Man's wife, Sue Dibny, is murdered. In a now iconic illustration by artist Rags Morales, Elongated Man cradles his wife's body, as he loses control of his own. In text boxes, Dibny realizes that he is too late to save her: "I stretch as fast as I can. . . . But I'm still not fast enough."[37] If the stretchy powers of these superhero characters often figure into narratives of whimsically elastic crime prevention, *Identity Crisis* twists this absurd flexibility into uncontrollable grief. Dibny's body becomes expressive of his inner state, no longer a superpower but an exaggeration of suffering. *Identity Crisis* follows clearly in the path of DC's gritty reframing of superheroes, and its Elongated Man pietà registers loss even on the plastic bodies that represent consumerist fantasy within a secure social order.

In this moment in *Identity Crisis,* Elongated Man's powers operate in a different, unintended way, signaling grief rather than heroic action. Similar to Kamala Khan's local interest, this revision of the plastic superhero points to a different use of plastics, a framework around them that does not emphasize their magical ephemerality but instead their persistence, integration within our ecologies and bodies, and material resilience. As Heather Davis has argued, the age of plastics—what she refers to as a "plastisphere"—requires us to "learn to accept strange lifeforms, both human and nonhuman."[38] Looking at plastics in new ways—not as a transparent packaging or a means of engaging in a mundane action like toting groceries—means, in part, being mindful of how plastics have shaped us and our behaviors, from conscious choices to unconscious habits. Plastic superheroes articulate petrochemical fantasies of flexibility and action, of expansion beyond limits. Yet, in the case of Elongated Man's grief, they may also illustrate the ways that plastics have proliferated beyond the limits of human control. This realization could, perhaps, be the occasion for a humble approach to living with and among the plastics that are already here with us.

Writing about plasmatic animation, Eisenstein posits that in Disney's cartoons "essence and form are dissected."[39] In "the contour of a neck elongating beyond the neck itself," he argues, "the unity of an object and the form of its representation" ruptures.[40] This stretching and breaking of form and content has been normalized in superhero narratives. The ubiquity of the plastic imaginary and its attendant fantasies of freedom and power is both a key ideology of our consumer society and a reason to look for new ways of being in relation to the plastics that surround us and embolden us. Eisenstein valued the estrangement of form and content in plasmatic cartoons because it reconnected viewers to an animistic nature. What for Eisenstein triggered animistic fantasies might, for us today, clarify how plastics coextend with, and indeed have simply become part of, what we call "nature."

NOTES

1. See Sergei Eisenstein, *On Disney*, ed. Jay Leyda, trans. Alan Upchurch (New York: Seagull, 1986).
2. Eisenstein, *On Disney*, 7.
3. Christophe Bonneuil and Jean-Baptiste Fressoz, *The Shock of the Anthropocene: The Earth, History, and Us*, trans. David Fernbach (New York: Verso, 2017), 289.

4. Ursula K. Heise, "Plastic Nature: Environmentalism and Animated Film," *Public Culture* 26, no. 2 (2014): 305.
5. Heise, "Plastic Nature."
6. Scott Bukatman, *The Poetics of Slumberland: Animated Spirits and the Animating Spirit* (Berkeley: University of California Press, 2012), 13.
7. Bart Beaty, "Superhero Comics," *Fueling Culture: 101 Words for Energy and Environment,* ed. Imre Szeman, Jennifer Wenzel, and Patricia Yaeger (New York: Fordham University Press, 2017), 337.
8. Amanda Boetzkes and Andrew Pendakis, "Visions of Eternity: Plastics and the Ontology of Oil," *e-flux* 47 (September 2013), https://www.e-flux.com/journal/47/60052/visions-of-eternity-plastic-and-the-ontology-of-oil/.
9. Jeffrey L. Meikle, *American Plastic: A Cultural History* (New Brunswick, N.J.: Rutgers University Press, 1997), 64, 68, 67.
10. Jerome Siegel and Joe Shuster, "Superman," *Actions Comics* 1 (June 1938). This issue can be accessed online at https://www.cgccomics.com/1134755001/.
11. J. R. McNeill and Peter Engelke, *The Great Acceleration: An Environmental History of the Anthropocene Since 1945* (Cambridge, Mass.: Harvard University Press, 2014), 137.
12. Bukatman, *Poetics of Slumberland,* 19.
13. Art Spiegelman and Chip Kidd, *Jack Cole and Plastic Man: Forms Stretched to Their Limits* (New York: Chronicle, 2001), 37. Spiegelman's profile of Plastic Man creator Jack Cole originally appeared as "Forms Stretched to Their Limits," *New Yorker* (April 19, 1999), https://www.newyorker.com/magazine/1999/04/19/forms-stretched-to-their-limits-2.
14. Barnett Newman, "The Plasmic Image," in *Barnett Newman: Selected Writings and Interviews,* ed. John P. O'Neill (Berkeley: University of California Press, 1990), 141.
15. Spiegelman, *Jack Cole and Plastic Man,* 15.
16. The United States Rubber Company Advertisement, "Take a Tip from a Navy Torpedo," appears as the penultimate page in *Police Comics* 1 (1941). The comic is available at https://digitalcomicmuseum.com.
17. Jack Cole, "Plastic Man," *Police Comics* 1 (1941), 32. Available at https://digitalcomicmuseum.com.
18. Cole, "Plastic Man," 34.
19. "The Evil Dr. Volt," *Plastic Man* 7 (1947), 5. Available at https://digitalcomicsmuseum.com. In both the Digital Comics Museum and the Grand Comics Database (http://comics.org), this story is attributed to the writer Joe Millard and the artist John Spranger, though the story itself contains no indication of the writer and artist. This is typical of comic books from this period.
20. "The Evil Dr. Volt," 12.
21. "The Evil Dr. Volt," 12.
22. "A Whale of a Tale," *Plastic Man* 3 (1946). Available at https://digitalcomicsmuseum.com. This story is signed by Jack Cole, though the Digital Comics

Museum and the Grand Comics Database (http://comics.org) name the writer as Gwen Hansen, and the artist as Jack Cole.

23. "Plague of Plastic People," *Plastic Man* 22 (1950). Available at https://digitalcomicsmuseum.com. This story is not signed, but the Digital Comics Museum and the Grand Comics Database (http://comics.org) attribute the art to Jack Cole.
24. "Plague of Plastic People," 13.
25. Sianne Ngai, *Our Aesthetic Categories: Zany, Cute, Interesting* (Cambridge, Mass.: Harvard University Press, 2012), 197.
26. Kyle Baker, *Plastic Man* 1 (2004). This issue has been collected in Kyle Baker, *Plastic Man: On the Lam!* (New York: DC Comics, 2005).
27. Amanda Boetzkes, *Plastic Capitalism: Contemporary Art and the Drive to Waste* (Cambridge, Mass.: MIT Press, 2019), 184.
28. The Elongated Man first appears in "The Mystery of the Elongated Man!," *Flash* 112 (1960). The story is attributed to writer John Broome, penciler Carmine Infantino, inker Joe Giella, and letterer Gaspar Saladino by the Grand Comics Database (http://comics.org). This story has been collected most recently in *Flash: The Silver Age Omnibus,* Vol. 1 (Burbank, Calif.: DC Comics, 2018).
29. "The Elongated Man's Secret Weapon!," *Flash* 115 (1960), 3. The story is attributed to writer John Broome, penciler Carmine Infantino, inker Murphy Anderson, and letterer Gaspar Saladino by the Grand Comics Database (http://comics.org). This story has also been collected most recently in *Flash: The Silver Age Omnibus,* Vol. 1 (Burbank, Calif.: DC Comics, 2018).
30. Stephen L. Harp's history of rubber documents that material's crucial role in the making of consumer capitalism: "During the late nineteenth- and early twentieth-century consumer-oriented industrialization—often called the Second Industrial Revolution—rubber was what sugar and cotton had been to the early, or 'first,' Industrial Revolution." Stephen L. Harp, *A World History of Rubber: Empire, Industry, and the Everyday* (Malden, Mass.: Wiley & Sons, 2016), 4.
31. The Fantastic Four were originally cocreated by Jack Kirby and Stan Lee. The superhero team first appeared in *Fantastic Four* 1 (1961). The first issues of the series have been collected recently in Stan Lee and Jack Kirby, *The Fantastic Four Omnibus,* Vol. 1 (New York: Marvel Comics, 2013).
32. "Fantastic Four Feature Page," *Fantastic Four* 16 (1963). According to the Grand Comics Database (http://comics.org), this page was written by Stan Lee, penciled by Jack Kirby, inked by Sol Brodsky, colored by Stan Goldberg, and lettered by Art Simek. It has been collected in Stan Lee and Jack Kirby, *The Fantastic Four Omnibus,* Vol. 1 (New York: Marvel Comics, 2013), 419.
33. Ms. Marvel, aka Kamala Khan, first appeared in *Captain Marvel* 14 (2013), and the *Ms. Marvel* series featuring her began in 2014.
34. *Ms. Marvel* 11 (2015). The issue has been collected in *Ms. Marvel,* Vol. 2:

Generation Why (New York: Marvel Comics, 2015). The story was written by G. Willow Wilson, drawn by Adrian Alphone, colored by Ian Herring, and lettered by Joe Caramagna.

35. Sarah Gibbons, "'I Don't Exactly Have Quiet, Pretty Powers': Flexibility and Alterity in *Ms. Marvel*," *Journal of Graphic Novels and Comics* 8, no. 5 (2017): 450.
36. Amanda Boetzkes, *Plastic Capitalism*, 214.
37. Brad Meltzer and Rags Morales, *Identity Crisis* (Burbank, Calif.: DC Comics, 2016). This moment originally appeared in *Identity Crisis* 1 (2004). The series was written by Brad Meltzer, penciled by Rags Morales, inked by Michael Bair, colored by Alex Sinclair, and lettered by Ken Lopez.
38. Heather Davis, "Imperceptibility and Accumulation: Political Strategies of Plastic," *Camera Obscura* 92 (2016): 192.
39. Eisenstein, *On Disney*, 104.
40. Eisenstein, *On Disney*, 105.

6

Organic Form, Plastic Forms

The Nature of Plastic in Contemporary Ecopoetics

Margaret Ronda

In "The Age of Plastic," a poem published in a recent anthology on the poetry of climate change, Chamorro poet Craig Santos Perez catalogs the innumerable ways plastics are embedded in contemporary life.[1] Like many contemporary poets writing about global ecological crisis and its unevenly distributed effects, Perez—an important writer in the rapidly developing field of ecopoetics—turns to plastic as a key material through which to meditate on these broader socio-ecological transformations. Found in household goods and medical products, technological and transportation networks, bodily interiors and industrial processes, this synthetic material plays an enabling role in virtually all spheres of human activity. In the first half of the poem, Perez highlights these beneficial, life-sustaining applications of plastic, focusing particular attention on the way this material has become vital to bodily health, warmth, and nourishment:

> plastic keeps food fresh—
> delivers medication and clean water—
> forms cable and clothes—
> ropes and nets—even
> stops bullets—
> *"plastic is the perfect creation*
> *because it never dies"*—[2]

These lines chronicle how plastic facilitates the healthy function of the human body, serving as a material supplement that extends the body's natural workings. Perez's long dashes, extending the end of the line and connecting each image to the next, reflect the expansive reach of plastic as it preserves and increases corporeal flourishing. Plastic prolongs and even saves human lives, Perez suggests, imbuing anthropogenic bodily processes with the more "perfect" capacities of the synthetic. As a substance uniquely suited to inhabit, redirect, and expand bodily capacities, plastic exemplifies a sense of care embedded in objects such as food, clothes, and medication, such lines indicate. At the same time, Perez suggests that plastic is a "perfect creation" because unlike the organic bodily processes and capacities it facilitates, this material "never dies"; instead, it extends this "immortal" materiality into the natural forms with which it is imbricated.

Yet alongside its portrayal of the essentially positive dimensions of plastic as an extension of human agency and a material expression of compassion for bodily being, Perez's poem bears a profoundly ambivalent relation to the uncannily animate and deathless capacities of plastic. This aspect emerges in Perez's portrayal of the role plastics play in his own family's reproductive dynamics. Exploring how plastics aid the prenatal development, birth, and newborn care of his infant daughter, Perez evokes several scenes of medical care and domestic intimacy in which plastic plays a formative role:

> the doctor presses the plastic probe
> onto my wife's belly—ultrasound
> waves pulse between fluid, tissue, and
> bone, echoing into an embryo
> of hope—"*plastic makes*
> *this possible*"— (164)

Subsequent stanzas describe the birth tub in which the mother-to-be labors, the Ziploc bag holding the placenta, the plastic nipple that feeds the baby milk. Drawing together this personal description of plastic's role in his daughter's birth with portrayals of the larger imbrications of plastic in everyday existence, Perez conveys plastic as an intimate container for and enabler of reproductive futurity.[3] We can see here a real fathoming with the forms of "hope" that plastic provides, a sense of wonder at its powers to shape and even animate human life, even as it itself remains nonsusceptible to its ravages. Plastic's seemingly inexhaustible capacities afford new senses of the "possible," as if contained in the material itself are new dimensions of human vitality and bodily being. It is as if the substance bears an internal secret to the workings of life itself—a secret upon which human sustenance now depends.

Yet as he wryly contrasts the unsettling endurance of this synthetic substance against the delicate, vulnerable bodies of new baby and mother, Perez registers the powerful disturbance of such a recognition. What would it mean for plastic to make life itself "possible"? What are the consequences of our shared, seemingly bottomless dependency on this substance? Perez's poem goes on to chart plastic's devastating impacts on ocean ecologies and its negative health effects for various creatures:

> in the oceans, there exists three tons
> of fish for every ton of plastic—
> *leaches estrogenic and toxic*
> *chemicals, disrupts hormonal*
> *and endocrine systems*—eight million
> tons of discarded plastic swim
> into the sea every year—
> *causes cancer, infertility, and miscarriage*—
>   multiplies into smaller pieces—
>   plankton, shrimp, fish, whales, and
>   birds confuse plastic with food—
>   absorbs poisons—will plastic make
> life impossible? (164–65)

Laden with toxic chemicals and circulating in oceanic and bodily systems, plastic's material presence no longer facilitates nourishment, health, and reproductive capacities but instead produces illness and pollution. Here, plastic's ubiquity, its toxic constitution, and its imperviousness to decay renders it a threat to the very systems it was designed to preserve. Plastic emerges as a *pharmakon* in Perez's poem, at once life giving and poisonous, its vital interconnection with other beings and processes entailing both sustenance and destruction.[4]

With its short lines and long dashes, its metonymic movement among objects and processes facilitated by plastic, and its figurative emphasis on motion and prosthetic activity, Perez's poem points toward its own acts of *poiesis* and to poetry's broader plasticity as an art form.[5] Poetry, like plastic, bears an intimate capacity to intuit and reflect dimensions of bodily being, bringing the reader inside the workings of the body—breathing, laboring, being ill, giving birth. And both poetry and plastic not only inhabit but also surpass these natural contexts, *living on* in unexpected ways. As cultural studies scholar Heather Davis writes of plastic's capacity to endure: "This quality of the undead is what plastic is often used for: to package and preserve, to seal off bacteria and other organisms to prevent the decay of fruits, vegetables and other matter."[6] Poetry, too, often elaborates tropes of survival beyond its immediate contexts. Central to Perez's meditation on plastic as a medium, then, is a metapoetic attention to poetry as itself a dynamic and life-altering form, placed into a complex analogical relation to the durable material of plastic. If the poem explores the reciprocal dynamics between plastic as a material and the embodied forms that it engages, it also meditates on its own affordances, its forms of *poiesis,* its capacity to endure. At the same time, it offers a means of reflecting on what Davis calls the "accidental or incidental aesthetics" and material effects that develop through plastic's transformative capacities.[7]

In this chapter, I consider the way a series of contemporary ecopoetics texts engage with the material of plastic to explore these questions of *poeisis,* aesthetic and petrochemical. As Canadian ecopoet Adam Dickinson writes of plastic in his recent book, *The Polymers*: "Its pervasiveness, as a tool and as physical and chemical pollution, makes it an organizing principle (a poetics) for recurring forms of language, for obsessive conduct, and for the macromolecular arrangements of people and waste in geopolitical space."[8]

Writing in an era of sustained ecological crisis, ecopoets such as Perez, Dickinson, Allison Cobb, Orchid Tierney, and Divya Victor explore plastic as a resource for approaching the broad dynamics of environmental transformation and the unintended effects of postwar technological ingenuity. These poets all share an experimental orientation in their work, attentive to the ways poetry can be approached as a site of inquiry into the complex relays between language, form, and the material world. They attend to the materiality of plastic itself, the forms it takes, the larger limits and possibilities it enacts, its dynamic interactions with broader ecological systems. Their work explores how, as Jennifer Gabrys, Gay Hawkins, and Mike Michaels write in their collection on the cultural and ecological itineraries of plastic, this entity in its various manifestations "provides particular ways of thinking about and advancing understandings of materiality *as process*."[9] Drawing on and reformulating midcentury process-based poetics, these writers consider how the properties of plastic might necessitate new conceptions of poetic form, contemplating new dimensions of the organic and inorganic, the generative and the toxic, the transient and the enduring.

Plastics and Ecopoetics

Across a half century, Perez's consideration of the ubiquity and miraculous nature of plastics echoes philosopher Roland Barthes's meditation in his classic study of postwar Western culture, *Mythologies*. This text is notable, not only for its innovative reflections on modern mass media and cultural ideologies, but also for its examination of the particular substances, textures, and somatic experiences of the era's burgeoning consumer capitalism. Writing in 1957, Barthes describes detergents and soap powders, the texture of foam, the tactility of wooden and plastic toys, the streamlined design of the Citröen, luminous images of food and movie star faces in the media. In his chapter on plastic, Barthes highlights the versatile properties of this material, writing of its unique capacity for transformation and its life-bearing ability:

> So, more than a substance, plastic is the very idea of its transformation; as its everyday name states, it is ubiquity made visible. And it is this, in fact, which makes it a miraculous

> substance: a miracle is always a sudden transformation of nature. Plastic remains impregnated throughout with this wonder: it is less a thing than the trace of a movement.[10]

Barthes's language bespeaks a sense of plastic not as a material substance but a medium characterized by its transformative capacities. "Less a thing than the trace of a movement," plastic's metamorphic qualities allow it both to inhabit and to radically alter natural forms. Drawing on images of generation and reproduction, Barthes imbues plastic with a creative and miraculous capacity. "The whole world *can* be plasticized, and even life itself, since, we are told, they are beginning to make plastic aortas," he declares (99). Even the human heart will become "plasticized," Barthes suggests, demonstrating plastic's capacities to inhabit and animate life itself. For Barthes, plastic's miraculous properties are a mark of anthropogenic power, revealing a newfound ability to recast natural forms according to our desires and needs: "the very itinerary of plastic gives [humans] the euphoria of prestigious freewheeling through Nature" (98).

While plastics were first developed in the early twentieth century, their production expanded rapidly during the 1950s and early 1960s with new technological advances. Chemical firms turned attention to consumer markets, developing plastic products to fulfill myriad needs and functions. As Susan Freinkel details in her history of plastics, *Plastic: A Toxic Love Story,* this wide array of affordable plastic products created a powerful new sense of consumer identity and possibility, particularly for middle-class Americans. Barthes's exuberant portrayal of the miraculous power and seemingly limitless potential of plastic, in turn, is characteristic of general sentiments about this substance during this period. The material itself seemed to promise this flexibility, as Freinkel writes: "Plastics heralded a new era of material freedom, liberation from nature's stinginess. In the plastic age, raw materials would not be in short supply or constrained by their innate properties. . . . Plastic, admirers predicted, would deliver us into a cleaner, brighter world in which all would enjoy a 'universal state of democratic luxury.'"[11] These early conceptions of plastic frame this substance as the emblematic material of human potential, embodying and expanding human sentience, capacities, and freedoms. Such humanist optimism about plastic's capabilities is indelibly linked, here, to the ideological commitments of a consumerist and expansionist Cold War culture.

Emerging alongside this postwar plastics boom were new aesthetic interests in questions of materials, form, and process in American poetry. Reimagining Modernist interests in impersonality, abstraction, and sculptural aesthetics, postwar poets turned to more personal explorations of the somatic and processual nature of poetic making. Black Mountain poets Charles Olson, Robert Duncan, M. C. Richards, Robert Creeley, and Denise Levertov developed a process-based poetics emphasizing the perceptual encounter with materials and the development of poetic form immanent to this encounter, connecting these processes to broader ecological dynamics.[12] Perhaps the two most influential reformulations of these ideas are Levertov's 1965 "Some Notes on Organic Form" and Olson's 1950 "Projective Verse" manifesto.[13] Both poets develop these ideas about poetry as what Levertov calls a "revelation" of its materials as an extension of their broader beliefs in systemic interconnection. Olson, who came to be powerfully influenced by Alfred North Whitehead's process philosophy and systems-thinking, develops what ecocritic Jonathan Skinner terms a "visceral poetics" that connects body, matter, and system in dynamic interaction.[14] In his essay on "Projective Verse," Olson argues for a process-based model of poetry that graphs the energy and forms of perceptions as they unfold. The poem is an active, experimental enactment of the interweaving of body, breath, and poetic material (syllable, line, syntax, objects) with external perception and experience. Olson envisions the poem as a process of "composition by field," a kinetic experience of shaping and being shaped by the materials at hand. Levertov's poetics is broadly positioned against the destructiveness of nuclear war and environmental imbalance, conceiving of the forms and processes of poetry as a generative space of imagination and wholeness amid an age of "chaos."[15] Her "Some Notes on Organic Form" discusses "exploratory" poetry that involves an "intuitive interaction between all the elements involved" toward the creation of the "rhythm of the whole."

These poetics renovate the Romantic concept of organic form, with its emphasis on living systems and its fundamental analogy between aesthetic creation and natural processes, for the postwar era. As Greg Ellermann points out in a penetrating essay on the legacies of Coleridge's organicist aesthetics, for Coleridge and other theorists of organic form, the principle shared in common between natural entities and the form of an aesthetic work such as a poem is *plasticity*: "In Coleridge, plasticity is a universal principle of formation that links artworks with natural things, and each moment of artistic creation with the dynamic unfolding of organic life."[16] These postwar experimental poets follow this Coleridgean sense of poetry as a "plastic" form: as Black Mountain poet and potter M. C. Richards writes in her well-known book on aesthetic making, *Centering in Pottery, Poetry, and the Person,* "Poetry is probably the most plastic of all materials," the most receptive to creative imprint.[17]

Such techniques of composition by field, breath-based poetics, and attention to material interrelation have been crucially influential to the development of ecopoetics as a contemporary field of poetic practice.[18] Yet while midcentury writers such as Levertov, Olson, Duncan, and Richards consider poetic form in relation to natural materials (plants, cells, and animal life, as well as wood, clay, and stone) and portray systematicity through ideas of unity, wholeness, and balance, practitioners of contemporary ecopoetics enact these portrayals of systems under the sign of toxicity, pollution, and global climate change. CAConrad, a well-known ecopoetics writer who composes "somatic rituals" to create restorative connections to their sustaining environment, at once draws on and reformulates the ideas of organic form in their "The Right to Manifest Manifesto":

> I cannot stress enough how much this mechanistic world . . . has required me to FIND MY BODY to FIND MY PLANET in order to find my poetry. If I am an extension of this world then I am an extension of garbage, shit, pesticides, bombed and smoldering cities, microchips, cyber, astral and biological pollution, BUT ALSO the beauty of an unspoiled patch of sand.[19]

As Conrad's catalog conveys, ecopoetics experiments draw connections between body, planet, and poetry and insist on the irreducible relation between the toxic and the natural under industrialized capitalism. They often highlight the way life-sustaining elements—water, soil, air—often come to contain life-threatening qualities at a variety of scales, a *pharmakon* of the damaged present. And they point to the ways our interfusion with and dependency on these elements necessitates new conceptions of embodied being that reshape organicist aesthetic modes. One key site of such ecopoetic explorations is the material of plastic—its affordances, its relational capacities, its ecological implications—and the broader interpenetration of the organic and the synthetic that plastic entails. As the profound scale of plastic's environmental impacts has become more widely recognized over the past decade, plastic has become a particularly central locus of ecopoetic meditation and an extension, in new directions, of these conceptions of organic form. As Lynn Keller writes in a chapter on plastics and ecopoetic writing in her recent *Recomposing Ecopoetics,* plastics have elicited contemporary poetic explorations of the "imbrication of nature and culture or the natural and the artificial; the permeability between what has conventionally been considered the bounded inside and outside; and the thorough interrelation of living things with one another and with substances in their environments, including human-devised toxins."[20] Turning to plastic facilitates particularly nuanced engagements with these broader themes in ecologically oriented poetry.

In her recent book, *Plastic: An Autobiography,* Allison Cobb retells one history of the rise of plastics and explores the nature of its material forms. Cobb is a Portland-based poet who employs documentary techniques, drawing on interviews, photojournalism, personal history, and experimental biography in this hybrid poetic prose text to investigate the nature of plastic. In *Plastic: An Autobiography,* she turns to plastic in its appearances as an intimate, alienated, historically embedded and globally circuitous entity. Offering extended meditations on the author's discovery of a car part, a photo of an albatross body filled with plastic, and the creation of the thermonuclear bomb, Cobb's experimental poetic prose highlights the imbrication of plastic into human and nonhuman forms, material histories, and ecosystemic degradation. If Barthes's essay praises the innocuous and almost wholly mysterious birth of plastic in labs, Cobb reveals the darker origins of plastic in military use, revealing that polyethylene was a key component of atomic weaponry. She writes of the decision to use plastic in the plutonium bomb by atomic scientists:

> They needed some other material to intervene, a material of low atomic weight that would not interfere with the reactions. They chose polyethylene, just carbon and hydrogen, made from the bodies of ancient sea creatures, out of the same molecules that make up every living being. . . .
>
> When the atomic bomb goes off, it heats the plastic to a million degrees in an instant, creating a plasma that expands explosively, squeezing the deuterium and igniting a thermonuclear fire.[21]

For Cobb, charting this itinerary of plastic back to its source is to connect with the deepest initial perceptions of these scientists as they engaged in nuclear and plastic *poiesis*. Of their first fathomings of atomic energy and plastic materiality, she writes: "To see as if // to touch. To see, an inside // sense, a sort // of felt thought" (49–50). Scattering these phrases across the page, Cobb evokes a sense of the imaginative, intuitive energies of making that went into the creation of these materials; such a moment might be termed an instance of what critic Peter Middleton calls "physics envy."[22] Cobb portrays these histories and moments of creative inspiration in order to understand her own connections to this material. As Cobb points out, to write a lyric prose poem about plastic is to write "an autobiography." "Anything alive could write this book," she writes. "The autobiography of plastic is the autobiography of everything" (vi).

Across the text, Cobb considers in an extended way a car part she finds on her fence, using it to meditate on the fundamental somatic needs that plastic addresses. The unwieldy car part is unnoticed in its daily function: it is, Cobb writes, "the perfect cover." Brought out of its functional context and into Cobb's living room and then bedroom, it becomes a palpable site for reflecting on plastic's often invisible omnipresence in our lives and on what plastic covers and covers over: "indeterminate, no whiff of industrial blood on it, featureless, flawless, eternal." Through this extended somatic experiment, Cobb explores the intimacy with plastic central to contemporary life, connecting plastic's broader atomic history with her own daily perceptions and bodily experiences. Made of the same chemical compound, polyethylene, as the material in the bomb, the car part emblematizes the uncanny organic unity of plastic as a substance that dynamically connects past and present, living and inanimate entities, itself made of the "molecules that connect every living being."

Plastic *Poiesis*

While Cobb highlights the history and ubiquity of plastic through her expanded-field meditation on a single exemplary object, Adam Dickinson focuses sustained attention on the broader *poiesis* of polymers and petrochemicals in his recent works of poetry, *The Polymers* and *Anatomic.*[23] Dickinson's work often explores the interplay between poetic and scientific logics and practices, and it might be best characterized as conceptual: guided by procedure or structuring concept.[24] For Dickinson, the biosemiotic dimensions of plastic—the way it inscribes itself into the hormones and chemicals in bodies, terrestrial and aquatic ecosystems, and even the fossil record—necessitate expanded ways of conceiving of anthropogenic making, while raising new, unsettling conceptions of the dynamic form and action of these materials. Plastic reads and writes us as we read and write it, Dickinson asserts in *The Polymers:* "Our chains reread us precipitously" (3). As Dickinson examines the interconnected nature of plastic as a material, he takes the polymeric chain—the repetitive structure of polymers and their connective dynamics—as a key formal principle, registering in his compositional methods how the plastic nature of poetic language and design makes palpable these broader biosemiotic expressions. At the same time, his work points attention back to the ways plastic itself facilitates our bodily existences and creative endeavors alike: "This entire book was typed on plastic keys," Dickinson writes (111).

In *The Polymers,* Dickinson develops playful, unexpected techniques from plastic's composition of molecules to develop a poetics shaped from this material: a plastic *poiesis.* Each poem offers a new formal framework for embodying the properties of plastic, whether in a piece that draws on the "Resin Identification Code" developed by the plastics industry to meditate on the myriad appearances of plastic, or a poem that uses anagrams of one polymer ("Halter Top [Translating Translating a Polyester]"), or a piece called "Cigar? Toss It in a Can. It Is So Tragic." that plays with what Dickinson calls "linguistic isomers," or orthographic neighbors and malapropisms: "For all intensive purposes, the fire distinguishers / are pigments of the imagination" (23). Another poem, "Coca-Cola Dasani," is at once an abecedarian and, according to Dickinson's "Materials and Methods" primer, "a perfect anagram of all constituent elements of section 64 of the Canadian Environmental Protection Act": "a a a alps and applicable at at before best beverages bicarbonates bottle bottled calcium chlorides clean collection commerce composition content cool dissolved . . ." (107, 42). Across these poems, Dickinson develops linguistic and poetic patterns that replicate the structural logics of polymers (repetition, associative chains, anaphora), while highlighting the flexibility and multiple guises of plastic as a material. The language, at once lively and structured, repetitive and defamiliarizing, *enacts* (rather than simply representing) the patterns and dynamics of plastics. Plastic appears here as a profoundly generative and social medium, imbricated in and formally expressive of human desires, behaviors, social systems, hierarchies, forms of freedom, and modes of exploitation. We live in and through plastics, Dickinson writes, constitutive as it is of our most intimate relations and corporeal experiences: "Lunch boxes and lipsticks / are our mothers" (14).

Dickinson's most recent book, *Anatomic,* extends this consideration of the somatic dimensions of plastic further through a fascinating and disturbing corporeal experiment. Dickinson had his blood, sweat, and urine tested for a wide array of substances: "Phthalates, Dioxin-like chemicals, PCBS, PFCS, OCPS, PAHS, HBCDS, Parabens, BPA, Triclosan, additional pesticides, and twenty-eight heavy metals."[25] He writes, "I am a spectacular and horrifying crowd. How can I read me? How can I write me?" (9). The book interweaves diaristic entries ("specimen reports") about Dickinson's lengthy biomonitoring regime with poems evoking this petrochemical biosemiosis, as

Dickinson discovers that his body is inscribed by various environmental toxins and synthetic chemicals, some introduced via plastic products (particularly bisphenol A and phthalates). Across *Anatomic,* Dickinson draws on the dynamics of hormones and bodily processes to generate what he calls a "prosody of metabolism," exploring the various ways these chemicals interact with and alter bodies. In a prose poem, "Disruptors," Dickinson meditates on the textures and flexibility of phthalates, exploring how it makes its way into bodily interiors: "The softness of phthalates is the softness of squeeze toys, pacifiers, and laboratory tubes. . . . The softness of phthalates is the softness of transparent packaging crumpled in a fist. When released it springs outward from memory" (77). Through both these ecopoetic meditations on plastic's chemical and material properties, Dickinson creates new forms of composition by field, connecting body, matter, and energy system in and through the plastic forms of poetry. His work develops a dynamic, uncanny language—a plastic biosemiotics—that evokes the imbrication of this material within and across life forms and systems.

Plastic Waste, Toxic Bodies

In his celebratory midcentury portrait of plastics, Barthes did not foresee the devastating ecological implications of this material's natural "itinerary." He lists a series of objects built for long-term use—"suitcase, brush, car-body, toy, fabric, tube, basin"—but increasingly, the petrochemical industry embarked on a more profitable venture in its development of plastics: disposable products and packaging. Today, fully half of all plastics manufactured become trash in under a year, according to a recent study.[26] The production of plastics by the petrochemical industry is energy intensive and fossil fuel dependent. For each ounce of polyethylene produced, according to the EPA, an ounce of carbon dioxide is emitted. And if the components of plastic production bear a significant carbon footprint, the ongoing presence of plastic after consumer use bears an even more weighty environmental impact. Only around 9 percent of plastic goods are recycled, and the remainder ends up in landfills, decomposing over about five hundred years and leaching harmful pollutants into soil and waterways. Vast quantities of plastic can be found in the earth's oceans, accumulating in garbage patches and riverways and threatening aquatic life. As media studies critic Sy Taffel puts it, "One of the materials most commonly associated with a throwaway consumer culture in fact produces environmental effects measured in millions of years."[27] BPA and other chemicals in plastics have been linked to various harmful effects on human health as well, as Perez's "Age of Plastic" and Dickinson's *Anatomic* detail. It is to these itineraries and their biotic implications that contemporary ecopoetics often turns, meditating on the novel forms and patterns that this metamorphosing material takes after it is "empty of [humane] awareness."

Cobb's reflections on plastic emerge from a photograph she saw of a dead albatross chick filled with plastic trash, taken by Susan Middleton on Kure Atoll in the Northern Hawaiian Islands in 2004 and published in *National Geographic* in 2005.[28] Cobb evokes the beautiful flight patterns of the albatross and its strong, delicate, airborne frame: "*In-spire.* The albatross is filled with air—tiny sacs pack the vault of its ribs, curving around its organs and extending through the narrow bones of its wings that span six feet, eight feet, eleven, the longest of any creature" (24–25). Alongside such portrayals of the kinesthetic motion and lightness of the albatross, Cobb juxtaposes the disturbing contents of the cut-open albatross chick in the photo: "The cut reveals a black cylinder of plastic, a bottle / cap, a toy top. // Plastic erupts from inside the chick" (13). Inside the body of the bird, plastic circulates and accumulates, enmeshed in and obstructing its internal workings, functioning as the opposite of air. In her meditations on this image, Cobb draws a connection to Coleridge's "Rime of the Ancient Mariner" and its figure of the dead albatross that haunts the mariner. After the mariner kills the albatross, Cobb writes, "All / that breathes is monstrous" (17). Here the material of plastic becomes the figure of monstrous ongoingness and dynamism, as the plastic "erupts" from the corpse, strangely vital. In its metamorphic appearances and activity, plastic emerges here as an uncanny kind of organic form, its shape and presence "proceeding" rather than "superinduced," processual rather than imposed.[29]

Another recent book of ecopoetics that explores the new entanglements of life forms and the "monstrous" processes generated by plastic waste through its inner formal workings is Orchid Tierney's spare, haunting *ocean plastic.* This text's formal plasticity conveys the accumulative presence of plastic in ocean ecosystems as it reshapes these systemic dynamics. In Tierney's work, we glimpse what critic Patricia Yaeger calls the "techno-ocean," which "subtracts sea creatures and adds trash."[30] As Yaeger writes, the techno-ocean reminds us that "the ocean as *oikos* or home rolls under, beneath, and inside the edicts of state and free market capitalism"; the plastic debris swirling in ocean gyres demonstrates the fateful presence of these imperatives.[31] Tierney's *ocean plastic* begins with short fragments that mirror the small bits of plastic that find their way into the ocean: "gritty grains gauge soft oyster flesh | / airy spines spun with sea gull stomachs."[32] The repeated sounds call to mind the material encounter between ocean creatures and plastic, the hard *g* sounds against the sibilant *s,* while the vertical bar suggests obstructions and channels through and around which these entities form.[33] Each page accumulates more of these fragments, recombining the words and phrases into new arrangements. Unsettling and recomposing, its accretive form conveys the swirling mass of the marine gyre:

> an amputated sea welts | soft | gull stomachs | guppy globsters |
> thicken | moss piglets | airy spines spun with | urchin
>   wraith-skins |
> blue sea burrs buried in | polymermaid tears | gritty grains
>   gauge |
> gummy squidding hydrophobic cthulhu | on scud currents | red
> gossamer fleece | oyster flesh | tumbling over | transparent fish |
>   gill
> filters | partial polyghosts soupify | sympathy | in garbage
>   gyres (18)

Tierney's fragments halt and progress, enacting blockages and movement, limit and fluidity. The words themselves register uncanny new forms, an enmeshed array of textures and matter: "polyghosts," "guppy globsters," "gummy squidding," "a herd of nurdles / grazing." What is living and nonliving blurs in these fluid combinations, as beings occupy liminal and transforming forms of animacy.[34]

Through this transforming flow, we glimpse, in motion, the effects of the development of the ocean as arena of capitalist extraction and as dumping ground, as consumer goods and waste from industrial fishing operations reappear in uncanny forms, swirling alongside uncanny sea creatures. The poem renders the processes by which organisms interact, offering a portrait of what marine biologists have called the "plastic soup" of oceanic pollution. As Jennifer Gabrys writes, "this plastic soup is a site of continual metamorphosis and intra-actions, so that new or previously unrecognized corporeal relations emerge in the newly constituted spaces of the oceans."[35] As the text draws attention to these violently unmade and recombinant forms, it also highlights its own capacity to convey such processes through its patterns of repetition, fragmentation, and recombination. Drawing the reader into a scene of transfiguring materials, the poem activates a complex field of perceptions of textures, sound, touch, and friction. The dynamic capacities of field poetics here convey the motions and changing proportions of this transforming oceanic entity, enacting, as Levertov puts it, the "rhythm of the whole" in all its disturbing, animate force.

Plastic Futures in Countertranslation

The end of Perez's poem, "The Age of Plastic," returns to an image of the speaker feeding his infant daughter and articulating a poignant, if disconcerting, wish:

> i press the plastic nipple of
> the warmed bottle to
> my daughter's small lips—for a moment,
> i wish she was made of plastic
> so that she, too, would survive
> our wasteful hands—so that she,
> too, will have a "great future." (166)

With these closing lines, the poem raises difficult questions: What and who will "survive" this "age of plastic"? What will a "great future" consist of—and for whom? Perez's closing lines immediately follow his evocation of the Great Pacific Garbage Patch and its forms of harm inflicted on Pacific marine life. In this light, these final lines can be read as a response to the particular threats plastic poses to the island habitats and communities that sustain his family. Born in Guam but currently living in Hawai'i, Perez draws attention in his books of poetry to the forms of "survivance" characteristic of Pacific Islander communities, while highlighting the interlocking systems of colonialism and racial capitalism that threaten them.[36] Pacific Islander populations and marine ecologies are "frontline communities" in relation to various forms of ecological crisis including global plastic pollution, facing dramatically disproportionate impacts to health and ecosystemic flourishing.[37] Perez's expanded field poetics highlight the lifeways of indigenous ecologies and the ways social forces transform these ecologies. As he writes in a recent lyric essay on colonialism and the toxic history of Pacific plastics, "Our Sea of Plastic": "The plasticity of colonialism can be felt in how its toxic presence crashes against the shore of these fragments and floats on (and below) the surface of the poem. The plastic ocean is in us. It molds our bodies and stories."[38] Perez underscores how islander communities often emblematize what Macarena Gómez-Barris calls an "extractive zone"—sites of intensified extraction and waste that also unearths "a differently perceivable world, an intangible space of emergence."[39]

These dynamics—formal, ecological, intergenerational—are brought into further focus through a recent "countertranslation" of Perez's "The Age of Plastic" by Indian-American poet Divya Victor, first into Tamil and then back into English. Victor's countertranslation appears in *The Margins* blog of the Asian American Writers' Workshop, as part of a larger series of countertranslations that aim to "destabilize notions of mastery" and "open possibilities of exchange beyond the frames of English" by creating new engagements with a poetic text.[40] Victor's countertranslation of Perez's poem calls attention to what is passed down and what is lost, what is made and what is rendered disposable. As she writes in her author's note, Victor drew on the assistance of her mother, grandmother, and aunt to generate this translation. Drawing on Perez's images of reproductive dynamics, Victor's countertranslation develops by calling forth a maternal linguistic legacy—a "mother tongue"—to collectively create this piece. In this way, Victor's own process of translation as a form of active *poeisis* recasts Perez's meditations on reproductive futurity in an age of plastics, highlighting the way poetic language becomes a means of bearing, carrying on, or losing cultural heritage, as well as being a dynamic material to shape and transform.

Plastic—as material and subject—becomes the locus of meditation on these questions of language, making, inheritance, loss, and waste. Victor's translation, borne across languages, cultures, and geographical terrain, subtly alters the figurative landscape of Perez's piece. Victor pares down its catalogs of information about plastic and develops spare, surreal images from his descriptions. She writes:

எங்கள் மகள்
Our daughter

தொட்டிலில் தூங்குகிறாள்
பிளாஸ்டிக் பூக்கள்
sleeps in a crib. She eats
சாப்பிடுகிறாள்
plastic flowers.[41]

From Perez's more straightforward descriptions of the infant's nourishment and care comes this eerie, fairy-tale-like image of a small child eating plastic flowers. At poem's end, Victor plays on Perez's images of plastic's emptiness to conjure a meditation on disposability in human and nonhuman forms:

இந்த வெறுமை என்ன?
What is this emptiness?

பிறந்தோம், சுரண்டப்பட்டோம், எறியப்பட்டோம்
We were born, were exploited, were thrown away.

In Victor's countertranslation, the "we" refers both to plastic and human lives rendered disposable. The attention to human disposability is particularly underscored by the word "exploited," drawing forth the more subtle implications in Perez's poem about the susceptibility of precarious populations. Victor's version closes, then, by reminding readers of the governing capitalist ethos of exploitation and disposability that governs these dynamics, and highlights the unfathomable "emptiness" that this ethos produces at multiple scales, for humans, creaturely life, and biotic processes.

Shored against this emptiness, there is what Victor calls the "mudbank" of poetic language, gathered to protect, to restore, to hold together. Victor writes in her author's note of her poetic process: "From [Perez's] metaphor of salt water emerges my story of mud, land, muddled, *lang syne,* language made into a mudbank—as archaic and as new as a womb at the bottom of the sea, where plastic blooms and takes us back into the grasp of its collapsing calyx." Across these ecopoetic texts, poetry becomes a means of thinking through this medium, examining plastic's forms of vitality and force, tracing its patterns of interconnection and its toxic "blooms," holding open the emptiness it generates. Laying bare the violence and the power of these seemingly benign materials, these poems portray plastic as a vital planetary form bearing creative and destructive potential, living within and beyond organic lifespans. These works draw attention, as well, to the poem's own medium as a means of imagining with and against plastic's affordances—a form of countertranslation that holds forth other possibilities. As Perez writes in "Our Sea of Plastic": "The poem proves that if you are reading its currents of words, then you have survived, and it is not too late to re-shape our future."

NOTES

1. Portions of this chapter originally appeared on the Stanford University Press blog, March 2018: https://stanfordpress.typepad.com/blog/2018/04/plastic-pollution-and-poetry.html.
2. Craig Santos Perez, "The Age of Plastic," in *Big Energy Poets: Poets Think Climate Change,* ed. Amy King and Heidi Lynn Staples (Buffalo, N.Y.: BlazeVOX, 2018), 164–67.

3. For a powerful personal and theoretical meditation on plastics, reproduction, and disability, see Jody Roberts's essay on his daughter's birth and diagnosis with cerebral palsy, "Reflections of an Unrepentant Plastiphobe: An Essay on Plasticity and the STS Life," in *Accumulations: The Material Politics of Plastic*, ed. Jennifer Gabrys, Gay Hawkins, and Mike Michael (London: Routledge, 2013), 121–33.
4. In "Plato's Pharmacy," Jacques Derrida charts the various meanings of *pharmakon* that appear in Plato's dialogues. *Pharmakon*, Derrida suggests, "acts as both remedy and poison" and "can be—alternatively or simultaneously—beneficent or maleficent." *Pharmakon* might be seen as a particularly amenable concept in relation to the materials and cultural meanings of plastic, both in terms of its fundamental ambivalence and duality, and also in the way it emblematizes what Derrida calls "antisubstance itself: that which resists any philosopheme, indefinitely exceeding its bounds as nonidentity, nonessence, nonsubstance." Jacques Derrida, "Plato's Pharmacy," in *Dissemination*, trans. Barbara Johnson (Chicago: University of Chicago Press), 70.
5. As Greg Ellermann writes, plasticity can be defined as the "susceptibility of matter to receive beautiful form as well as to the creative power or impulse that gives form. Plastic arts are defined by the process of shaping, by form's simultaneous imposition on and emergence from a given material" (199). Greg Ellermann, "Plasticity, Poetry, and the End of Art: Malabou, Hegel, Keats," in *Romanticism and Speculative Realism*, ed. Chris Washington and Anne McCarthy (London: Bloomsbury, 2019).
6. Heather Davis, "Life and Death in the Anthropocene: A Short History of Plastic," *Art in the Anthropocene: Encounters Among Aesthetics, Politics, Environments, and Epistemologies*, ed. Heather Davis and Etienne Turpin (London: Open Humanities Press, 2015), 352.
7. Davis, "Life and Death in the Anthropocene," 348.
8. Adam Dickinson, *The Polymers* (Toronto: House of Anansi, 2013), x.
9. Jennifer Gabrys, Gay Hawkins, and Mike Michael, "Introduction: From Materiality to Plasticity," *Accumulation: The Material Politics of Plastic* (London: Routledge, 2013), 3.
10. Roland Barthes, *Mythologies*, trans. Annette Lavers (New York: Noonday, 1972), 97.
11. Susan Freinkel, *Plastic: A Toxic Love Story* (New York: Houghton Mifflin, 2011), 8.
12. See Edward Halsey Foster, *Understanding the Black Mountain Poets* (Columbia: University of South Carolina Press, 1994), Helen Molesworth, *Leap Before You Look: Black Mountain College 1933–1957* (New Haven, Conn.: Yale University Press, 2015), and Mary Emma Harris, *The Arts at Black Mountain College* (Cambridge, Mass.: MIT Press, 1987) for discussions of Black Mountain poetics and the interarts experiments associated with this college.
13. Denise Levertov, "Some Notes on Organic Form," in *New and Collected Es-*

says (New York: New Directions, 1973); Charles Olson, "Projective Verse," in *Collected Prose,* ed. Donald Allen and Benjamin Friedlander (Berkeley: University of California Press, 1997).

14. Jonathan Skinner, "Visceral Ecopoetics in Charles Olson and Michael McClure: Proprioception, Biology, and the Writing Body," in *Ecopoetics: Essays in the Field,* ed. Angela Hume and Gillian Osborne (Iowa City: University of Iowa Press, 2018), 65–83.
15. Denise Levertov, "A Note on the Work of Imagination," *The Poet in the World* (New York: New Directions, 1974), 200.
16. Greg Ellermann, "Plasticity, Poetry, and the End of Art," 200.
17. M. C. Richards, *Centering in Pottery, Poetry, and the Person* (Middletown, Conn.: Wesleyan University Press, 1987), 67. Richards draws extensively on Coleridge's ideas of organic form throughout this book.
18. For one key discussion of these legacies, see the "Introduction" to the recent edited volume *Ecopoetics: Essays in the Field* (Iowa City: University of Iowa Press, 2018). Editors Angela Hume and Gillian Osborne point out that their subtitle gestures to the centrality of these midcentury poetic practices to contemporary ecopoetics.
19. CAConrad, *A Beautiful Marsupian Afternoon: New Soma(tics)* (Seattle: Wave, 2012), 1.
20. Lynn Keller, *Recomposing Ecopoetics: North American Poetry of the Self-Conscious Anthropocene* (Charlottesville: University of Virginia Press, 2017), 61.
21. Allison Cobb, *Plastic: An Autobiography* (New York: Essay, 2016), 69. Susan Freinkel discusses the military history of plastics in her *Plastic: A Toxic Love Story.*
22. Peter Middleton, *Physics Envy: American Poetry and Science in the Cold War and After* (Chicago: University of Chicago Press, 2015).
23. Another key ecopoetics text that engages with plastic as a material and develops a mode of plastic *poeisis* is Evelyn Reilly, *Styrofoam* (New York: Roof, 2009). Two insightful critical considerations of this book and its ecopoetics are Lynn Keller's discussion of Reilly in her chapter on plastics in *Recomposing Ecopoetics* and Heather Milne's chapter on Reilly in *Poetic Matterings: Neoliberalism, Affect, and the Posthuman in Twenty-First Century North American Feminist Poetics* (Iowa City: University of Iowa Press, 2018), 133–51.
24. For a reading of Dickinson's *The Polymers* as a work of conceptual ecopoetics, see Joshua Schuster, "Reading the Environs: Toward a Conceptual Ecopoetics," *Ecopoetics: Essays in the Field,* ed. Angela Hume and Gillian Osborne (Iowa City: University of Iowa Press, 2018), 208–27.
25. Adam Dickinson, *Anatomic* (Toronto: Coach House, 2018), 9.
26. See Sharon Lerner, "Waste Only: The Plastic Industry's Fight to Keep Polluting the World," *The Intercept,* July 20, 2019, https://theintercept.com/2019/07/20/plastics-industry-plastic-recycling/.

27. Sy Taffel, "Technofossils of the Anthropocene: Media, Geology, and Plastics," in *Cultural Politics* 12, no. 3 (November 2016): 355–75.
28. This famous photo was printed in *National Geographic* and then reprinted widely, including in a 2015 online *Audubon Society* article about plastic's effects on seabirds. Purbita Saha, *Audubon,* September 15, 2015. "99 Percent of Seabird Species Could Be Tainted with Plastic by 2050, Science Says," https://www.audubon.org/news/99-percent-seabird-species-could-be-tainted plastic-2050-science-says.
29. Samuel Taylor Coleridge, *Biographia Literaria* (Oxford: Oxford University Press, 1973), 262.
30. Patricia Yaeger, "Sea Trash, Dark Pools, and the Tragedy of the Commons." *PMLA* 125, no. 3 (May 2010): 530.
31. Yaeger, "Sea Trash," 529.
32. Orchid Tierney, *ocean plastic* (Kenmore, N.Y.: BlazeVOX, 2019), 10.
33. In her notes, Tierney suggests that the vertical line represents the pipes through which plastic enters marine ecosystems (24).
34. For an essential intellectual genealogy and innovative theoretical deployment of the term *animacy,* see Mel Y. Chen, *Animacies: Biopolitics, Racial Mattering, and Queer Affect* (Durham, N.C.: Duke University Press, 2012).
35. Jennifer Gabrys, "Plastic and the Work of the Biodegradable," in *Accumulation: The Material Politics of Plastic,* ed. Jennifer Gabrys, Gay Hawkins, and Mike Michael (London: Routledge, 2013), 217.
36. The term "survivance" is from Gerald Vizenor, *Survivance: Narratives of Native Presence* (Lincoln: University of Nebraska Press, 2008).
37. Thom Davies, "Toxic Space and Time: Slow Violence, Necropolitics, and Petrochemical Pollution," *Annals of the American Association of Geographers* 108, no. 6 (2018): 1537–53, doi:10.1080/ 24694452.2018.1470924.
38. Craig Santos Perez, "Our Sea of Plastic," *Kenyon Review Blog,* February 1, 2013, https://www.kenyonreview.org/2013/02/our-sea-of-plastic/.
39. Macarena Gómez-Barris, *The Extractive Zone: Social Ecologies and Decolonial Perspectives* (Durham, N.C.: Duke University Press, 2017), xx.
40. Santos Perez, "The Age of Plastic," and Divya Victor, "Countertranslation," in *The Margins: Asian American Writers' Workshop,* November 1, 2018, https://aaww.org/the-age-of-plastic/.
41. Victor, "Countertranslation."

7

On the Beach

Porous Plasticity, Migration Art, and the *Objet Trouvé* of the Wasteocene

Maurizia Boscagli

Since the moment of its invention in the early twentieth century, plastic has been considered the matter of modernity, and as such it has heralded creativity, progress, futurity, and the new. Plastic's utopian qualities have been acknowledged by Roland Barthes,[1] and more recently by Catherine Malabou.[2] In particular Malabou opposes flexibility, the quality that neoliberalism demands of its subject, to plasticity, the capability to take and give form, and recognizes plasticity as the point of departure for political innovation and dissent. This essay addresses the ways a possible politics of denunciation and resistance to neoliberal capital is carried on today by an aesthetic appropriation of plastic. I study plastic artifacts that appear on beaches around the world as traces of two contemporary epochal events: the planetary climate crisis and global migration. Each of these is profoundly related to the economic and social conditions put in place by late capitalism; millions of war, poverty, and climate refugees move from the South to the North of the world. The artifacts I discuss are, first, the plastiglomerate, a conglomerate of plastic debris and sand or molten rock that geologists Charles Moore and Patricia Corcoran and artist Kelly Jazvac found in 2006 on Kamilo Beach, in Hawai'i, and, second, the plastic life vests and inflatable boats that migrants abandon on the beach upon their arrival in Greece or Italy, and that the Chinese artist Ai Weiwei has in recent years exhibited in various installations throughout Europe. The relocation of these objects in the art gallery or museum offers the critic the opportunity to interrogate the function and the power of plastic art and in particular of the *objet trouvé* in the post-avant-garde period. As ordinary found objects and, in the case of the life vests, objects of everyday use, the plastic artifacts I analyze are de facto ready-mades. From the early twentieth-century Surrealist object, "found" and collected by André Breton and Marcel Duchamp, to the work of Arman and Piero Manzoni in the 1960s, to the appropriation of quotidian materiality by Italian Arte Povera artists in the same period, the *objet trouvé* has always been a vector of the avant-garde's iconoclastic provocation, meant to attack the art institution's way of producing aesthetic value. Does contemporary plastic art and its aesthetic transformation of everyday objects maintain the same iconoclasm and provocation aimed for by the avant-garde? Is the shock of seeing the life vest in the museum or in a public space, as well as the unexpected presence of the plastiglomerate in an art gallery, still alive? Do these objects jolt the viewer into recognition, or are they another exciting *trouvaille,* an exercise in surprise simply by virtue of being situated, unexpectedly, in a space traditionally reserved for art? Do they produce critical consciousness or aestheticized forgetfulness? To begin to answer these questions, and in order to further elaborate the dialectical relation of art and reality, pleasure and critique, that this plastic art suggests, I turn first to two contemporary art works: Damien Hirst's *Treasures from the Shipwreck of the Unbelievable,* from the 2017 Venice Biennale, and Christoph Büchel's *Barca Nostra* (Our Boat), shown at the 2019 Venice Biennale. The two installations, even though plastic appears only in Hirst's work, put into focus the problematic suggested by plastic art: the question of the symbolic and political power of plastic waste once it is turned into art. Does the repositioning of plastic waste in the museum or in the art gallery make the discarded auratic? How does the meaning and function of the aura change when it reappears with the most antiauratic, artificial, and human-made material, plastic itself?[3]

Two Shipwrecks

In 2017 the British artist Damien Hirst mounted two interrelated major exhibitions in two Venetian museums, the Palazzo Grassi and the Punta della Dogana. Both of these venues are owned by the millionaire Francois Pinault, who is also the owner of Christie's art auction house, a major collector of Hirst's art, and the cofinancer of both exhibitions. Since all of Hirst's work in the shows was (discreetly) for sale, the "reality" or "truth" of the global art market complicated, or perhaps simplified, Hirst's creative exuberance, his evident pleasure in playing with what is and what is not believable, fictional, and real. The shows displayed a vast number of carefully crafted artifacts, statues, jewels, and so on,[4] all purportedly objets d'art found, during the archeological excavation of a sunken ancient Roman galley, at the bottom of the sea. All were in fact art made by Hirst.

The whole exhibition was a fantastic fake, presented to the viewer as the result of an archeological excavation. The premise of the exhibitions was that Hirst personally financed the excavation that brought the "treasures" to Venice. At the Dogana, past the ticket office and a door surmounted by the inscription "Somewhere between lies and truth lies the truth," the audience was first presented with a film that documented the salvaging of the artifacts from a Roman ship that had been shipwrecked two thousand years ago. Hirstian history maintains that a freed slave of the first century, Cif Amotan II (an anagram of "I am fiction") accumulated a fortune and became an art collector. Everything was lost when the ship transporting the "treasures" sank in the Indian Ocean. The ship's name was *Apistos,* Greek for "unbelievable," hence the title of the exhibitions. The artifacts recovered from the ocean are encrusted with human-made corals, barnacles, and various patinas, while some claim to be copies of lost originals. Made from of an array of different materials, from lapis lazuli to bronze, to malachite, to resin, the objects include female torsos with a Barbie body, a Greek goddess with the head of a fly, a "Calendar Stone" similar to that kept in the National Anthropology Museum in Mexico City, and other pre-Hispanic objects that could certainly not have been carried in a Roman ship. Other kitsch mixtures of the classical and contemporary pop culture abound: Kate Moss and Rihanna loan their features to Egyptian deities, and various Disney characters are exhibited together with more "historically correct" figures (Figure 7.1). In Palazzo Grassi a gigantic statue of "Demon with a Bowl" loomed, many stories high, in the atrium: the sixty-foot-tall sculpture was made of resin painted to resemble bronze, evoking the image of

FIGURE 7.1. Damien Hirst, "The Collector and Friend," from *Treasures from the Wreck of the Unbelievable*, (2017). Fred Romero on Flickr, Creative Commons, Attribution 2.0, Generic License. https://www.flickr.com.

the Colossus of Rhodes (Figure 7.2). When, during a visit, I asked a guard how they had managed to bring it inside the museum, she explained that the colossus had been brought in as a number of pieces, and then assembled inside the palace.

Critical reception of the joint exhibitions has included both en-

FIGURE 7.2. Damien Hirst, "Demon with a Bowl," from *Treasures from the Wreck of the Unbelievable* (2017). Fred Romero on Flickr, Creative Commons, Attribution 2.0, Generic License. https://www.flickr.com.

thusiastic and highly critical voices.[5] Hirst's approach to all these fake ready-mades is ludic. His comedy was tempered only by the seriousness of money: what many critics saw as an aesthetic failure was poised to be, and became, an economic success. Nonetheless, Hirst's work asks its audience to reflect on the relation between art as both fiction and reality, and on the willingness—and perhaps the need—of the viewer to believe in the authenticity of what is obviously a fake. Through this meditation on belief and truth, fiction becomes real by becoming art. A tall tale materializes through Hirst's pieces, and reality exists only as the stories told by the objects on show. In this unresolvable negotiation between truth and untruth, reality and fiction, the *objet trouvé,* here born as the artist's own creation, does not shock the viewer but rather makes the unfamiliar and the unbelievable familiar and believable once again.

This is not the case with *Barca Nostra,* an exhibit two years later of another lost ship, also shown at perhaps the world's preeminent art exhibition, the Venice Biennale. This exhibition traces the opposite process to that of Hirst's treasures. While Hirst's audience is asked to lose itself in the twilight zone of manufactured reality and its ludic pleasures, and be surprised by the real fiction of the art works it is consuming, the audience of *Barca Nostra* encounters reality in its most unadorned and brutal aspect. The Swiss-Icelandic artist Christopher Büchel's installation was the most controversial exhibit at the Venice Biennale of 2019. As his contribution, Büchel brought to Venice the damaged ninety-foot-long fishing boat that had sank on April 18, 2015, 193 kilometers south of the Sicilian island of Lampedusa, crowded with refugees, most of whom lost their lives. Lampedusa is one of the key points of arrival for migrants from Africa to Europe; it is 296 kilometers off the coast of Libya, the ship's point of departure. Due to the incompetence of its captain, now in prison charged with manslaughter and trafficking, the ship collided with another boat that was coming to rescue the migrants. This was the worst shipwreck in the Sicilian channel in memory: between 800 and 1,100 migrants drowned when the ship capsized.[6] The Italian authorities ordered the recovery of the wreck, which was towed to the naval base of Melilli; bodies caught in the hold were identified, so that their families could be notified. Büchel went to great lengths to get permission to take the boat to Venice, since legally in Italy shipwrecks are destroyed.

The installation *Barca Nostra* is a collaborative project between Büchel and the Sicilian town council of Augusta. The decision to bring the ship to one of the world's most prominent international art gatherings was made at the time when the right-wing government in Italy closed Italian ports to migrant boats. Büchel's collaborator, Maria Chiara di Trapani, declared to *The Guardian*: "We are living in a tragic moment without memory. We all look at the news and it all seems so far away: someone is dead at sea and we change the channel." Di Trapani felt that the actual presence of the boat could change that, hoping that the visitors seeing *Barca Nostra* "will feel respect for it and look at it in silence—just keep two minutes of silence to listen and reflect."[7] In reality, the reactions of both visitors and critics have been varied, and, in the case of the throngs of visitors, unpredictable. Some saw the boat as the source of pure shock value: for the critic Lorenzo Tondo the artistic context in which the wreck is situated deprives it of its power as a political denunciation, so that mere provocation takes over the possibility to sensitize the viewer.[8] In this perspective art appears to irrevocably aestheticize any real event and therefore deprive the artifact of its denunciatory intent. Ralph Rugoff, this year's Biennale director, commented thus on his decision to include the boat in the exhibition: "It's a thing to see an image in a newspaper or on television, but when you confront the physical thing, you have a whole other group of sensations. You feel it in a different way; you are processing the information in a different way, and hopefully that leads you to think in a different way."[9]

A number of commentators criticized the lack of context in which the boat was exhibited.[10] Büchel refused to put any explanatory text or caption near the vessel. The organizers of the show wrote a commentary, but Büchel insisted on its removal, choosing instead to maintain the brutal effect of the thing itself, its rusty hull with the great hole near the bow raised onto dry land on a wharf of the former Venetian boatyard, the Arsenale. The history of death and danger, of marginality and risk the vessel conveyed was spelled out in the catalog of the Biennale, an expensive publication that not many visitors purchase. Although Büchel also refused to comment on the various reactions of the critics, his spokeswoman, voicing the opinion of the entire team who organized the exhibit, released a statement about the choice of excluding any on-site explanatory text. The team, she explained, looked forward to exhibiting an interactive work of response and interpretation from the public and with the public: "Public responses, including press articles, actual essays and social media posts are integral to the overall concept. Büchel's work comprises process and unmediated interactions. . . . Again, the fishing boat is not the artwork; instead the ongoing process and its journey are the artwork."[11] In other words: the process of encountering the ship, the reactions it elicits in different groups of recipients, and the way these reactions are circulated through the media are what constitutes the work of art.

Yet the boat may still be simply perceived as a piece of reality that does not belong in the art space, or as reality "tamed" and made innocuous exactly by the context in which it is placed, the art exhibition. If Hirst's shipwreck is fiction that materializes into reality thanks to art, once reality is situated in the space of art, or it is presented as art, it may be interpreted, once again, as auratic. The question of the return of the aura in the case of the contemporary plastic ready-made is, therefore, key to our inquiry. This potential for the belated return of the auratic sparks a number of questions about the impact of the aura of the postmodern and post-avant-garde ready-made. Its contemporary cultural inscriptions possess an affective and emotional charge, rather than a merely contemplative one, as Walter Benjamin famously claims in his 1936 essay "The Work of Art in the Age of Mechanical Reproduction." It's the shock power of the *objet trouvé* that paradoxically gives the artifact its aura, this time experienced by the viewer as affective engagement rather than contemplative distance. For Benjamin, the aestheticism of the aura and the passivity it engendered were countered by a call to engagement with both art and reality, an engagement that the proximity and tactility of technology seemed to guarantee. Today, instead, the affective and emotional charge of the plastic object on show seems to be what shocks the viewer into an agentic and critical position. For Benjamin, this emotional absorption, experienced through closeness rather than distance from the art object, is dangerous, because it replicates the oceanic, "aesthetic" closeness of the individual to the fascist spectacle. Is the affective charge of the newly auratic plastic art a form of tactility, capable of sparking an engaged discursivity from the audience, or is it yet again, as Benjamin affirmed, an anaesthetic? The question of the contextualization of the ready-made is important, but whether the textual and ideological "anchoring" of the object through its caption is enough to make evident its political, more than iconoclastic charge remains to be assessed.

Plastiglomerate versus the Life Vest

Is making the *object trouvé* an art object a way of remembering or of forgetting? Is aesthetics always a matter of aestheticizing reality? The questions that Hirst's treasures and Büchel's choice to send the shipwrecked refugee boat to Venice help formulate are further elucidated by some examples of contemporary plastic art. Both the plastiglomerate and Ai Weiwei's installations of migrants' rubber boats and life vests in various European cities have been circulated in museums and art galleries as ready-mades, or have become public art. What is the effect of moving plastic debris into these spaces? Is their shock effect still alive or have the objects been reified into mere fetishes, into a spectacle similar to that of the commodity, which always erases the memory of its past? Do they affect the viewer, to produce critical consciousness of the reality they evoke?

The artifacts I am going to examine in this section, Corcoran's and Jazvac's plastiglomerate, Fereniki Tsamparli's *The Chessboard of the World* (2016), and Ai Weiwei's migrant art, provide different answers to my questions. While they are all indexical of a close entanglement of human and nonhuman, natural and artifactual, it's when they foreground their connection to the human body, to the migrant and refugee and her story, that they become more effective means of denunciation and resistance.

In 2006 the oceanographer and plastic pollution activist Charles Moore found on Kamilo Beach, Hawai'i, a hybrid conglomerate of stone and beach debris. In 2013 the artist Kelly Jazvac went to a talk by Moore at Western University of Ontario, Canada, where she met Patricia Corcoran, an earth studies professor with whom Jazvac would conduct field work in Hawai'i. The until-then-unnamed material Moore had discovered was called "plastiglomerate," and defined by Moore, Corcoran, and Jazvac as

> an indurated, multicomposite material made hard by agglutination of rock and molten plastic. The material is subdivided into an *in situ* type, in which plastic is adhered to rock outcrops, and a clastic type, in which combinations of basalt, coral, shell and local woody debris are cemented with grains of sand in a plastic matrix. . . . Partially melted polymers adhered to basalt outcrops included fishing nets, piping, bottle caps, and rubber ties.[12]

The heat that soldered together stones and plastic was not of volcanic origin, but rather its sources were the bonfires that visitors lit on the beach when camping. Kamilo Beach, on the southeastern tip of the Big Island of Hawai'i, is one of its most polluted; the currents in the Pacific Ocean and the vortexes created by the earth's rotation bring debris from the Great Pacific Garbage Patch to the coast.

Corcoran and Moore read plastiglomerate as evidence of the Anthropocene, an evidence that fully confirms that we are, as we have been for some time, in a new, post-Holocene geological era. The plastic fragments incorporated into the rocks have been formed anthropogenetically, and as such they warn about the dangers of producing plastic waste as well as leaving this debris in the open: the chemical substances released by deteriorating plastic ("carbon monoxide, polycyclic aromatic hydrocarbons, and dioxins,"[13]) can cause cancer, hormonal disruptions, and neurological disorders. Furthermore this new "fossil of the future" endures: sunken in the sands of Kamilo Beach, it remains unaffected by the action of the wind and the water. In other words, it potentially becomes eternal.

This dark and most threatening image of a human-made material hybridized into nature is only the latest chapter in the history of plastic, a material that has come to be identified with twentieth-century modernity.[14] The utopian quality of plastic, a material that Roland Barthes writing in 1957 considered as an alchemic "transmutation of matter,"[15] was made comic in the French director Jacques Tati's film *Mon Oncle* of the same year, in the unforgettable scene of the factory production of "plastic sausages." Barthes's relatively utopian and benign image also fades away rapidly when we take into account plastic's direct participation in colonialism and in human and nature exploitation, that is, when we take into full consideration its comprehensive contribution to the history of modern capital.[16] Heather Davis, among others, points out the destructive and contaminating power of plastic,[17] whose production has multiplied exponentially since the 1970s[18] and whose connection with the extraction of oil is key: in her words, "a staggering percent of the world's oil production goes into the manufacture and production of plastic."[19] The disposal of plastic artifacts, as the plastiglomerate on Kamilo Beach also makes evident, is highly problematic: plastic is expected to last thousands of years before breaking down into smaller, but still dangerous, molecules. This is the history that the plastiglomerate evokes.

After samples were collected, analyzed, and classified by Corcoran and Moore, portions of the plastiglomerate from Kamilo Beach have been turned into an art exhibition by Kelly Jazvac. Since 2013 they have been displayed in university museums, from the University of Toronto to the Peabody Museum at Yale University, and art galleries, from the Het Nieuwe Institut, Rotterdam, and Natura Artis Magistra, Amsterdam, to the David Fierman Gallery in Manhattan. They were shown at the Milan Triennale in 2019. In a recent interview Jazvac affirms that, as art, plastiglomerate constitutes first of all a visible marker of the effects of the Anthropocene and of its impact on the environment, by showing "the permanence of the disposable."[20] Second, she attributes to her ready-mades the power of what she terms "Art's transgressive aesthetics in the presence of political and social change. . . . [Art] can help visualize things that are very hard to visualize—in this case the magnitude and intensity of the pollution and contamination of the earth." Jazvac then quotes the environmental critic and activist Zoe Todd, to point out the uneven way in which different classes have contributed to, and profited from, the production of plastic debris and other contaminants.[21]

In another interview, this time with Gunseli Yalcinkaya,[22] Jazvac recognizes that these "fossils of the future" generate curiosity in the viewer, at first because of their aesthetic, sculptural quality: "I find them beautiful and horrific at the same time."[23] The affective element of pleasure and play made available by plastic, and the tactility and sensuousness of its colors and textures, is what draws the viewer close to the stones, until their identity as scientific and cultural evidence of environmental contamination is disclosed. The way the viewer will look at the plastiglomerate is volatile and ultimately quite undecidable: will she read them for the way "they physically embody cycles of production, consumption, and disposal,"[24] or will she embrace them exactly as what the theorist Jane Bennett terms "vibrant matter"?[25] The critic Kirsty Robertson comments on "the aesthetic vibrancy of the artefacts," which becomes sculptural and realistic by their incorporation of objects, cigarette lighters, can lids, ropes, and so on. "The combination of rock sediment and plastic creates a charismatic object, a near luminous granite, pockmarked with color. . . . Plastiglomerate is made by a series of anthropogenic gestures that create fascinating, disquieting objects."[26] The function of this luminosity and the charismatic quality of the rocks remain to be defined: will their aesthetic quality occlude and obscure their history of collusion with capitalism and its violence? Robertson tries to attach a caption to these artifacts but reconstructs their history only at the individual level, just as a history of consumption:[27] "Whose lighter was it? A smoker in Los Angeles? Possibly in Tokyo, maybe in Ojai?"[28] This perspective has the effect of romanticizing and personalizing the artifacts. Vis-à-vis both Jazvac's and Robertson's claim that the plastiglomerate makes visible a problem otherwise too vast and too distant to be understood, their reading of the rocks telescopes between a universalist perspective, centered on "the human," and its opposite, a personalized and individualized reading of minutiae that lets us imagine the identity of the consumer of the plastic debris. In so doing both Jazvac and Robertson fail to mention the most important part of plastiglomerate's past, its participation in a historical and structural conjuncture that remains invisible.

The fascination with the "accidentally or incidentally aesthetic"[29] quality of plastiglomerate remains to be studied and analyzed, and so does the auratic ("charismatic" in Robertson's words), quality of the rocks once they are situated in the museum. While spelling out a clear warning against the dangerous effects of the Wasteocene, Jazvac's findings may resemble too closely the perfect curios for the late capitalist *Wunderkammer.* The objects stand as a warning for the museum or gallery goers, those who produce, potentially, the plastic debris; yet no narrative is provided for the people who are excluded from the conspicuous consumption of plastic and instead have their lives and habitats threatened by it. As "vibrant matter" these "disquieting objects" remain slightly specious, if not suspicious, as they are always verging on the side of the fetishistic animism of the talisman. Their "charisma" needs to be appropriately contextualized, and given a collective, rather than individual history, in order to produce awareness of the historical and economic, not only geological, forces that created the plastiglomerates. As the Anthropocene, in Marco Armerio's and Massimo de Angelis's critique of the current use of the term, refers primarily not to "Anthropos" but to capitalism, so must the interpretation of Kamilo Beach ready-mades shed both the scientific objectivity or the "humanistic" universalism that make up their interpretations, to reveal instead their materialist history. However, it is the aesthetic quality and affective tactility of these objects, with their capability to address the viewer at an unmediated, almost corporeal level, that could shift the meaning of these artifacts away from either science or from the neoliberal grand narrative of universal shared human suffering. Differently captioned, the plastiglomerate could help reframe the current environmental discourse by asking the viewer not simply, in the best neoliberal fashion, to take *individual* responsibility for the plastic waste and contamination. Rather, Kamilo Beach hybrid rocks might ask us to think of waste and contamination as a structural problem, articulated along the lines of class struggle and of uneven local and global power relations. Newly situated within this historical narrative, the geological ready-mades Jazvac brought to the museum cease to be curios and become, potentially, instead a means for creating a knowledge alternative to the logic of the Anthropocene. This alternative knowledge would question, rather than asking the individual to fix, the capitalist system itself. Even more, by becoming a tool for repoliticizing the Anthropocene, plastiglomerates could become the conduit to imagine new forms of communing and of struggle.

If Jazvac's hybrid rocks occupy an unstable and undecidable space between politics and aesthetics, science and affect, resistance and acquiescence to the logic of neoliberalism, Ai Weiwei's plastic art uses migrants' life jackets to make a more directly denunciatory statement.[30]

There is another story of plastic pollution that needs to be told, this time taking place on beaches on the other side of the world from Hawai'i, on the Greek islands of Lesbos, Chio, and Samos. In particular the island of Lesbos has recently become the point of arrival for hundreds of thousands of migrants and refugees (450,000 passed by Lesbos in 2015 alone) in their attempts to reach Europe from Syria, Somalia, Afghanistan, Iraq, and Pakistan, among other countries. Once they reach the island, the migrants abandon the rubber boats on which they arrived—when the boats are not washed to the coast as shipwrecks—and discard the life vests they wore during the passage from Turkey. This in itself has created an environmental problem for the ecosystem of Lesbos. The flow of migrants then contributes to the problem of plastic pollution by a further, predictable, means. The refugee camps, where the refugees are placed by the Greek authorities after their arrival, from which they hope to continue their journey to other countries or fear being sent back, produce more debris: discarded plastic containers for meals and water pile up on several points of the island (last year, for example, three meals a day for 9,000 people produced 27,000 pieces of plastic trash per day).[31] Lesbos has become the epicenter of plastic pollution between Turkey and Greece; this, in turn, affects tourism, upon which the Greek economy increasingly depends since the financial crisis of 2008.

The problem of plastic recycling has not yet been solved, but it has been addressed by the migrants themselves, who since 2016 have been collecting life vests, inflatable boats, and other plastic debris on the beaches of Lesbos. Supported by local and international nonprofit organizations, the refugees, together with low-income and vulnerable Greek citizens, cut and sewed bags out of the plastic debris for the Safe Passage Bag Project. The Lesbos Solidarity Bags have been selling through the Hathaway Contemporary Art gallery in Atlanta, Georgia, for $40 or $60 each, all proceeds going to support the workers in Greece. The bags create some jobs and potential economic sustainability for both refugees and locals. At the same time this work of upcycling becomes one means to deal with the lack of adequate recycling centers on the island.

While the production of the Solidarity Bags is carried on through a collaboration between locals, refugees, and international nonprofit organizations, in order to create *The Chessboard of the World,* a public art installation also realized through the recycling of plastic debris left on the beach, in 2016 artist and professor Fereniki Tsamparli collaborated with her students and other faculty at the Aegean University in Lesbos.[32] The chessboard was conceived as art that would memorialize the passage of the migrants and the loss of their lives. Each chess piece, about a meter and a half high, was hand built by students and faculty with the foam extracted from the life vests, successively piled up to form the chess pawns. The pawns were then cemented into shape by papier-mâché made from discarded academic papers, to signify an act of fusion and solidarity between academics and migrants. The pieces could be moved, and Tsamparli, besides lining them up upon a large chess board also made of discarded plastic, set some on the beach close to the point where drowned migrants bodies had washed ashore. Tsamparli's installation is both a memorial to the migrants' passage and a ludic means of acknowledging the refugee crisis as it is experienced by the various stakeholders on the island.

An even more incisive example of plastic art concerned with the epochal event of migration is provided by the work of the Chinese artist Ai Weiwei. For the past three years Ai, himself since 2015 an exile from China for political dissidence, has collected a great number of life vests from Greece and turned them into a political tool of denunciation and sensitization for the inhabitants of three European cities, Florence, Berlin, and Copenhagen. The artist's commitment to making visible the refugee crisis has attracted both praise and vehement criticism; even though less overtly provocative than some of Ai's other work on the refugee crisis, for instance his restaging of the photo of the three-year-old drowned Syrian boy Aylan Kurdi, or his handing around thermal blankets at a gala soiree, three installations have attracted both the public's and the critics' attention. Yet Ai's work is not mere provocation for the sake of provocation. He is incredibly clear about the task of the artist and the rationale of his artistic production. Asked what he thinks about the criticism his work has received, he replied: "As artists we are not decorating their [the audience and the critics] aesthetic views, we are always working in a dangerous area and questioning existing judgements, [whether] moral, philosophical, or aesthetic. You cannot always have so-called good taste. I don't understand why that sort of comfort is important. Art has to be relevant. Relevant means making the people whose life and moral judgements are so fake, at least feel uncomfortable about it. If I cannot make them feel uncomfortable I am a total failure, and I will feel sad about why I am still doing this."[33]

In this spirit, Ai has continued to mount a campaign to express solidarity with refugees. His 2017 two-hour film *Human Flow* received two nominations at the 2017 Venice Film festival, while one of his installations, *Laundromat* (2012), showing thousands of clothing items worn by Syrian refugees, was featured in London and in Doha, Qatar.[34] Ai visited the refugee camps of Lesbos in December

2018. He was deeply struck by the remains of the rubber boats, and the piles of discarded life vests he saw on the beach. He took 14,000 with him to Europe, to mount three art installations. In February 2016 he used some of the vests to cover six columns on the facade of the Berlin Konzerthaus; he also situated a rubber dinghy over the building's entrance with the title of the installation, *Safe Passage* (Figure 7.3). In 2017 he used 3,500 salvaged life jackets to cover the windows of Copenhagen's Kunsthal Charlottenborg, for an installation called *Soleil Levant*. While the title cites one of Claude Monet's most famous paintings, *Impression soleil levant,* the installation itself cites the space of the refugee tent in the camps: the life vests cover the windows of the museum and close its space to the light of the sun, as in a prison. Furthermore, with its reference to Monet's painting of 1872, the installation also makes an allusion to the period when European industrialization and colonialism exploded, setting the stage for the capitalist development that created wars and economic exploitation at home and abroad. In October 2016, when a retrospective of Ai Weiwei was mounted inside Palazzo Strozzi in Florence, the artist hung a highly visible orange rubber dinghy over each of the second floor windows of the Renaissance palace, calling the installation *Reframe* (Figure 7.4). Seen from inside the museum, the boats obstruct the view of the city and of the street, and, as in Copenhagen, they produce the effect of being inside a prison. From the street they surprise and shock the passers-by with their loud color and their out-of-placedness. In Florence, as in Berlin and Copenhagen, the migrants' objects occupy a liminal position between city space and art space. This liminality is striking and significant: neither inside nor outside the museum, the life vests and the inflatable boats reclaim for themselves the right to be art, and as such acquire an aura that, far from isolating them from the everyday in the contemplative space of aesthetics, demand and call the public's attention to the event that they memorialize.

The artifacts in Ai Weiwei's installations share much of the urgency and the jarring power of *Barca Nostra,* as well as some of the sensuousness of both the plastiglomerate and of Hirst's treasures. They attract the viewer's gaze with their color, texture, and sheer, excessive quantity. This excess, when located in the middle of Florence,

FIGURE 7.3. Ai Weiwei, Berlin Konzerthaus Installation, NWY69, Creative Commons, Attribution No Derives, Generic License. https://www.flickr.com/.

FIGURE 7.4. Ai Weiwei, Florence Palazzo Strozzi Installation *Reframe* (2016), manuelarosi, Creative Commons, Attribution Share Alike 3.0 Unported. https://commons.wikimedia.org.

Berlin, and Copenhagen, speaks of the magnitude of contemporary migration flows, the vast numbers of the refugees,[35] and at the same time makes visible, and palpable, the individuality of each of the users of the life vests. Their out-of-placedness as ready-mades, debris found on the beach, singles out each of these plastic found objects as exceptional, and yet gives each of them an aura free of the incantatory power of the fetish. Their aura, the aura they possess as works of art, is not undercut, but rather, and rather paradoxically from a Benjaminian point of view, bolstered by the shock they produce, the shock of an elsewhere grafted onto the everyday of a European city. This is the form that the aura takes up in postauratic and post-Fordist late modernity.[36] In this context, Benjamin's famous definition of the aura in "The Art Work" essay can no longer capture and explain the dissemination of auratic experiences and textualities in postmodernity. His remains a modernist theorization that does not fit the contemporary cultural panorama. Benjamin connects the aesthetic absorption and contemplation experienced by the viewer of art with the anaesthetic effect of fascist aestheticized politics, which, with its spectacularity, presents itself as auratic. Today, rather than being disactivated by technology, as Benjamin claimed in the case of cinema, the aura is dispersed into, and reverberates through, different and new media. This same discursive multiplication produces the meaning of *Barca Nostra* (Figure 7.5) as the organizers of the installation explain in their press release. The work of art is not the material object itself, but rather the mediated multidiscursivity and reactions it produces through different media. The aura is now understood as a process, and as "a catalyst of historical memory"[37] exactly through the affective impact that the shock of the new plastic *object trouvé* is capable of producing.

If its contemporary cultural inscriptions show that the aura is no longer conceivable as a pretechnological vestige of religion and of the sacrality of art, then also the opposition between the aesthetic and the rational, or, to use Benjamin's image, between the magician and the engineer, no longer stands: the first moment of sensuous absorption in the work of art, pace Benjamin, does not create distance and passive awe in the viewer, but rather is itself a form of tactility that draws the viewer into it, and at the same time does not exclude

FIGURE 7.5. *Barca Nostra,* Venice Biennale 2019, Jean-Pierre Dalbéra, Creative Commons, Attribution 2.0, Generic. https://en.wikipedia.org.

the rational moment of critique and recognition. In a post-Fordist information society, the emotional intensity created by the aura of the work of art—here the affective and affecting shock of the life vest—does not exclude the possibility of critique and the reconquering of memory in the midst of contemporary amnesia. The contemporary inscriptions of the aura, as we have seen in the case of Ai Weiwei's recycling of migrants' life vests into art, make memory accessible again exactly through, rather than through the exclusion of, the dense materiality of a tactile and sensuous experience.

As a newly auratic object, the contemporary ready-made of plastic art can spark a process of awareness of the space elsewhere, as well as a process of recognition of one's subjectivity in relation to alterity. This is what the portions of the plastiglomerate, and even more Ai Weiwei's life vests, can provide: an affective semiosis meant to interpellate the viewer, the person in the street. Because of the contemporary altered structure and function of the aura, this presentation of the migrant object as *objet trouvé* does not perform the act of anesthetization and "beautification" of reality that Benjamin, in 1934, attributed to the art of the German *Neue Sachlichkeit,* when he critiqued how "it has succeeded in transforming even abject poverty—by apprehending it in a fashionably perfected manner—into an object of enjoyment."[38] Rather, the plastic objects themselves may well work as a path to memory and to the awareness of an epochal event that, even though experienced differently, is happening to everybody.

Plastic Porosity

The power of the auratic sensuousness of the plastiglomerate, which Moore and Corcoran do not quite take into account and which Robertson appears to overlook, returns prominently and powerfully in Ai Weiwei's rubber inflatable boats and life vests. Their hybridity as artwork and waste with a story is only one aspect of their liminality: simultaneously inside and outside the museum, beckoning the passer-by with a tactility capable of generating awareness, they also signify the uncertain threshold that connects the nation, represented by the national monuments on which the vests are displayed, and the postnationality of the migrants, a postnationality that signals, and is signaled by, the porosity of the national borders they traverse.

The life vest and the rubber boat tell a person's story, and through this story they challenge, and change, the very concept of nation and of borders. The plastic, foam-filled life vest remains on the beach as a trace of a passage, of an identity that cannot be named, and that refuses to be called national. As such, the undocumented migrant bends and transforms the rigidity of both border and nation, makes them porous, and imparts a plastic quality to both. This is the very plasticity Catherine Malabou theorizes: the migrants receive and give form to the spaces and to those they encounter. As such their story imparts to plastic a quality that it does not possess in reality: porosity. This porosity is at the center of the Pakistani author's Mohsin Hamid's 2017 novel *Exit West*. In the novel Nadia and Saeed are two war refugees who migrate from an unnamed city in the Middle East first to Lesbos, then to London, and finally to California. The plot, centered on Nadia's and Saeed's vicissitudes as refugees, is also a palimpsest of the stories of many other migrants, coming from different countries and disseminated all over the world, from Australia to Japan, from the Netherlands to Spain. Hamid's characters move from one country to another by passing through "doors," passages they are guided to after paying for the journey. Although the realistic figure of the *passeur* is maintained in Hamid's narrative, as well as the risk of giving money to a person who may not do what he promised, Hamid chooses not to represent the harrowing hardships of crossing borders in realistic terms, but rather through magical realism: crossing borders, before being caught, for some migrants temporarily, for other indefinitely, in another plastic world, that of tents in refugee encampments, is presented in the novel as "emerging." "It was said in those days that the passage was like dying and being born, and indeed Nadia experienced a kind of extinguishing as she entered the blackness [of the door], and a gasping struggle as she fought to exit it. . . . Saeed was emerging and Nadia crawled forward to give him space."[39] To emerge, here, means to come up to the surface, to pass a limit, to move between two points, to make it through a restraint, to be able to breathe again. It means, literally, to emerge from the sea, surviving drowning and death, to emerge on the beach and shed one's life vest as a carapace no longer useful to a new life predicated upon the relinquishing, but not the forgetting, of the past. Left on the beach, this past materialized into a piece of plastic, in order to become visible and memorable to those who were not there, who have not seen, and need to understand. The life vests relocated in the city are a testimony to this passage, but also to the instability of the idea of the nation, to the porosity and plasticity of the border, to desperation and the need to emerge into a second chance in life.

July, 2:00 pm, at the Arsenale, Venice Biennale 2019

The afternoon heat is suffocating. In the dusty silence I look for a place to sit in the shade. The wreck is mounted on a sort of pedestal; it does not touch the water of the lagoon. From whatever direction you are coming, it cannot be missed. Seen from below it is huge, and yet not big enough for all the people who died in it, most of them trapped in the hold. A human cargo who had to pay to be trafficked. Some visitors—Art lovers? Art consumers?—pass by. Others hurry toward some air-conditioned building, where hundreds of years ago ships were built that went east and south, heralding Venetian trade and economic power. These visitors hardly look at the wreck. Others arrive in small groups, and take a selfie with the ship. Some smile in the picture, the memento they'll share to say "I was there." None of us was there when the boat sank. Does this piece of reality forced into art make one think? Remember? Understand? Want to do something?

Sitting on a step, I look at art, I look at a mass grave. I feel I am trespassing. I am angry. I am ashamed. I mourn.

NOTES

1. Roland Barthes, "Plastic," in *Mythologies* (New York: Farrar, Straus, and Giroux, 1972).
2. Catherine Malabou, *What Should We Do with Our Brains?* (New York: Fordham University Press, 2008).
3. Some of these questions are addressed also by Jane Kuenz in her essay, "The Plastic You: Plastination and the Post-Mortal Self," in this volume. What our essays share is the concern with the hybridity of natural and artifactual that plastic produces when it comes in contact with the human body, as well as the interest in the spectacle of the plastic hybrid object when this object is situated in the space of the museum and of the exhibition. However, while Kuenz focuses on the ethical aspect of the spectacle and commodification of plastinated bodies, I interrogate the effect of the aestheticization of plastic, as well as the permanence of the aura of the displayed plastic artifact.
4. "Two museums: 54,000 square feet of exhibition space; 198 art works, including 100 sculptures, one of them 60 feet high; 21 cabinets filled with small objects." Scott Reyburn, "Venice Is a Stage for Damian Hirst's 'Treasures' (and a Biennale, too)," *New York Times*, May 12, 2017.
5. See Elizabeth S. Greene and Justin Leidwanger, "Damien Hirst's Tale of Shipwreck and Salvaged Treasure," *Online Museum Review*, AJA Open Access, January 2018, https://www.ajaonlaine.org/online-museum-review/3581; Tiernan Morgan, "Damien Hirst's Shipwreck Fantasy Sinks in Venice," *Hyperallergic*, August 10, 2017, https://hyperallergic.com/301158/damien-hirst-treasures-from-the-wreck-of-the-unbelievable-venice-punta-della-dogana-palazzo-grassi/; and Laura Cumming, "Damien Hirst: Treasures from the Wreck of the Unbelievable Review—Beautiful and Monstrous," *The Guardian*, April 16, 2017, https//:www.theguardian.com/artanddesign/2017/apr/16/Damien-hirst-treasures-from-the-wreck-of-the-unbelievable-review-venice.
6. Charlotte Higgins, "Boat in Which Hundreds of Migrants Died Displayed at

the Venice Biennale," *The Guardian,* May 7, 2019, https://theguardian.com/artanddesign/2019/may/07/boat-in/which-hundreds-of-migrants-died-displayed-at-venice-biennale.

7. Higgins, "Boat in Which Hundreds of Migrants Died," 4.
8. Cristina Ruiz, "Fierce Debate over Christoph Buchel's Venice Biennale Display of Boat that Sank with Hundreds Locked in Hull," *The Art Newspaper,* May 14, 2019, https://www.theartnewspaper.com/news/christoph-buechel.
9. Ruiz, "Fierce Debate," 2.
10. See the editorial "*The Guardian* View on the Venice Biennale's Migrant Boat: Pushing the Limits of Art," *The Guardian,* May 17, 2019, https://www.theguardian.com/commentisfree/2019/may/17/the-guardian-view-on-the-venice-biennale-migrant-boat-pushing-the-limits-of-art.
11. "As with all of Christoph Büchel's work, on-site explanatory text was never intended to be part of the ongoing BARCA NOSTRA project's presence at the [Venice Biennale]. Here, as with all of his previous projects, public response—including press articles, critical essays, and social media posts—is integral to the overall concept. Büchel's work comprises process and unmediated interactions. . . . Again, the fishing vessel is not the art work; instead, the ongoing project and its journey are the artwork. For the appearance of the 18 April shipwreck in Venice, the BARCA NOSTRA team has from the outset strongly encouraged the Biennale to include a project summary text written by [the curator] Nina Magnusdottir, in the exhibition catalog. The team has also suggested that the full project press release be posted on the Biennale website, so that journalists and members of the general public alike can have access to the necessary information." Ruiz, "Fierce Debate," 4.
12. Patricia L. Corcoran, Charles J. Moore, and Kelly Jazvac, "An Anthropogenic Marker Horizon in the Future Rock Record," *GSA Today* 24, no. 6 (June 2014): 3. https://www.geosociety.org/archive/24/6/article/i1052-5173-24-6-4.htm.
13. Corcoran, Moore, and Jazvac, "An Anthropogenic Marker Horizon," 5.
14. See Susan Freinkel, *Plastic: A Toxic Love Story* (New York: Houghton, Mifflin, and Harcourt Publishing, 2011); Jeffrey Meikle, *American Plastic: A Cultural History* (New Brunswick, N.J.: Rutgers University Press, 1995); Stephen Fenichell, *Plastic: The Making of a Synthetic Century* (New York: HarperBusiness, 1996).
15. Barthes, "Plastic," 110.
16. Marco Armiero and Massimo de Angelis, "Anthropocene: Victims, Narrators, and Revolutionaries," *South Atlantic Quarterly* 116, no. 2 (April 2017): 345–62.
17. Heather Davis, "Life and Death in the Anthropocene: A Short History of Plastic," in *Art in the Anthropocene: Encounters Among Aesthetics, Politics, Environments, and Epistemologies,* ed. Heather Davis and Etienne Turpin (London: Open Humanities, 2015).

18. Andrés Cózar, Fidel Echevarría, J. Ignacio González-Gordillo, Xabier Irigoien, Bárbara Úbeda, Santiago Hernández-León, Álvaro T. Palma, et al., "Plastic Debris in the Open Ocean," PNAS 111, no. 28 (July 15, 2014): 10239–44.
19. Kirsty Robertson, "Plastiglomerate," *e-flux journal* #78, December 2016.
20. Ben Valentine, "Plastiglomerate, the Anthropocene's New Stone," *Hyperallergic,* November 25, 2015, hpps://hyperallergic.com/249396/plastiglomerate-the-anthropocene-new-stone.
21. Zoe Todd, "Indigenizing the Anthropocene," in *Art in the Anthropocene: Encounters Among Aesthetics, Politics, Environments, and Epistemologies,* ed. Heather Davis and Etienne Turpin (London: Open Humanities, 2015); see also Rob Nixon, *Slow Violence and the Environmentalism of the Poor* (Cambridge, Mass.: Harvard University Press, 2013).
22. Gunseli Yalcinkaya, "Kelly Jazvac Presents 'Beautiful and Horrific' Plastiglomerate Lumps at Milan Triennale," *Dezeen,* April 21, 2019.
23. Yalcinkaya, "Kelly Jazvac Presents," 2.
24. Yalcinkaya, "Kelly Jazvac Presents," 4.
25. This concept is elaborated by Jane Bennett in *Vibrant Matter: A Political Ecology of Things* (Durham, N.C.: Duke University Press, 2010).
26. Robertson, "Plastiglomerate," 5.
27. This is a point of contention for Armerio and de Angelis, in their critique of the term "Anthropocene": "In the Wasteocene as in the Anthropocene, instead of speaking of capitalism and injustice, the mainstream narrative focuses on consumerism—'everybody is responsible'—and technology—'experts can do this'" (Armerio and de Angelis, "Anthropocene," 116).
28. Robertson, "Plastiglomerate," 7.
29. Davis, "Life and Death in the Anthropocene."
30. While I concentrate on Ai Weiwei's work, much critical attention has been dedicated to the relation of art and the environment, in particular to art made with recycled waste. See Amanda Boetzkes, *Plastic Capitalism: Contemporary Art and the Drive to Waste* (Cambridge, Mass.: MIT Press, 2019); Thomas J. Demos, *Decolonizing Nature: Contemporary Arts and the Politics of Ecology* (Berlin: Sternberg Press, 2016); Anna Lowenhaupt Tsing, *Arts of Living on a Damaged Planet: Ghosts and Monsters of the Anthropocene* (Minneapolis: University of Minnesota Press, 2017); and the already mentioned *Art in the Anthropocene* edited by Davis and Turpin.
31. Fahrinisa Campana, "Greece's Refugee Crisis Creates a Strain on an Already Fragile Ecosystem," *PRI,* November 27, 2018, https://www.pri.org/stories/2018-11-27/greece-refugee-crisis-creates-strain-already-fragile-ecosystem.
32. Elyse Wanshel, "This Giant Chessboard Is Made of Refugees and Migrants' Life Jackets," *HuffPost,* June 9, 2016; https://www.huffpost.com/entry/university-of-the-aegean-lesbos-greece-giant-chess-board-refugees_n_57586657e4b0ced23ca6ba25.
33. Aimee Dawson, "Ai Weiwei: 'I'm Like a High-End Refugee' Interview," *Art*

Newspaper, March 27, 2018, https://www.theartnewspaper.com/interview/ai-weiwei-i-m-like-a-high-end-refugee.

34. Kate Brown, "Ai Weiwei Will Make the Refugee Crisis Personal in His Upcoming Qatar Show," *News Artnet,* March 16, 2018, https://news.artnet.com/art-world/ai-weiwei-qatar-1237127.
35. "According to the UNHCR, 1,277,349 individuals arrived in Europe via sea in 2015 and 2016. In the same period 8,000 individuals have died or disappeared attempting the journey," from the Kunsthal Charlottenborg, Copenhagen, website, quoted in D. J. Pangburn, "3,500 Salvaged Life Jackets Storm Danemark for Ai Weiwei's Latest," *Vice,* June 26, 2017, https://www.vice.com/en/article/payj4z/ai-weiwei-3500-salvaged-life-jackets-copenhagen.
36. Lutz Koepnick, "Aura Reconsidered: Benjamin and Contemporary Visual Culture," in *Benjamin's Ghosts: Interventions in Contemporary Literary and Cultural Theory,* ed. Gerhard Richter (Stanford, Calif.: Stanford University Press, 2002).
37. Koepnick, "Aura Reconsidered," 99; on the question of the postmodern aura and memory, see also Andreas Huyssen, "Escape from Amnesia: The Museum as Mass Medium," in *Twilight Memories: Making Time in a Culture of Amnesia* (New York: Routledge, 1995).
38. Walter Benjamin, "The Author as Producer," (1934), in *Walter Benjamin. Selected Writings Volume 2, Part 2, 1931–1934,* ed. Michael W. Jennings, Howard Eiland, and Gary Smith; trans. Rodney Livingstone et al. (Cambridge, Mass.: Harvard University Press, 1999), 775.
39. Mohsin Hamid, *Exit West* (New York: Riverhead, 2017), 104.

◊♦◊ **PART III** ◊♦◊

Plastic's Capitalism

8

"Refuge of Ignorance"

A Prehistory of "Plastic"

Crystal Bartolovich

As the Bakelite Corporation was developing synthetic polymers commercially early in the twentieth century, it commissioned a film, *The Fourth Kingdom* (1937), to introduce "plastic" to the public as a substance so novel that it unsettled the classical taxonomy of animal, vegetable, and mineral. Its opening frame displays three iris shots in pyramid formation—cows grazing (on top), trees being logged, and a prospecting pan being sloshed over a stream—before segueing to a montage of an automobile-thronged urban street, followed by a speeding train, then a tilting-upward pan of a skyscraper, and, finally, an airplane with propellers awhirl, while the voice-over narration explains that the three previously known kingdoms have proved "inadequate" to "our modern complex industrial world." The solution? *Plastic.* An avuncular "chemist" appears onscreen to produce a synthetic polymer resin before our eyes, explaining the ingredients, the tools, and the process. We then visit factories, where machines spew out an enormous array of plastic components, whose assembled form we later follow into shops and homes, as diegetic merchants and voice-overs tout their admirable properties: plastic explained, demystified.

Or is it? At the same time as such displays disseminate information, they also can encourage awed astonishment, in part because of the "singular of its [plastic's] origin and the plural of its effects"—as Roland Barthes muses in an essay on another plastic "exhibition."[1] To be sure, the Bakelite Corporation appears to remove the sign from the factory gate ("No admittance except on business") to which

Marx playfully calls our attention when he shifts from describing the "surface" of the commodity to explaining its "production"; *these* factories are no "hidden abode"![2] The film emphatically foregrounds a network of relations usually invisible to, say, a parent making breakfast with a plastic juicer. On the other hand, though, its very detail can be mystifying, and not only because we are confronted with myriad wildly different things—telephones, radios, jewelry, funnels, dentures—all seemingly generated from the same resin we see conjured up at the beginning of the film by the "scientist" surrounded by beakers and test tubes, his acknowledged allies. Given the massive evidence of acknowledgement of certain nonhumans—often *over* humans—in countless sites such as this, I have always found the new materialist insistence that humans are utterly unaware of nonhumans as "actants" perplexing, not only because of corporate puffery like this industrial film, but also as evidenced in everyday life. Who *doesn't* think an aspirin, or other medicine, or food will "do" something when humans take them in, or, for that matter, doubts that an injection of growth hormone does something to a cow, or compost to a plant? Jane Bennet's claim, following Latour, that only new materialists have noticed that nonhumans "do things" (her words) is preposterous. And even if it *were* true, it is unclear how such recognition would lead, on its own, as she suggests, to "wiser interventions," under capitalist *conditions* of existence that impose a propertarian attitude toward "nature" and humans, conditions that promote and constrain actions (human and nonhuman) so vehemently.[3] To be convincing, new materialists would have to have something more convincing to say about that than what they have put forth so far. While the Bakelite film suggests, along with Barthes, that "the whole world, even life itself, can be plasticized," it can *celebrate* this plastic world, while Barthes decries it, not least because despite the film's frank and admiring attention to the nonhuman, key aspects of the "miracle of polymerization" (as the film calls it) remain unexplained. As long as the *conditions* in which all the networks, all the tracings, transpire are, as Theodor Adorno put it, "wrong," no amount of network tracing can suffice to either elucidate or ameliorate what ails the world.[4] From Adorno's perspective, the film simply *displays* a "second nature" triumphant over the first, including humans, normalizing it.[5]

Meanwhile, invisible shareholders and capital and property relations continue to assert mastery not only over "nature" but, too, *most* humans, who are utterly subordinated to plastic (and the relations of production that give rise to it) in the film's vision. After the opening frame, grass and trees appear hardly at all, and as mere backgrounds to factories and plastic commodities such as golf balls, the stars of the show. The only animals we see are human, and they often get reduced to appendages (disembodied hands, encased in thick gloves) manipulating plastic things or tending the machines from which they emerge. In short, seeming to expose plastic production—which no one would deny can only occur with the massive assistance of nonhumans—the film *still* obscures how *capitalism* works, which is what Marx was getting at when he undertook to explain the commodity form. The film reveals plastic things being made in an *explicit* human–nonhuman collaboration, which "flattens" workers, at least, with nonhumans, but does not ask if all humans and nonhumans experience the pleasures and bear the burdens of this production evenly and fairly. Indeed, it takes for granted that they won't, since the hierarchized organizing force of unequal private property held by corporations like Bakelite remains uninterrogated and normalized. The film is a site of information, then, but, at the same time, it serves as what a seventeenth-century commentator on plastic called a "refuge of ignorance," *even though* it elaborately exposes human–machine–chemical collaborations to view.[6]

Yes: *seventeenth* century. Before "plastic" named a particular set of things, it was a *concept* that called attention to the problem of human knowledge—a history worth exploring. The charge that "plastic" offered a "refuge of ignorance" emerged with capitalism in the seventeenth century, as part of a struggle over what *matter* could and would mean. Unsettled by the implications of the Cartesian matter–spirit dualism, natural historians—trying to understand how (to use Barthes's terms) the "singular" substance of, say, semen could give rise to the "plural" effects of vastly different organs and bodies, or how fossilized shells could turn up far from the sea—attributed these effects to an organizing, formative process they called "plastic power."[7] Others dismissed such moves as a "refuge of ignorance," since *how* plastic power worked remained unknown, though its deniers couldn't offer an explanation for the effects it described either. From the hindsight provided by modern knowledge of genetic code and evolution, this debate can seem quaint, but I call attention to it because it foregrounds how knowledge and ignorance, science and myth, rise up together in a manner specific to *capitalist* Modernity, as not only Barthes but also Horkheimer and Adorno have shown, arguments worth remembering at a time in which counter-narratives of the emergence of modernity, such as Bruno Latour's, are ascendant.[8] This essay explores the prehistory of modern "plastic" to suggest that Latour's rewriting of the emergence of "modernity" in terms of "science" rather than "capitalism" works like *The Fourth Kingdom*: Latour *seems* to explain why "modernity" is catastrophic by pointing to a supposedly neglected "middle" of networked relations among humans and nonhumans that everyone, except new materialists, supposedly fails to see, while *he* denies the mediations imposed by capitalist property. Is this a problem? For Marxists, the answer is yes, and Latour's account of modernity offers a catastrophic "refuge of ignorance" to humans who hope to preserve capitalism and—impossibly—the planet as well.

Plastick

How *does* "modernity" happen? Latour's version of the tale in *We Have Never Been Modern*—which has become as much a master narrative (Latour is no Lyotardian) as any put forth by Marxists—proposes that a catastrophic divide occurs between "nature" and "society" in the seventeenth century. Thus far, he is in total agreement with Horkheimer and Adorno. But for Latour "science," and the division of labor it negotiates with "politics"—*not* capitalism—plays the starring role in forcing this binary, a process in which he takes the dispute between Hobbes and Boyle on the air pump to be "exemplary." Because Hobbes and Boyle are also key figures in the "plastic" debate I introduced above, that debate offers an intriguing site in which to assess Latour's claims.

Etymologically, "plastick" entered English from Latin and Italian in the sixteenth century, designating molding arts, the persons who engaged in them (especially potters), and the substances (typically clay or wax) on which they worked, as well as the end result of their labor. Until the seventeenth century, the craft signification was the sole use of the word in English. First considered a "hard word," it turns up in early dictionaries, beginning with Thomas Elyot's 1542 *Bibliotheca*, where "plastice" is defined as "the crafte of warkynge in erthe." By the early seventeenth century, the term was sufficiently familiar, however, to find its way into stage plays and other "popular" sites, typically referring to body transformative practices, such as using cosmetics, which moralists disparaged for calling God's "plastick" abilities into question, adulterating his work.[9] It accumulated other analogical uses as well, some approving. James Harrington viewed education as the application of "plastick art" on the ostensibly claylike malleability of a child's mind.[10] Jeremy Taylor attributes to preaching the "plastick power to forme men into Christians."[11] "Plastick," thus, came to describe not only making nonhuman things, but also making humans, at a moment in which human relations to "erthe" were changing because of enclosure and the generalization of private property relations.[12]

By the mid-seventeenth century, as new "mechanistic" theories asserting the primacy and independence of "matter," displacing or bracketing "spirit," proliferated, not least in England by way of Hobbes, "plastick" became a particularly heated site of controversy. Armed with the biblical assertion that God not only "formed" Adam out of the "dust of the ground" but also "breathed into his nostrils the breath of life," "plastic" philosophers insisted that a creative *spiritual* force animated matter, releasing it from mechanical determinism, and explaining how wholes, like bodies, exceeded the sum of their physical parts.[13] "Plastic philosophers" saw themselves continuing an ancient conversation (some reworked Plato's *anima mundi*) concerning the problem of order and wholes, while responding to the challenge of emergent empiricism and mechanical materialism. Speaking for the latter, Robert Hooke protested that transformations of matter currently attributed to a spiritual "plastick faculty" by some of his contemporaries were actually effects of mechanical causes yet unknown, the typical rejoinder. Seeds were "small machines of nature" that appeared to be mysterious in their workings now, but, as microscopic and other experimental knowledge increased, they would be no more inexplicable than is the knowledge of how tapestries are woven to those who know how looms work.[14] Others, however, used *the same* argument of increasing knowledge, to argue *for* metaphysical "plastic power." Eschewing the "wild Epicurean doctrine" that "an accidental and blind concourse of atoms" could give rise to the "textures of bodies" and the movement of history in all its spectacular complexity, many thinkers insisted that there must be a "plastic Faber"—significantly, a workman rather than a machine—guiding seeds into forming bodies of all kinds, and also keeping the universe from descending into chaos.[15] They contrasted random mechanical unfolding, which could only be traced in a chain of direct immediate material relations, with "plastick power," which operated systemically from the moment of the Earth's creation, informing all matter imminently, albeit not self-consciously.

Two points are worth underscoring here: first, the various participants in the seventeenth-century debate on plastic were concerned with different levels of causation; the advocates of plastic power ultimately concerned themselves with *wholes,* while the mechanical philosophers repeatedly pulled these speculations down to immediately observable relations, traceable in immediate connections of one entity to another. Second, both groups realized that their approaches gave rise to *knowledge,* but also, crucially, to *ignorance.* Indeed, the seventeenth-century antagonists on "plastick power" frequently accused each other of *cultivating* ignorance. Robert Boyle, whose early work tentatively allowed the possible exercise of "plastick power" that he later rejected, is "epitomized" by the end of the century as suggesting that "an advantage in our hypothesis is that it flies not to an unknown Power, as a *Plastick* one, or an *Anima Mundi,* whose Operation is not known, but gives us a Mechanical Account of Things."[16] Boyle himself had asserted: "I endeavour'd . . . to explain the *Phaenomena* exhibited in our Engine . . . without recourse to a *Fuga Vacui,* or the *Anima Mundi,* or any such unphysical Principle."[17] This approach, he insists, is superior to a "plastick" one, which "gives no more Satisfaction, than if one were told, that a Watch tells the Hours of the Day, because made by such a Man; whereas the true Reason is, because the Parts so plac'd together are in Motion."[18] To achieve "satisfaction," though, Boyle and his followers had to *bracket* the kinds of questions that most concerned their critics: What keeps the *wholes* in motion in particular ways beyond mechanical dynamics? Why are there watches at all instead of chaos? Boyle explicitly recuses himself from speculating about questions of "Gravity in general," and the like. The problem remains, then, as Mathew Hale points out, that a "plastick" account might not give "satisfaction," but it is difficult to discount entirely because there are pressing points on which the "mechanical" view does not give satisfaction either.[19]

Ralph Cudworth, for example, complained that what the mechanists refer to as "laws" of Nature are actually the very "plastic power" that they deny: "They do but unskillfully and unawares establish that very thing which in words they oppose." He refutes the accusation that "plastic power" is "occult" by pointing out that its workings are apparent in the effect of "harmony of disagreeing things" that it brings to pass. Order, for him, is the proof of "plastick power." He fulminates: "He that asserts a plastic nature assigns a determinate and proper cause, nay the only intelligible cause of . . . the orderly, regular and artificial frame of things in the universe, which the mechanic philosophers . . . assign no cause at all."[20] Tracing physical existents in direct and immediate causal networks, mechanical philosophers left to the side "macro" questions, except *inductively* derived "laws," while at the other extreme a plastic approach proposed that the organizing complexity of the whole required a force greater than the sum of their parts, even if its workings remained obscure.

I lay out this debate *not* to declare a winner, since, from the perspective of the related debate today concerning networks (or "assemblages") versus totality, neither are sufficient.[21] *Both* the move to localize questions to those whose answers could be immediately observed, as the mechanists insisted, *and* the resort to a metaphysical "plastic power" understood as "harmony of disagreeing things" secured, ultimately, by a deity, permitted nagging questions of *totality* in its later, secular, Marxist, sense to be evaded. For Marxists, not only is a mode of production, such as capitalism, greater than the sum of its parts, but *contradiction* and *conflict*—not "harmony"—characterize that whole so long as the parts are unjustly articulated. Furthermore, the process is entirely worldly and material.[22] *Dialectical* totalities for Marxists are not stable or homogenous; they are a heuristic, a freeze-frame view of a system necessarily in constant motion *because* riven by contradiction. What if the "Man" who makes Boyle's watch is a slave? Are "freemen" really "free"? How do racism and sexism arise and endure? Is it sufficient to give cows or trees "rights" to protect them from human rapacity? These are questions that require, for many, a consideration of systemic processes: "Structures of stewardship, care . . . and legal personhood for land are not, in and of themselves, definitive solutions" to ecological or other challenges today, Robert Nichols rightly observes, *because* "a field of power" is always already in place, impinging on all entities, whether Latour acknowledges it or not.[23] Dialectical attention to this "field" explains why history *tends* to unfold as it does: that is, demonstrably, in the interests of relatively few humans, *not* purely accidentally, which does not mean that there is either a "Great Dispatcher" (who Latour repeatedly conjures up as if Marxists, much less Marx, believed in any such individual or collective conspiracy) or a Telos.[24] Dialectics simply recognizes that there are *systemic* effects of property relations and their unevenness that cannot be *ignored* when bringing together "entities" to compose a collective.

This distinction brings me to *mediation*. Latour defines it as "the creation of a link that did not exist before and that to some degree modifies two elements or agents." He objects to the claim "Man flies," because "flying is a property of the whole association of entities that includes airports and planes, launch pads and ticket counters."[25] What this list omits is as telling as what it includes.[26] While states and corporations *own* the airlines under conditions of capitalist globalization, demonstrably unequal, racist, and privileging the global North, such a list could never suffice to explain who can afford to fly and not, how comfortably, and with what ability to ignore the ecological effects on not only humans but nonhumans. Latour nevertheless insists that one need not go beyond any given network to explain the distributed action within it: "Networks are immersed in nothing."[27] Marxists define mediation very differently. Fredric Jameson asserts that everything is *always already* part of a *totality,* "a seamless web, a single inconceivable and transindividual process, in which there is no need to invent ways of linking language events and social upheavals or economic contradictions because on that level they were never separate from one another."[28] For Latour, there is no such "level" at all: only networks, with "nothing" between.

Indeed, referring obliquely to the plastic debates, he asserts: "We do not need a mysterious ether for them [networks] to propagate themselves." His reference to "ether" here has little to do with Hobbes's understanding of it (an all-pervasive substance that enabled distant objects to move each other).[29] Latour's target with "ether," rather, displaces it from its historical meaning to his own purposes: using it to critique a reliance on "social context" in *Leviathan and the Air Pump,* Latour dismisses social context as a "mysterious" force "between" networks, in an intriguing reprise of a typical move in the "plastick" debate. Marxists, of course, deny that the forces of capitalism are "mysterious." At issue are different understandings of "mediation" that have significant effects for how the world is understood, what is relegated to the unknown, and why.

Latour rejects "totality" as not only theoretically false, but also politically disabling because, in his view, it "renders its practitioners powerless in the face of the enemy, whom it endows with fantastic properties."[30] The Marxist injunction to overturn "totality" makes the task appear *too hard,* he argues, leading to despair, which is unnecessary, he says, since change is readily achievable in networks, once they are viewed as unconstrained by totality. Would that this were so! Latour takes as evidence of capitalism's fragility, for example, that "powerful CEOs" can suddenly have the "impulse to strap on golden parachutes and leap from their skyscrapers."[31] Marxists, however, emphasize that *capitalism* as a systemic force never blinks because of such *individual* leaps, so long as the uneven total distribution of capital that secures it remains intact (any more than sexism is dismantled when Harvey Weinstein goes to jail so long as the financial and legal structures that uphold gender inequality persist). The political choice here is clear: *if* capitalist property relations implicate *every* part of capitalist totality with inequality and injustice (Jameson's definition of "mediation") then we don't *have* to engage constantly in "empirical studies of the networks" in order to diagnose the problem with the current order of things, as Latour's "mediation" proposes.[32] Latour, conversely, doesn't recognize uneven property as a problem at all. His proposed alternative to revolution, the "Parliament of Things," thus welcomes corporations like Monsanto (!) to the table as if they are actually capable of engaging in significant ecological repair given the constraints of capitalism, and he insists that sufficient change is possible without revolution.[33] More recently, participants in an experimental "parliament" he helped organize—funded by major corporations, which he apparently saw in no way as a problem—realized they could never implement their plan of action without a *prior* transformation of society as a whole—that is, *revolution*—a concern on their part that Latour's account fails to mention.[34]

The crucial point: both "network" and "totality" give rise to ignorance as well as knowledge—as does every theory; the question is, which ignorance is the more costly to the goal of making an ecologically and socially just planet? It is certainly the case that tracing networks can offer useful knowledge. Corporate analysts and numerous others engage in it all the time when they do "commodity chain analysis," for example; Marxism, too, has its analyses that explore the role of the nonhuman, but with the significant difference that Marxist "networks" are always situated in capitalist totality, not treated as if they act *completely* independently and *only* contingently as they do for new materialists. While dialectics provides mechanisms for confronting particulars, contradictions, *and* totality, then, the reverse is not the case. Having rejected totality, Latour cannot assess, as a Marxist must, the pressure of systemic forces—most importantly, the *mode of production*. He simply ignores it, never asking, for example, where the *funding* for Boyle's air pump came from. Let's take a look and see if "context" matters or not.

Richard Boyle, Robert's father, made his fortune in colonial Ireland as a deputy escheator (legal representative responsible for determining ownership and arranging transfers of landed property), which offered him "many chances for legitimate and illicit gains," which he pursued "energetically," amassing enormous holdings in Munster.[35] Having acquired numerous estates, he administered them with entrepreneurial zeal, implementing "improvements" (the term used to justify the social and ecological costs of establishing the dominance of capitalist private property), manufacturing (textiles, glass), and the exploitation of natural "resources," such as timber, sometimes to exhaustion.[36] Brutal colonial dispossession, then, as well as exploitation of human labor and nonhuman "resources" provided the funding for what Latour calls "Big Science." The money that paid for the air pump and Boyle's other equipment, as well as his leisure to work with it, is, irreducibly, bound up in the "cost" of emergent capitalism, of which "Big Science" is an *effect* as well as a participant, a perspective that Latour eschews, which encourages in his followers an ongoing "sanctioned ignorance" about how capitalism works systemically. Acknowledging the *capital* accumulation that pays for the air pump—a process that exacts very palpable costs—indicates a more robust and accurate way to tell the story of modernity if we actually desire a *better* world, rather than preserving the world according to Monsanto and its ilk, who are the progeny of the very mode of accumulation that made the air pump possible.

"Big Science" was—and is—no accident: it was built on the capital provided by rapacious capitalist colonialism and the dispossession of most people so that capital accumulated in a few hands. Just as important: emergent capitalism favors some "networks" over others; it is the "ether" that Latour denies persistently, but that has left loose ends for his story of the emergence of the Modern: *why this way?* From a Marxist perspective, Latour's method encourages ignorance of what we most need to know in order to act effectively in the face of ecological destruction and social inequality and remediable suffering: the totality of forces in which we find ourselves inserted, unevenly. *We Have Never Been Modern* was written in the heyday of capitalist triumphalism following the collapse of the USSR, a triumphalism in which Latour participates as he lauds the "miraculous year 1989."[37] He emphatically denounces "those modernists par excellence, the Marxists": "On the basis of the fragile heterogeneous networks that collectivities have always formed, the critics have elaborated homogeneous totalities that could not be touched unless they were totally revolutionized. And because this subversion was impossible, but they tried it anyway, they have gone from one crime to another. . . . Might the belief in a radical and total modernity then lead to immorality?"[38] This is, of course, an entirely false description of Marxist theoretical practice, which *cannot* "homogenize" totality, given that it is riven by contradiction and struggle for hegemony among heterogenous elements. What makes them "propagate" in the *specific* way that they do? Latour can suggest nothing beyond contingency, like the other antirevolutionary revisionists, such as Francis Furet, from whom he derives his understanding of "history."[39] He has never relinquished the perspective that aspirations to totalizing transformation are politically disabling—the opposite view to Jameson's, which offers us a clear choice.

Crucially, with Boyle and the emergence of "modernity," accumulated capital has no meaning or "agency" outside the total historical conditions from which it emerges; Boyle's "money" is not "tainted" at the individual level as if there were "clean" money elsewhere that he could have used instead for the air pump; the point, rather, is that a *pile of pounds* cannot be added as a "thing" to a "network" without carrying with them the *total historical process that gave rise to and maintains their power,* a force that, necessarily, operates "between" all the networks—a "middle" that Latour ignores.[40] Money has no meaning, or force, as capital without it. *Dialectic of Enlightenment* thus points out that Bacon's fantasy of mastery over nature is *underwritten* by the rise of private property and capital, which enables systemically privileged humans to assert their right to control "nature" and other humans, while claiming, insidiously, to set them "free." *Capitalist* mastery cannot be undone without abolishing the property relation that secures it; this is not an epistemological problem, but a material one. Iyko Day suggests as much when she points out the lamentable effects of the failure of so many theorists today to think *dialectically* in the face of appeals to privilege the "concrete" ("the tree in your backyard, the dusty work boots by the door, the reliable pickup truck in the driveway")—*over* the "abstract" ("capital accumulation, surplus value, and money").[41] To extend Day's point in Horkheimer and Adorno's terms, capitalist property relations *require* not only inequality among humans, but *also* between humans and nonhumans, that cannot be understood without dialectic, or overcome while preserving capitalist private property.

Fighting Sanctioned Ignorance

Networks or cognitive mapping? Which offers the best guide toward preventing ecological disaster, a goal that Marxists and Latourians avowedly share, and one from which, as this volume attests, we cannot dissociate plastic? New Materialists such as Latour envision a solution to impending catastrophe in which private property and corporations can persist, and so no revolution is required. As native theorists as well as Eco-Marxists have forcefully argued, however, a propertarian relation to land and "resources"—without which there can be no capitalism—negates the possibility of healing the planet.[42] Even Latour's supporters have wondered if his approach "allows insufficient room for sub-revolutionary change that would still be significant" given the challenges we face.[43]

As my reading of the Bakelite Corporation's *Fourth Kingdom* suggested, elaborate empirical detailing of local connections among humans and things, like the "scientist" with his equipment, simply *cannot* tell the whole story of plastic or anything else, while capitalism remains uninterrogated as the conditions in which *all* such "mediations" unfold. No matter how far we extend the network, it won't explain or address inequality and ongoing remediable suffering. Furthermore, putting all the emphasis on networks distracts us from the systemic forces that must be transformed if we are to have an ecologically and socially just world. The main point: *Only* undoing property relations can create the alternative material *conditions* that would give rise to the possibility of ecological repair. Latour's theoretical refusal to engage with these systemic conditions provides a "refuge of ignorance" for those who don't want to acknowledge how deeply capitalism does indeed structure existence, human and nonhuman.

NOTES

1. Roland Barthes, *Mythologies,* trans. Richard Howard and Annette Lanvers (New York: Hill and Wang, 2012), 193–94.
2. Karl Marx, *Capital,* vol. 1, trans. Ben Fowkes (London: Penguin, 1990), 280.
3. Jane Bennet, *Vibrant Matter* (Durham, N.C.: Duke University Press, 2010), viii, 4.
4. Theodor Adorno, *Minima Moralia,* trans. E. F. N. Jephcott (London: Verso, 1974), 39.
5. Barthes, *Mythologies,* 195; on "second nature," see Carl Cassegard, "Eco-Marxism and the Critical Theory of Nature," *Distinktion* 18, no. 3 (2017): 314–32.
6. Stephen Blankaart, *A Physical Dictionary* (London, 1684), 232: "plastical virtus is . . . [a] Refuge of Ignorance, for what the ancients could not explain they called a plastic Virtue."
7. Peter Anstey, Sarah Hutton, Domenico Meli, and Jasper Reid, among others, have published more recently on aspects of the debate, but the most focused overview of the debate in England remains William B. Hunter, "The Seventeenth Century Doctrine of Plastic Nature," *Harvard Theological Review* 43, no. 3 (1950): 197–213.
8. Max Horkheimer and Theodor Adorno, *Dialectic of Enlightenment,* trans. Edmund Jephcott (Stanford, Calif.: Stanford University Press, 2002); Bruno Latour, *We Have Never Been Modern,* trans. Catherine Porter (Cambridge, Mass.: Harvard University Press, 1993).
9. John Marston's *The Malcontent* (London, 1604) refers to an aging Madam as an "olde peece of plastick"—that is, transformed by cosmetics.
10. James Harrington, *Commonwealth of Oceana* (London, 1656), 208.
11. Jeremy Taylor, *Of the Sacred Order* (London, 1647), 385.
12. Jason Moore, *Capitalism in the Web of Life* (London: Verso, 2015) makes a compelling case for viewing the emergence of capitalism as establishing the foundation for the ecological crisis that we find ourselves in today, a timeline and claim I entirely agree with, though I sometimes find his attempt to make concessions to new materialism to be in conflict with his recognition of capitalism as a structuring force.
13. In Isaiah (64:8) the figure is explicitly associated with pottery: "We are the clay, and thou our potter; and we all are the work of thy hand."
14. Robert Hooke, *Micrographia* (London, 1665).
15. W. Simpson, *Philosophical Dialogues* (London, 1677), 32, 35.
16. Richard Boulton, *The Works of the Honorable Robert Boyle* (London, 1699).
17. Robert Boyle, *Tracts* (London, 1672), 10.
18. Jessica Riskin, *The Restless Clock* (Chicago: University of Chicago Press, 2016).
19. Matthew Hale, *Observations Touching the Principles of Natural Motions* (London, 1677), 26–31.

20. Ralph Cudworth, *True Intellectual System of the Universe* (London, 1678), 154.
21. Manuel DeLanda's *New Philosophy of Society* (London: Continuum, 2006) offers an influential "assemblages against totalities" view, though his account is profoundly crippled by not raising, much less accounting for, dialectical *contradiction*. He can see easily enough that "emergent properties"—the whole being greater than the sum of the parts—operate at the level of individual assemblages, but, like Latour, assumes that, at the level of totality, emergent properties do not arise. This theoretical refusal of totality has a mystifying effect today. Latour is right: focusing on the "middle" matters more than ever for confronting the ecological devastation of the planet and human failure to act in relation to it, but he is also wrong: there is more than one middle, and we must attend to both not only "assemblages," but what operates *between* them.
22. For a recent defense of "totality," along the lines I engage here, see Alberto Toscano, "Seeing it Whole," *Sociological Review* 60, no. 1 (2012): 64–83.
23. Robert Nichols, *Theft is Property!* (Durham, N.C.: Duke University Press, 2020), 158.
24. I don't always agree with McKenzie Wark, but that Latour's view of "totality" is extremely selective and narrow and has little relation to Marxist understanding of it—and especially that Latour's "Great Dispatcher" is a straw man—we are in complete accord. See "Bruno Latour: Occupy Earth," https://www.versobooks.com/blogs/3425-bruno-latour-occupy-earth.
25. Bruno Latour, "On Technical Mediation," *Common Knowledge* 3, no. 2 (1994): 29–64.
26. New materialists sometimes attempt to "fix" this problem by simply listing structuring forces as one actant among others, as if all existed on the same "level" and were somehow invented in the assemblage adduced. So keen is Bennet to "prove" that assemblages are not impinged from "without" by any "external purpose," that she claims that "the electrical grid is better understood as a volatile mix of coal, sweat, electromagnetic fields, computer programs, electron streams, profit motives, heat, lifestyles, nuclear fuel, plastic, fantasies of mastery, static, legislation, water, economic theory, wire and wood—to name just some of the actants" (25). She does not explain how "actants" that are NOT restricted to the "electrical grid" on this list can possibly be equated with the items that are more grid specific (though none of the items are only part of electrical grids). Certainly the "profit motive," etc. were not generated *by the grid itself* as Bennett fantastically proposes, but demonstrably preexist the existence of *any* such grids and impinge on *all* of them. The differences in "scales" among these putative "actants" must be explained, not merely finessed *rhetorically* by throwing all the items in the same list side by side. Important work on racism, for example, has had to argue again and again

that all such attempts to reduce oppressions to mere local attitudes and interactions is to misunderstand their *structuring force* entirely; see, for example, Ibram X. Kendi, *How to Be an Anti-Racist* (New York: One World, 2019), which argues that racism can only be dismantled *structurally* (with capitalism) and that all other approaches help *keep it in place.*

27. See chapter 2 of Latour, *We Have Never.*
28. Fredric Jameson, *Political Unconscious* (Ithaca, N.Y.: Cornell University Press, 1981), 40.
29. Latour's source for "ether" is also the target of his analogical deployment of it: Steven Shapin and Simon Schaffer, *Leviathan and the Air Pump* (Princeton, N.J.: Princeton University Press, 1985), which does not discuss the "plastick" debate per se.
30. Latour, *We Have Never,* 125.
31. Bruno Latour, *An Inquiry into Modes of Existence,* trans. Catherine Porter (Cambridge, Mass.: Harvard University Press, 2013), 416.
32. Latour, *We Have Never,* 46.
33. Latour, *We Have Never,* 144.
34. See my "The Common, Force and the Capitalocene," *Minnesota Review* 93 (2019), where I discuss Latour's experimental "parliament" in more detail.
35. Toby Barnard, "Boyle, Richard, first earl of Cork" ODNB (2008); Terance O. Ranger, "Richard Boyle and the Making of an Irish Fortune," *Irish Historical Studies* 10, no. 39 (1957): 257–97.
36. Richard Drayton, *Nature's Government* (New Haven, Conn.: Yale University Press, 2000).
37. Latour, *We Have Never,* 145.
38. Latour, *We Have Never,* 126.
39. Latour, *We Have Never,* 40.
40. Contrast Latour with Jason Moore, *Capitalism in the Web of Life* (London: Verso, 2015).
41. Iyko Day, *Alien Capital* (Durham, N.C.: Duke University Press, 2016), 10–11.
42. See Nichols, *Theft is Property!.*
43. Graham Harman, *Bruno Latour: Reassembling the Political* (London: Pluto, 2014), 120.

9

The Petrochemical Unconscious

Destructive Plasticities in Richard Powers's *Gain*

Christopher Breu

In the context of the world-ecology, climate change can perhaps best be theorized in terms of what Catherine Malabou defines as *destructive plasticity.* She defines it as "a plasticity that does not repair, a plasticity without recompense or scar, one that cuts the thread of life in two or more segments that no longer meet."[1] Malabou's emphasis here is equally on destruction as absolute loss and on the violence it does to systemic connections. She is theorizing this primarily in a postphenomenological framework that emphasizes human perception and experience of illness, loss, and death, but I find it similarly helpful for thinking about macronarratives of capitalist-driven exploitation, creative destruction, and the ecosystemic decimation produced by climate change. Richard Powers's *Gain* is similarly split between micro- and macronarratives, one telling the story of Laura Bodey's death from ovarian cancer in the fictional small Illinois town of Lacewood and the other telling a large-scale story of the 150-year transformation of the Clare company from a Boston soap company to a multinational, partly headquartered in Lacewood, which produces a range of petrochemical products (one or more of which probably caused Laura's cancer). Written in the waning years of the twentieth century and set in downstate Illinois, a historical cancer belt as Sandra Steingraber has noted, Powers's novel takes on an added urgency in our twenty-first-century moment of capitalist-produced toxicity, inequality, resource exhaustion, and climate change.[2]

Climate change is a destructive plasticity, one ironically enough, produced, in part, by the ever-growing production, disposal, and destruction of plastic itself, which is one part of the petrochemical economy that has been central to post–World War II global capitalism and the preeminent position of the United States within it. This petrochemical economy includes the production of synthetic polymers from gas and nonrenewable energy through the vast panoply of consumer goods and packaging, the use of petrochemical products in preproduction, and what Jason Moore, citing Richard Walker, terms "the petrochemical-hybrid complex" that drove the green revolution of the second half of the twentieth century.[3] Produced by humans but not fully controlled by them, this destructive plasticity inheres in the very productive plasticities of postwar and contemporary life. What seemed like productive plasticities from a certain privileged vantage have now emerged as fully destructive ones, "where the repertory of viable forms has reached exhaustion and has nothing else to propose."[4] We find ourselves precisely at the limits of transformation undertaken by the long and finally ecocidal history of capitalism. For Marx, capitalism was always about contradictions and the joining of new and powerful forms of productivity with new forms of exploitation, destruction, and immiseration. If such destruction was always part of capitalism's plasticity, then the destructive part in our own moment of climate change outstrips any productive return.

Yet, how do we experience the destructive plasticity of the present? How do we begin to account for the relationship between the vast workings of what Amanda Boetzkes terms the "oil economy," with its plastic manifestations at all levels of the world ecology from production, through distribution, and consumption, with our specific and phenomenological encounters with plastic and waste?[5] How can we map the human perceptual scale with the vision of plastic as "new material of the Anthropocene par excellence, extending the pathways of the global oil economy in all directions, permeating substances and ultimately becoming a source of fuel in and of itself, even as its ecological effects become increasingly unruly"?[6] The concept of the Anthropocene has of course been one way of mapping such macro-scale workings of climate change and the global oil economy more generally. Yet, as others have noted, the concept of the Anthropocene has its limitations. Moore argues that the Anthropocene as a framework seems to place the blame for climate change on the mere fact of human existence, rather than interactions between the capitalist world system and what Moore nicely terms the "world ecology." While, Moore has coined the alternate term "capitalocene," I want to propose a different notion for the way that, as Boetzkes puts it, "capitalism has become plastic."[7]

The term I propose instead of the Anthropocene in this essay is the *petrochemical unconscious*. The petrochemical unconscious can be thought in ways parallel with the Jamesonian notion of the political unconscious.[8] I choose this term because it captures the unruly, complex, multiscalar, and multitemporal dimension of the relationship of oil capitalism to the climate crisis and human perception. I also use it because so much of our relationship to petrochemicals is unconscious, from our lack of awareness of how much petrochemical waste is present in capitalist production before commodities hit the market, to the presence of petrochemicals in all sorts of areas that we don't think about from agriculture to medicine, to the spatiotemporal scale of petrochemical waste and its storage around the world. I also use the term because it foregrounds the question of representation. As Jameson argues in relationship to the capitalist world system in *The Geopolitical Aesthetic*, the whole of the impact of petrocapitalism on contemporary life, human and otherwise, is unrepresentable in its totality within human representational forms.[9] Yet, this is not to argue that representation isn't crucial. Representation, and its forms, become necessary for precisely doing the work of mediation and transformation that climate change demands. Moreover, as David Herman has recently argued, representation is not sealed on the level of the human, but opens out in all sorts of ways to the nonhuman, including the petrochemical.[10] I use the term *unconscious* rather than N. Katherine Hayles's recent, powerful argument for the importance of thinking the "nonconscious" dimensions of contemporary life, because petrochemicals aren't merely *absent* from conscious knowledge.[11] They are more properly understood as *repressed*. We know on some level that they structure our daily lives, inform the desire that organizes consumer capitalism, and are central to the growing climate emergency, yet, like the psychoanalytic unconscious, we repress this knowledge most of the time. The petrochemical unconscious, with its link to commodity desire and the growing threat of extinction, is also shaped by collective forms of drive (erotic and deathly) in the present.

Gain, Inflexibility, and Representation

Given the centrality of representation in engaging the petrochemical unconscious, questions of literary form and aesthetic practices become paramount. In contrast to hierarchical conceptions of the aesthetic, I draw on Stephanie LeMenager's definition of "the word 'aesthetic'" as "deriving meaning from its most basic etymological root in how we sense and perceive and form what have been called ideologies of the aesthetic, forms of representation a value expressed by means of display, spectacle, concealment, and stealth."[12] Within such a framework, one also present in the work of Sianne Ngai, the aesthetic is not the province of high culture but attaches to all forms of social and natural production.[13] The question of ideology returns in this account of the aesthetic, as does the question of forms and their affordances as Caroline Levine posits it.[14]

Such an attention to the political question of form animates the novels of Richard Powers, which change form depending on their subject matter. With the recent publication of the Pulitzer-Prize-winning *The Overstory,* Powers has emerged as perhaps our leading novelist of environmental catastrophe. If *The Overstory* represents his most celebrated ecological novel, his 1998 novel, *Gain,* represents a crucial precursor to it. *The Overstory* is noted for the vastness of its narrative canvas, which includes both human and nonhuman actors; *Gain* is the novel where the relationship between ecological violence and capitalism is spelled out most explicitly. As Stephen J. Burn and Peter Dempsey have argued, *Gain* was written in order to chart the "impact of the modern corporation on modern life."[15] Thus, while all of Powers's works are a mix of realist and postmodern aesthetics (marking him, as Joseph Dewey suggests, as part of the generation of so-called post-postmodernists), *Gain* is one of his most straightforwardly realist novels.[16] It is an embrace of realism, but realism with a difference. One of the challenges with the return to realism is the question of scale. No matter how plastic realism becomes, it has trouble being flexible or capacious enough to be adequate to the petrochemical unconscious and the forms of economic, ecological, and social life tethered to it.

Gain takes this inadequacy as its springboard. As Derek Woods argues, "Throughout the novel, the macroform of both narratives interacts with its rhetorical microform through tropes that substitute one body for another, for example by using the swarm as a figure for the corporation or the synthetic molecule or the person as a figure for the corporation."[17] Rather than trying to provide a language flexible and capacious enough to fully integrate the two narratives, Powers constructs two divergent narratives that link by the kinds of figurations described by Woods but never fully connect (except in one visionary moment we will address below). While Powers's novels, such as *The Gold Bug Variations*, are often organized around contrapuntal narrative structures, the musical scale rather than geophysical scale being the operative metaphor, *Gain* uses its disjunctive structure to emphasize the incompatibility of different spatial scales. Rather than presenting a narrative organized around flexible plasticity, where words are stretched, accumulated, and reworked so that they form a world of their own, as in Pynchon, Wallace, or Powers's own early fiction, the plasticity of *Gain* is willfully inflexible. Like what Elizabeth Mazzolini and Stephanie Foote describe as the "nonbiodegradable lumps of plastic, shedding bisphenol A and phthalates" present in landfills and oceanic garbage patches, Powers's novel refuses flexibility and stylistic transformation.[18] It suggests that the best way we can engage the petrochemical unconscious is by refusing to attempt to be adequate to it; instead we should foreground the problems of scale that come with any attempt to represent it.

Thus Powers creates a plastic narrative, but unlike the flexible plasticity of the postmodern word play, the modified realism used by Powers is organized around an inflexible but modular plasticity, in which the object can continue to grow, decline, or repeat itself, but it cannot reach out or connect in a fully coherent way to objects of a very different scale. The two narratives are organized primarily around different kinds of plasticity. The heroic arc of the Clare company's ascent to global power is narrated via productive plasticity, in which the negativities engaged by the narrative are finally recontained within its positive movement. Meanwhile the destructive plasticity of Laura's narrative finally reveals all positivities to be a version of what Lauren Berlant describes as "cruel optimism," or affirmative narratives that inhibit flourishing and cover over forms of systemic violence.[19] Of course, as critics Ralph Clare and Bruce Robbins note, the company Clare gains from Laura's losses.[20] Thus, the cruelest optimistic narrative adopted by Powers is the one attaching to what Greil Marcus, in his review of *Gain,* describes as the "Promethean messianism of corporate America."[21] While Clare's narrative is finally that of a transnational corporation, it is framed in the exceptionalist terms that have animated the liberal and imperial version of American history. In contrast and even counterpoint to this macronarrative is the decidedly minor narrative of Laura Bodey's decline and death.

Microrealism

Powers's writing in the Laura Bodey sections of the novel are the closest to conventional realism. Like the celebrated realisms of the nineteenth century, this part of *Gain* tracks the fate of a single, ordinary, yet somehow representative, bourgeois subject, in this case Laura Bodey, a real estate salesperson and divorced mother of two living in a generic downstate Illinois town, Lacewood, the only distinguishing feature of which is that it is one of the headquarters of Clare International. Yet, even more than the protagonists of the early and mid-nineteenth-century realisms of Austen, Dickens, and Balzac, who could act decisively in relationship to their social milieu, Laura echoes the protagonists of the naturalist novel, not only in the way in which her disease emphasizes the negative plasticity of her biological body (the centrality of which to the narrative is indicated, of course, by her last name), but also the way in which social and material forces appear altogether too large and opaque for her actions to be in any way heroic.

Yet, the realism or naturalism employed by Powers in the Laura sections of *Gain* is finally different from its nineteenth-century precursors. Rather than the larger forces of society visibly overwhelming or being in dialectical tension with the protagonist, she instead feels thoroughly disconnected to forces that remain obscure to her. Take, for example, an early scene, before Laura is diagnosed, when she sees a group of farmers at the store:

> She wouldn't know how to talk to these men if one turned around and chatted her up. All she can do is take from them. These boxes of multigrain cereal. The corndogs that Tim eats unheated, right out of the pouch. Ellen's tubes of fat-free whole wheat chips. The nonstick polyunsaturated maize oil spray. The squeezable enriched vegetable paste. The microwave tortillas. The endangered-species animal crackers. Everything in her cart, however enhanced and tangled its way here.[22]

The disconnection here is one between production and consumption, between the consumerist lifeworld of the neoliberal United States and the massive work of post-Fordist capitalist production (both agricultural and petrochemical) that sustains this lifeworld. This disconnection is emphasized by a series of misrecognitions. Laura thinks these farmers are distinct from agribusiness. In an adjacent passage, she talks about the kids of the farmers "selling out to the inevitable Agribiz" (27). Yet, if they are really the producers of the raw materials that are remade into the seemingly impossible and denatured products listed in the passage above, then their products are already profoundly intertwined with agribusiness, even if they are nominally independent as farmers. Laura also misrecognizes who does a lot of the production, on the level of chemical alteration, of the products she references. The agricultural division of Clare, which is located in Lacewood and provides a majority of its employment, does this work, yet the company is notable for its absence in the above passage. Finally, Laura also misrecognizes the forms of destructive plasticity (including the killing of the very endangered species referenced in the animal crackers) that is produced as so much fallout from the seemingly impossible (constructive) plasticity promised by the products above, which somehow wed gastronomic appeal and positive "enrichment" to the absence of negatives like fat, saturated and unsaturated. What emerges then from this passage is what Rachel Greenwald Smith describes as the compromise aesthetics of neoliberalism, in which private existence is marked as the most authentic experience that can be conveyed by the work of art.[23]

Yet, unlike most versions of compromise aesthetics, Laura's experience with cancer pushes her to look out toward larger social, ecological, and economic contexts. Still, she can seemingly do no more than note or begin to trace the larger context: "Everybody is battling cancer. Why did she never see these people before?" (242). Laura thus begins to see the scope of the epidemic, yet this recognition does not translate into agency or even definite knowledge. She is finally told by her ex-husband, Don, who is encouraging her to join a class action lawsuit against Clare, what the suspected exact cause of the epidemic is (a home weed killer that Laura uses for her favorite, seemingly ecofriendly pastime, gardening).

Even in this moment of revelation, she capitulates to the corporation completely: "And in the next blink: a weird dream of peace. It makes no difference whether this business has given her cancer. They have given her everything else. Taken her life and molded it in every way imaginable, plus six degrees beyond imagining. Changed her life so completely that not even cancer can change it more than halfway back" (364). Here the corporation takes on an almost divine stature. Clare giveth and Clare taketh away. And, as with most deities, one should not ask why, but accept the implacable will of the gods. Laura views Clare as the primary motive force of her existence, but one that is outside of rational or political engagement. After, imagining a moment of resistance, in which she and the other claimants can at least appear, however unequally and inadequately, on the same field of political struggle within the framework of liberal law (and she does finally agree to the lawsuit at the end of her life, the money from which ironically allows her son to start a corporation), she instead gives herself over to the will of the company that is imagined as all powerful. On one level, Laura's vision is an accurate depiction of how ubiquitous and fearsome, yet protean, the modern corporation is. As Clare Incorporated metastasizes, the critic Ralph Clare notes, the novel's metaphors for it become more "monstrous" and "inhuman."[24]

While Clare grows ever more global and ubiquitous, Laura is in turn sealed into a privatized, neoliberal world, in which, as Wendy Brown puts it, the subject as human capital is "in charge of itself, responsible for itself, yet an instrumentalizable and potentially dispensable element of the whole."[25] Rather than the collective being responsible for the individual, even as it shapes the individual more and more thoroughly, the individual is responsible for being worthy of increasingly privatized collective agents of investment. Laura has trouble comprehending the corporation as something other than a very powerful and dangerous person. This inability to imagine the large-scale working of the corporation and its relationship to the intimate workings of her dying body is a central manifestation of what I am calling the petrochemical unconscious, which can only be misrecognized (although in ways more or less enabling of anticapitalist and proenvironmental struggle) on the level of representation.

Within this neoliberal framework, it is striking, if unsurprising, that the two times Laura imagines an interaction with Clare, the company is personified. An ironic commentary, as Paul Maliszewski notes, on the status of the limited liability corporation as person and the kind of individualist representation central to the neoliberal cultural sphere, both these personifications rescript the profoundly asymmetrical relationship between Laura and Clare as a narrative between individual people.[26] The first, more empowering, vision is of having the president or chief come to Laura's house to explain "why this happened" (380). As much as this is a reassuring fantasy, it fundamentally misimagines the scale on which Clare operates. Even if the president did visit Laura in her room, he himself would probably not be able to give her the answers for which she is searching. Moreover, this imagined scene frames the problem as one of individual morality rather than collective action, transformation, and policy.

She imagines a similar, if more sinister, scene just before her death, in which Clare goes from being a romantic and handsome suitor to a date rapist: "But always, the night of romantic dancing turns by evening's end into desperate caresses, a brutal attack, date rape" (391). While it is always fraught to metaphorize rape, the metaphor, in this case, captures the embodied violence of what cancer and Clare as its agent have done to Laura. Here the text almost produces a language of allegory in which this encounter compellingly stands in for larger violence produced by a political economy and world ecology that put profits, innovation, and corporate plasticity over the health of ecosystems, people, and finally the planet itself. Yet, the allegory remains stubbornly fixed to a personal narrative here. It is a morphine-induced hallucination—a kind of displacement or condensation produced by the forces of the petrochemical unconscious. But this momentary narrative never opens out to a larger scene—at least not within the terms of the microrealism of the Laura Bodey sections of the novel. Date rape here, even as its violence is presented as repetitiously common, is seen as a matter of individuals, a contingent effect rather than the systematic form of violence it is.

Macrorealism

The other narrative presented by *Gain* is the seemingly endless rise of the Clare Corporation. If Laura's narrative is a micrological one of destructive plasticity, then, Clare's narrative is a macrological one of ostensibly productive plasticity, in which destructive plasticities of labor exploitation, imperial expansion, genocide, creative destruction, the violent effects of financialization, and large-scale ecological violence are all managed, shed, or externalized in the name of corporate growth and renewal. If in Laura's narrative Powers presents a version of neoliberal realism in which everything is reduced to the level of individual actors, the Clare sections of the narrative work in the opposite direction. While there are personified actors in this narrative as well, including the members of the Clare family and finally the corporation, Clare, itself, which, as Powers details, shifts from a mercantile firm to a soap manufacturing company, to a publicly held limited-liability corporation, in which Clare itself becomes a person under the law, the corporation is always presented as exceeding any potential personification. Such personifications are never anywhere adequate to the capitalist transformations narrated by the novel.

Powers marks this inadequacy on the level of narration. The Clare sections of the novel work primarily by using the voice of the pro-business American history textbook. Yet this stentorian, mock-heroic voice is often crosshatched with passages that sound like they are taken from different parts of Marx's *Capital*.[27] This voice captures the future orientation of capitalism as a mode of production, the way in which everything else is sacrificed, exploited, or appropriated for the future acquisition of profit. Take, for example, this passage about the way in which the Clares profit from the Civil War:

> As far as business made out, war was less crisis than its antidote. The Clares saw disaster's chance. Lard and cleanliness were the only suitable exchange for a society in cataclysm.... The Clares, with the luck that always accompanies an accommodating business, stood by, ready with straw to stable the Four Horsemen's mounts when those steeds blasted through town. (159)

Here futurity and capitalist growth are tied explicitly to large-scale destruction. The passage uses the language of inevitability, narrating from the point of view of business itself, and suggesting that the Clares are more lucky than enterprising. They are also presented as amoral war profiteers, the language of the Four Horsemen echoing the mock-biblical language that Marx uses to describe and condemn capitalist violence. Yet, what is most striking in passages like this is the way in which they dialectically complicate any personal, moral narrative. Certainly, the language of capitalist inevitability can function as an alibi, as it does in this passage. Yet, it also captures how the logic of capitalism colonizes the future. Within its logic, contingent events and choices take on a language of inevitability. It is this logic of inevitability, as a real abstraction, that becomes the power of narrative itself. The Clares aren't so much in control of this narrative as they are in thrall to it. Powers, like Marx, respects the material and rhetorical force of capitalism enough to narrate it from within its own logic even as he demonstrates the ultimate damage, destruction, and violence it produces in the name of progress. The narrative itself works to transmute the material contradictions of the present into the profit of tomorrow, even as the violence of the contradictions continues to grow.

The Clare narrative traces the viral (indeed cancerous) logic of capital accumulation and, in a condensed manner, the transformation of various stages of capitalism, from mercantilism through entrepreneurialism, industrial production, diversification, vertical and horizontal integration, becoming public, Taylorism, Fordism, the growth of finance, globalization, to greenwashing and beyond. In each context, "Clare's choice was a simple: grow or die" (267). Yet this growth itself is marked as what turns productive plasticity into destructive plasticity. Let us remember that cancer too is a form of productive plasticity within its own logic, yet it is destructive of the larger body of which it is a part. This is the implicit parallel put forward by Powers's novel.

Mapping the Petrochemical Unconscious

There is another form of discourse present in *Gain* that I have yet to discuss. These are the advertisements for Clare that regularly punctuate the novel, dividing the Laura and Clare sections. These ads range from the historical to the contemporary, with most of them parodying the kinds of ads that would bombard contemporary TV and radio at the time of *Gain*'s publication. If part of what the macrorealism of *Gain* attempts to address is the vast corporate, political-economic, and ecosystemic infrastructure that exceeds any single figuration, then the various ads are the user-friendly interface through which ordinary citizens, like Laura and Don, understand corporations. These interfaces are not just simplified; they are patently misleading, working to mask all kinds of things, including exploited labor, ecological damage, toxic products, wholescale appropriation, and the material production of the corporation itself by both human and extrahuman actors.

So, the novel leaves us with the question of how we can begin to map the political-economic and ecological infrastructure that seems to exceed any direct figuration of it. If the petrochemical unconscious is the product of this inability to represent the infrastructural completely, to bring it to consciousness in its dizzying complexity, then how do we begin to produce a representational praxis that will allow us to develop a literature and a politics that can move beyond happy interfaces of advertising and engage climate change and other degradations produced by contemporary capitalism? How do we link, in a politicized way, micro- and macrorealism?

Powers's novel provides an answer to this question in one of the closing sections of *Gain*. Given the impossibility of representing, in toto, the petrochemical unconscious, this textual moment charts instead a path through the infrastructural and systemic relationships that shape the world economy and world ecology. It does this through an aesthetic reworking of a conventional anticapitalist, pedagogical practice of tracing a commodity chain. Here, however, the figuration of the chain is less pragmatic and more sublime, demonstrating the materials of multiple continents, the complex chemical reactions, and forms of transnational labor that go into the making of a simple disposable plastic and cardboard camera, one that winds up discarded in a hospital drawer after Laura dies. As Ursula K. Heise notes, Powers's realism takes on a different resonance in this passage.[28] While she is more critical of the limits of the passage and Powers's realism, I want to argue that the passage can also be read as doing the important work of aesthetic disruption and scalar reorientation, rendering this seemingly humble, disposable object sublime in terms of the scale of labor, scientific innovation, and ecological forces that go into its production.

The passage begins with the complexity involved in producing something as deceptively simple as cardboard: "Somewhere on the coast of British Columbia, machines receive these trees. Pulper, bleacher, recovery plant, and mill synchronize to a staggering ballet, juggling inventory from calcium hypochlorite to nitrogen tetroxide, substances ranging from Georgia clays to the South Pacific guano" (393). Already, the simplest of materials is thoroughly transnational in its production. From its simplicity it reveals "a staggering ballet." This ballet is both human and posthuman, an ecological production, as much as economic and chemical one. The sublime dimensions of this passage, then, emerge not only from its contrasting scales but from the shift from the seeming simplicity of the camera ("All this for the box, the throwaway") to the complexity and vast scale of the production process itself: "The thing that Canada ships to Guangzhou for gluing is already an orchestral score." (394). Note the metaphor here. The comparison to music is especially notable in an author for whom it is a regular figuration of the aesthetic itself, whether in *The Gold Bug Variations* or *The Time of Our Singing*. Powers creates a kind of orchestral novelistic praxis in which the scope widens from the individual soloist to take in the massed orchestra, including the instruments, the symphony hall, the audience itself, and even perhaps the city of its performance.

The aesthetic here does not substitute for knowledge, but accompanies and affectively enriches it, even as it also marks the impossibility of fully knowing the petrochemical unconscious. In one of the final sections of the passage, plastic itself is invoked as precisely the knot at the center of the petrochemical unconscious: "Plastic happens; that is all we need to know on earth. History heads steadily for a place where things need not be grasped to be used" (395). Plastic here becomes a version of the commodity, functioning to mask and disavow the conditions of its production. Yet, more ambiguously, it also suggests both the necessity of transcending this commodity-based knowledge and the impossibility of full knowledge of what the world system and world ecology produce. We can only speculatively, with scientific, political, and aesthetic knowledge intertwined, attempt to map the petrochemical unconscious and the forms of infrastructural, political-economic, and political-ecological forces that shape it and upon which it depends.

Visionary Realism

Powers's *Gain* finally suggests a different understanding of realism than the one articulated by Leigh Clare La Berge and Alison Shonkwiler in their concept of a capitalist realist aesthetic, even as it too is engaged in representing global capitalism.[29] Instead, this realist aesthetic finds its apotheosis in the account of the camera that we have just analyzed. Here, objects and subjects (human and otherwise), including the laboring subject, would be the beginning (rather than the end-point) of representation. The representation would work against reification, commodification, and privatization to provide an aesthetic mapping of the world economy and ecology. Such a representation becomes visionary. It works to invoke the systemic and infrastructural dynamics that lie behind the spatial and temporal immediacies presented by conventional realism. Challenging capitalism's futurological orientation with its own, such a visionary realism transcends immediacy in the name of imagining the possibility of a better, resilient, and just future. In the contradictions of the present, visionary realism sees the possibilities of a different future. Such a realism is necessarily speculative—it cannot provide a positivist account of the entirety of the relations it invokes—but it provides an orientation for transforming our economic relations and the fundamental threat posed by climate change. It is both human and posthuman, attending to human relations, but also posthuman and ecological ones. Such a literary realism would be a worthy inheritor to nineteenth-century realism and a necessary aesthetic for our own moment of profound inequality, exhausted resources, species extinction, and ecocide. If we are going to survive the present, we will need a realist art of the most visionary sort. *Gain,* at its most powerful moments, suggests such a visionary realism.

NOTES

1. Catherine Malabou, *The Ontology of the Accident: An Essay on Destructive Plasticity,* trans. Carolyn Shread (Cambridge: Polity, 2012), 6.
2. Sandra Steingraber, *Living Downstream: An Ecologist's Personal Investigation of Cancer and the Environment,* 2nd ed. (New York: Da Capo, 2010). This essay is written from the very same cancer belt.
3. Jason W. Moore, *Capitalism in the Web of Life: Ecology and the Accumulation of Capital* (London: Verso, 2015).
4. Malabou, *Ontology of the Accident,* 54.
5. Amanda Boetzkes, *Plastic Capitalism: Contemporary Capitalism and the Drive to Waste* (Cambridge, Mass.: MIT Press, 2019), 184.
6. Boetzkes, *Plastic Capitalism,* 184.

7. Moore, *Capitalism,* 169; Boetzkes, *Plastic Capitalism,* 32.
8. Fredric Jameson, *The Political Unconscious: Narrative as a Socially Symbolic Act* (Ithaca, N.Y.: Cornell University Press, 1981), 9–14.
9. Fredric Jameson, *The Geopolitical Aesthetic: Cinema and Space in the World System* (Bloomington: Indiana University Press, 1992), 9–86.
10. David Herman, *Narratology beyond the Human: Storytelling and Animal Life* (Oxford: Oxford University Press, 2018), 263–94.
11. N. Katherine Hayles, *Unthought: The Power of the Cognitive Nonconscious* (Chicago: University of Chicago Press, 2017), 9–40.
12. Stephanie LeMenager, *Living Oil: Petroleum Culture in the American Century* (Oxford: Oxford University Press, 2016), 6.
13. Sianne Ngai, *Our Aesthetic Categories: Zany, Cute, Interesting* (Cambridge, Mass.: Harvard University Press, 2015).
14. Caroline Levine, *Forms: Whole, Rhythm, Hierarchy, Network* (Princeton, N.J.: Princeton University Press, 2017).
15. Stephen J. Burn, "Introduction," in *Intersections: Essays on Richard Powers,* ed. Stephen J. Burn and Peter Dempsey (Champaign, Ill.: Dalkey Archive, 2008), xxvi.
16. Joseph Dewey, *Understanding Richard Powers* (Columbia: University of South Carolina Press, 2008), 3.
17. Derek Woods, "Corporate Chemistry: A Biopolitics of Environment in Rachel Carson's *Silent Spring* and Richard Powers's *Gain,*" *American Literary History* 29, no. 1 (2017): 72–99.
18. Elizabeth Mazzolini and Stephanie Foote, "Introduction: Histories of the Dustheap," in *Histories of the Dustheap,* ed. Elizabeth Mazzolini and Stephanie Foote (Cambridge, Mass.: MIT Press, 2012), 2.
19. Lauren Berlant, *Cruel Optimism* (Durham, N.C.: Duke University Press, 2011), 1.
20. Ralph Clare, "Your Loss Is Their Gain: The Corporate Body and the Corporeal Body in Richard Powers' *Gain,*" *Critique: Studies in Contemporary Fiction* 54 (2013): 28–45.
21. Greil Marcus, "The Intersecting Fate of an Ordinary Woman and a Giant Corporation," *San Francisco Chronicle,* June 7, 1998, https://www.sfgate.com/books/article/The-Intersecting-Fate-of-an-Ordinary-Woman-and-a-3004456.php.
22. Richard Powers, *Gain* (New York: Picador, 1998), 27.
23. Rachel Greenwald Smith, "Six Propositions on Compromise Aesthetics," in *Postmodern/Postwar—and After: Rethinking American Literature,* ed. Jason Gladstone, Andrew Hoberek, and Daniel Worden (Iowa City: University of Iowa Press, 2016), 181–96.
24. Clare, "Your Loss Is Their Gain," 35; Bruce Robbins, "Homework: Richard Powers, Walt Whitman, and the Poetry of the Commodity," *Ariel* 34, no. 1 (2003): 77–92, https://www.questia.com/library/p408381/ariel.

25. Wendy Brown, *Undoing the Demos: Neoliberalism's Stealth Revolution* (New York: Zone, 2017), 38.
26. Paul Maliszewski, "The Business of Gain," in *Intersections: Essays on Richard Powers*, ed. Stephen J. Burn and Peter Dempsey (Champaign, Ill.: Dalkey Archive, 2008), 162–86.
27. Karl Marx, *Capital Volume One*, trans. Ben Fowkes (New York: Vintage, 1977).
28. Ursula K. Heise, "Toxins, Drugs, and Global Systems: Risk and Narrative in the Contemporary Novel," *American Literature* 74, no. 4 (December 2002): 747–78.
29. Alison Shonkwiler and Leigh Clare La Berge, "Introduction: A Theory of Capitalist Realism," in *Reading Capitalist Realism*, ed. Leigh Clare La Berge and Alison Shonkwiler (Iowa City: University of Iowa Press, 2014), 1–25.

10

The Impossible Figure of Oceanic Plastic

Sean Grattan

There has been a recent uptick in interest and awareness in oceanic plastic pollution. The central aim of this chapter is to investigate some ways that literary and artistic production tries to grasp the seemingly unrepresentable, monstrous, and undying nature of plastic. In doing so, I will consider representations of the Great Pacific Garbage Patch in three different aesthetic modes: photography, prose, and poetry. Underlying this investigation is a question about how literary and artistic texts might render the diffuse affects of climate change into actionable engagement with what is clearly a global crisis. In a world mostly peddling neoliberal individualism, what kinds of affective representations might illustrate the interconnectedness of global capitalism as rendered through one of its key waste products, plastic? In what follows I describe a particular ecological state—the Great Pacific Garbage Patch—as indicative of the difficulties in cognitively and affectively mapping the perils of plastic.

While its existence was predicted and modeled in 1988 by the National Oceanic and Atmospheric Administration, the Great Pacific Garbage Patch was first discovered by Charles Moore in 1997 as he returned home from the Transpacific Yacht Race. The Great Pacific Garbage Patch occupies somewhere between 270,000 and 5,800,000 square miles in the Pacific Ocean (which in its very large difference is interesting in and of itself). There is a lot of misinformation about the size, heft, density, and makeup of the patch, which is actually several areas that collect garbage in what is called the

North Pacific Gyre or the Pacific Garbage Vortex. There are approximately five major oceanic garbage patches, each emerging in different parts of the oceanic gyres. The global depredations at work and illuminated by garbage—and in particular plastic—cannot be uncoupled from global capitalism.[1] The nonnationality of garbage patches presents serious problems for cleanup efforts that, more often than not, rely on transnational cooperation. The transnationality of the Great Pacific Garbage Patch results in an evacuation of responsibility at both the national and corporate level. This evacuation, in turn, shifts responsibility down the ladder to individuals and their consumption choices.

Some Problems of Representation

For years an image of a man paddling a boat through heaps of garbage has been the generic representation of the Great Pacific Garbage Patch. He paddles, close to the water, with garbage looming above him. It is horrifying; it is shocking. It is also not the Great Pacific Garbage Patch, but is, instead, Manila Harbor. This image has a spectacular element to it, and that triggers an affective response: disgust perhaps—a revulsion at the idea of swimming, surfing, or boating in these waters. We think of our bodies moving through the ocean, having solid pieces of bobbing garbage slap and press against our skin. I want to argue that spectacular images like the man paddling through Manila Harbor often obfuscate the global reach of the plastisphere. Plastic is a particularly difficult site for thinking about scale and representation because of its simultaneous ubiquity and, in its smaller forms, opacity. Moreover, as Amanda Boetzkes argues, plastic is "an unprecedented and particular form of waste that is no waste at all, but rather an all-encompassing process of the world's autodestruction through its economy of self-expenditure."[2]

The Great Pacific Garbage Patch is the largest in the world, and it has dramatically increased in size since the 2011 Fukushima reactor disaster.[3] It is often described as "bigger than Texas," "at least the size of Texas," and so on. This gives rise to two things: 1) an unhealthy desire to measure things in units of Texas, and 2) the sense that floating in the Pacific Ocean off the coast of California is a solid mass of garbage that you can walk around on, rustle cattle on, and so forth. The Great Pacific Garbage Patch however, is primarily invisible; these images, though spectacular, do not capture anything but a part—and a small one at that—of the enormity of an interconnected system of production, refuse, and circulation. This circulation works both along human lines of traffic, but it also works through nonhuman actors. In other words, birds, crustaceans, water skimmers, an entire ecology that circulates without people; the ecology of the Garbage Patch also operates through currents, eddies, and a host of mostly inorganic materials and processes.[4] In *Vibrant Matter,* Jane Bennett attempts to redescribe the relationship between human and nonhuman forces. In attempting to develop a "vocabulary and syntax for, and thus a better discernment of, the active powers issuing from nonsubjects," Bennett emphasizes the importance of a language capacious enough to contend with the interconnectedness of subjects and nonsubjects.[5] This language needs to be both aesthetic and theoretical. Similarly, Mel Chen emphasizes the "animacy" of certain nonliving things like lead, mercury, or oil; however, for Chen these nonliving actors always circulate and reflect through and around human activity.[6] While Chen maintains a hierarchical relationship between human subjects and the object world, their work on toxicity, especially, demonstrates the porous boundaries between living and dead, which they describe as an energized form of "lifeliness."[7]

Of course the spectacular image sells: it moves units, it moves us. Therefore it is imperative to take the affective register of images seriously, but it is equally imperative to grapple with the ways large-scale global systems might be represented in forms that carry a similar affective heft. The near invisibility of plastic particles approaches a seeming immateriality, but these plastic particles' poisonous effects remain obdurately material. Rob Nixon has engaged with the struggle to represent unspectacular climate change under conditions of what he calls "slow violence." Slow violence is precisely the forms of ecological depredation that take nonhuman time to fully come into being. As a descriptive concept, slow violence is useful because it is precisely in the loss of immediacy that the conceptualization of threat is reduced through a logics of misdirection, obfuscation, and mystification. With plastic there is no spectacular moment; there is only the slow accretion of plastic waste. Nixon is particularly concerned with the limits of representation regarding slow violence, and the desire to produce and organize an affective response that can generate lasting resistance to what is an inarguably destructive global crisis. He writes, "the representational bias against slow violence has . . . a critically dangerous impact on what counts as a casualty in the first place."[8] Often eyes slide over slow violence; eyes are *encouraged* to slide over slow violence. Nixon describes the affective distance between ecological crises that are spectacular (like tsunamis) and the slow violence of less spectacular global issues like rising ocean temperatures as the "drama deficit of climate change."[9] Plastics in the Pacific is precisely the kind of slow and unspectacular violence that suffers a drama deficit. Plastic consumption and waste, in particular, as a form of slow violence also suffer from the pleasure of both consumption (in an orgiastic, over-the-top kind of way), and the pleasures of green capital consumption where the individual is called upon by corporations to do the right thing and buy a greener product. Yet individuals recycling their plastics does very little in the large scheme of things, nor do plans to clean up the oceans by individual investors stem the tide of plastic pollution.[10]

Charles Moore, one of the original observers of the Great Pacific Garbage Patch, points out some of the fallout from the intersections of transnational capital and ecological disaster when he writes in the *New York Times* that "the problem is compounded by the aquaculture industry, which uses enormous amounts of plastic in its floats, nets, lines and tubes . . . but no regulatory remedies exist to deal with tons of plastic equipment lost accidentally in storms."[11] Yet he also inadvertently points to the problem of representation that plagues the garbage patches. For every "oyster-buoy island" there are miles and miles of particles that don't photograph well and that rather than get the blood boiling, create, at best, a tepid response. The circulation, movement, and ubiquity of plastic waste require a reimagining of the nation-state, but also demand an interrogation of what modes of representation affect people and might produce both collective and individual action.

Another way of thinking about the drama deficit of climate change is as an affective exhaustion in the face of what Timothy Morton would call the "hyperobject" of environmental catastrophe.[12] In other words, the scalar difficulties in conceptualizing threat and response between individual action and global catastrophe often too easily mark boundaries along ideological, emotional, and sociopolitical planes, not to mention the rich interspecies and interobject worlds we actually inhabit. These intersections are where work in affective ecocriticism has sought to intervene. Heather Houser, for instance, writes that "it is emotion that can carry us from the micro-scale of the individual to the macro-scale of institutions, nations, and the planet."[13] Similarly, Kyle Bladow and Jennifer Ladino argue that affect theory offers "new, more compelling ways to foreground connections between environmental and social justice, and we must reach across ideological, species, and scalar boundaries to find common ground in this new geological epoch."[14] Orienting toward environmental affects, then, is one angle for approaching the epistemological and methodological challenges of scale during this contemporary ecological crisis.

Zombies, Birds, Anxiety, Diaries

Research by the 5 Gyres Institute describes the gyres as "shredders," which break down larger plastic into microplastic debris.[15] Descriptions of the action of the garbage patch as "shredding" plastic, and other garbage that drifts into its orbit surely implies, if not a sentience, an *action* that actively manipulates, destroys, and, at the very least, grasps; the act of shredding creates a seemingly vital and monstrous oceanic mass capable of interacting with its world. In these examples the metaphors of the gyres destabilize the hierarchical relationship between human and nonhuman actors. The vitality of the patch, and the way plastic circulates in and out, is the mise-en-scène of the texts I take up in this section. The affective and visual representations of environmental disaster constantly navigate the tricky line between the local and the global, or the particular and the universal. In what follows I will describe four different attempts at representing the Great Pacific Garbage Patch with a particular eye to the affective register that attempts to articulate a transformational politics. Margaret Ronda begins her *Remainders: American Poetry at Nature's End* by asking, "How does a poem make loss and extinction visible, or register new, disturbing presences, such as toxic sludge, oil spills, dead zones?"[16] In part, her answer rests on description and discovery—poetry must make global ecological crisis lively. Amitav Ghosh takes a dimmer view on the potential for poetry to speak to ecological disaster. He muses that since "the vocabulary that is associated with these substances: *naphtha, bitumen, petroleum, tar,* and *fossil fuels*" are so ugly that "no poet or singer could make these syllables fall lightly on the ear. And think of the substances themselves: coal and the sooty residue it leaves on everything it touches; and petroleum—viscous, foul smelling, repellant to all the senses."[17] Aside from the crude romanticization of what poetry might look like/be—yet perhaps arising from this simplification—Ghosh cannot see that it might be in the ugliness of the language and possibility of poetry inhabiting and embodying that ugliness that makes it a crucial site for literary engagement with climate change.

While the first text I look at does not necessarily name the Great Pacific Garbage Patch, it offers an incisive description of both the liveness of plastic and plastic's nearly immortal lifespan. Evelyn Reilly's 2009 book of poetry *Styrofoam* about the ubiquity of plastic is a slow meditation on the undying and zombified existence of plastic.[18] Reilly begins *Styrofoam* with an answer followed by a question: "Answer: Stryofoam deathlessness / Question: How long does it take? / . . . Answer: It is a misconception that materials / biodegrade in a meaningful time frame."[19] In this instance, a meaningful time frame is a human time frame. Margaret Ronda describes Reilly as revealing "an intensified problem of anthropocentrism" because the unintended effects of plastic morph into the "ankle bracelets of the birds" and the "ecstasy / of being / containers temporary or not."[20] The slow time of plastic cannot unfold over a human timescale, and what is left behind is inherently mutable. In *Ontology of the Accident* (2012), Catherine Malabou demands that "we must find a way to think a mutation that engages both form and being, a new form that is literally a form of being."[21] For Malabou "destructive plasticity enables the appearance or formation of alterity where the other is absolutely lacking."[22] Reilly renders plastics weird and more material by following the permutations of plasticity from one form to another. Seeping into the water, into the blood, and through the skin, plastic sticks around, but not in its original forms. Reilly explores the dispersed toxicity of plastics and the manner that they mutate from one form of being to another. It is the *ubiquity* of plastic that gives *Styrofoam* much of its affective heft. We are not only surrounded by plastic, but it is inside us as well. Each permutation of plastic animates in the way Mel Chen describes animacy as helping "us theorize current anxieties around the production of humanness . . . animacy activates new theoretical formations that trouble an undo stubborn binary systems of difference, including dynamism/stasis, life/death, subject/object, speech/nonspeech, human/animal, natural body/cyborg."[23] Plastic is precisely the kind of pliant and undying matter that troubles these binaries. Reilly writes, "POM, translucent, with good processing qualities / DEVELOPS A 'MEMORY' AND GRADUALLY/ CONFORMS TO THE USERS GRIP."[24] There is a liveness to plastic that Reilly makes explicit in the shifting scale of *Styrofoam* among the molecular makeup of different plastics, what they are used for, and the way these plastics circulate after they have been discarded as garbage.[25]

The monstrosity of plastic and plasticity—here perhaps most closely resembling Malabou's work—takes a clearer form when Reilly turns explicitly to John Carpenter's 1982 horror film *The Thing*. The plasticity of the monster in *The Thing* is able to imitate any live form, and in so doing destroys its newly animated host. Moving from body to body, the creature circulates and infects. Does the monster develop a memory like POM? And how does animating our own anxiety and fear toward the unknown, pliant, and constantly changing monster perhaps reorient our ability to engage with the idea that plastic pollution might be less than spectacularly visible, or that it is already inside us? Heather Houser argues that texts can work to produce affects that might "provide strategies for coping with the environmental and bodily threats that preoccupy artists as well as scientists, environmentalists, and policy experts."[26] For Houser some key affects for ecosickness fiction are "discord, wonder, disgust, and anxiety."[27] Reilly's use of *The Thing* insistently returns to the malleable monstrosity of undying plastic pollution, and in doing so activates a set of affective responses around horror and disgust.

The connection of bodies and the circulation of images is also central to Chris Jordan's stunning photography series he began in 2009, *Midway: Message from the Gyre.* Jordan's photography is a collection of images of decomposing albatrosses whose bodies have been filled with plastic.[28] Each image is an albatross with its stomach broken open to reveal kaleidoscopic plastic detritus. His artist statement describes the scene:

> On Midway Atoll, a remote cluster of islands more than 2000 miles from the nearest continent, the detritus of our mass consumption surfaces in an astonishing place: inside the stomachs of thousands of dead baby albatrosses. The nesting chicks are fed lethal quantities of plastic by their parents, who mistake the floating trash for food as they forage over the vast polluted Pacific Ocean.
>
> For me, kneeling over their carcasses is like looking into a macabre mirror. These birds reflect back an appallingly emblematic result of the collective trance of our consumerism and runaway industrial growth. Like the albatross, we first-world humans find ourselves lacking the ability to discern anymore what is nourishing from what is toxic to our lives and our spirits. Choked to death on our waste, the mythical albatross calls upon us to recognize that our greatest challenge lies not out there, but in here.[29]

While the images are certainly arresting, the decaying albatrosses function allegorically on a relatively straightforward level. First, the images demand that humans recognize that the inside of these birds are also our insides, and that fundamental species differences are here not much different than a canary in a coal mine. Second, the images make the wide circulation of plastics clear; the birds are in the middle of nowhere and dying from a glut of plastic in their guts. Finally, the albatross explicitly pulls readers toward Samuel Taylor Coleridge's cursed mariner, who has killed the albatross for no discernible reason and is then forced to tell his story to anyone who he senses is the correct listener. Above all, though, Jordan's images and subsequent film ask viewers to bear witness to the long life of plastic. In his indispensable reading of ecopoetical images, Ted Mathys writes that "these sorts of images often earn their affective heft and sizzle by working an insidious bait-n-switch: they suggest *something here does not belong,* and in suggesting as much, collapse back into the same dualistic 'nature over here, humans over there' thinking that they seek to upend."[30] As Mathys rightly notes, the affective heft and weight of these images rests on the juxtaposition of the natural with the unnatural: we are moved because we look at the undecayed plastic surrounded by decayed albatross meat and recognize the toxicity humans have created. Neither humans nor albatrosses are able to tell the difference between "the nourishing from what is toxic to our lives and spirits." We are like them; they are like us. The toxicity, which is not "out there" but "in here," signals the porousness of bodies and the unintended consequences of plastic waste.

The "affective heft and sizzle" is about more than just the bait and switch Mathys describes; it rests on Jordan's insistence on the maternal relationship between momma bird and chick. This familial relationship is what Jordan hopes will bridge the affective gap between albatross and human, and that when we see that "nesting chicks are fed lethal quantities of plastic by their parents, who mistake the floating trash for food as they forage over the vast polluted Pacific Ocean," there will be some kind of response. In the contemporary affect-saturated market, shock and disgust come to play a role in the attempt to break through the noise. But is something lost in the hope for relatability? In the trailer for *Albatross,* the voiceover intones, "Do we have the courage to face the realities of our time, and allow ourselves to feel deeply enough that it transforms us and our future?" Amanda Boetzkes describes the film as asking the viewer to experience "intimacy, frustration, and mourning."[31] Perhaps what is needed is an intimacy based entirely on not collapsing the strangeness of plastics nor the strangeness of albatrosses, but on an understanding of interconnectedness through, in Jason Moore's terms, a web of life that takes into account the ways capital accumulation is both structured by nature and structures nature.[32] As Boetzkes makes abundantly clear, the "visual scenario itself is a product of the entangled and speculative sense system that is becoming-environmental."[33] In other words, the close-up shots of the individual albatrosses can only show a minute fraction of the circulation of plastic waste, even if their remote location speaks to that circulation. The objects inside the birds—lighters, pens, bottle caps, etc.—are for the most part all clearly discernible products, and while this *does* help visualize why we might mourn these birds, it continues to represent only a very particular form of the plastisphere.

The anxiety of the garbage patch, however, is perhaps equally difficult to pin down. Diffuse and circulating—Jennifer Cooke captures this feeling in her 2012 poem "The Second Hand." Like Reilly's riff on *The Rime of the Ancient Mariner,* Cooke plays with the anxiety of William Butler Yeats's "The Second Coming" to interrogate the anxiety produced by the "widening gyre" of the garbage patch as it churns plastic "turning invisible to the eye in the pelagic plastics, the chemical sludge." "Awake at night," the garbage patch infiltrates Cooke's thoughts, driving her to distraction: "the internet is terrifying to me."[34] The affective weight of dread and anxiety circulate like the plastics causing it, and these intensities are felt in the body unable to sleep, sunk into an internet gyre collecting news items and trying to control something that seems uncontrollable with a "dreadful inevitability."[35] Again, this is a question of representation and individual solutions to a global problem that could only find resolution in a global response. Cooke lists various people attempting to call attention to the garbage patches—Richard Sundance Owen, Charles Moore, Curtis Ebbesmeyer, and Project Kaisai—and then asks: "But who will address you with passion / and intensity, apart from me, deliverer of watery revelations revolving / in the seascapes of your mind? I bet you don't even know what a nurdle is / but you wear it on your face. Shit. This is scaring me awake at 5.16 am."[36] In this final crescendo of anxiety, blame, and terse sarcasm, the forceful interjection of "shit" immediately anchors the poem in the affective immediacy of the moment. While the slow time of plastic breaking down in the Great Pacific Garbage Patch gyre, never actually disappearing but only becoming more opaque, unhinges the very idea of an individual subject on human time, the exclamatory and declarative "shit" focuses the vertiginous feelings of anxiety into a palpable exclamation. There is also the strident interpellation of the reader who doesn't "even know what a nurdle is" even though they might be wearing it on their faces. In other words, again like Coleridge's mariner, Cooke has to address someone who would rather be heading to a wedding than listening to a ghoulish mariner. Perhaps some of the anxiety arising in the poem is the understanding that the individual response, says the poet, is never enough in this global ecological crisis.

Finally, Ruth Ozeki's 2013 novel *A Tale for the Time Being* uses the Great Pacific Garbage Patch specifically as the mise-en-scène for a rumination on authorship, wonder, affect, history, and care.[37] Briefly, *A Tale for the Time Being* is about a writer named Ruth finding a Hello Kitty lunchbox that has washed onto the Canadian shoreline. The lunchbox has a diary inside written by a sixteen-year-old Japanese girl named Nao. Ruth and her husband Oliver surmise that the lunchbox washed away during the 2011 Japanese tsunami and Fukushima nuclear disaster.[38] Ozeki's masterful contrapuntal text narrates the interconnection of generations and nationalities through the circulatory power of the Great Pacific Garbage Patch.

A Tale for the Time Being is a step toward disheveling which bodies matter in a global ecology insofar as the gyre, rather than any particular human actors, sets the plot in motion. Ozeki's novel directly confronts the disconnection between scales of disaster and violence and how, affectively, disaster is consumed, understood, and remembered. Ozeki writes, "In the days following the earthquake and tsunami, Ruth sat in front of her computer screen, trawling the Internet for news of friends and family."[39] The internet offers up images recorded on cellphones of people running, panicked, but this gives way to a meditation on the temporality of disaster: "In the weeks following the earthquake, tsunami, and meltdown of the Fukushima nuclear reactors, we were all experts on radiation exposure and microsieverts and plate tectonics and subduction. But then the uprising in Libya and the tornado in Joplin superseded the quake, and the keyword cloud shifted to *revolution* and *drought* and *unstable air masses* as the tide of information from Japan receded."[40] In the rush of images and the tumbling speed of 24-hour news cycles, it is hard to keep even spectacular images circulating.

In the free indirect discourse of the narration, Ozeki asks: "Does the half-life of information correlate with the decay of our attention? Is the Internet a kind of temporal gyre, sucking up stories, like geodrift, into its orbit? What is its gyre memory? How do we measure the half-life of its drift?"[41] The analogy of the time spent in the gyre, the memory of the gyre, and the ability to hold onto events is apt especially as the gyre itself is slippery, hard to contain, and flits in and out of Ruth's focus. What does inhabiting the temporality of the gyre do to shift perception away from the boundaries and limits of human temporality? The lunchbox escapes the gyre's gravitational pull, but Ozeki maintains the slipperiness of conceptualizing the gyre. Forcing the eye to slip over, unbidden, the gyre seems impossible to capture, calculate, or imagine. Ozeki dramatizes the tension in attempting to imagine the thingness of the gyre. Ruth never seems completely comfortable with the nonhumanness of the gyre; for her the authenticity of the diary resonates and reverberates, but the relation between garbage and narrative is precisely a narrative attempt to navigate the materiality of the world. Heather Houser describes "ecosickness fiction" as a genre where "humans and the more-than-human world do not only interact, but more importantly are coconstitutive."[42] Ruth's inability to hold onto the Great Pacific Garbage Patch is, in part, indebted to the dual affects of wonder and anxiety produced by the existence of pollution that seems, almost inherently, out of representational reach.

I end with the brief readings of Reilly, Jordan, Cooke, and Ozeki as illustrations of the particular difficulties in representing the accretion of oceanic plastic. To grasp the danger of slow violence, to see what we can of the hyperobject for what it is, demands a vigorous reevaluation of the individual subject. Though in the contemporary moment humans have succeeded in making a permanent mark on the world, it is precisely this realization that forces us to think the subject otherwise. The present demands a nonhierarchical logic rather than hierarchical relations with nonhuman actors; the present demands a rich understanding of the interconnectedness of every *thing*. The present also demands taking into account the vast temporality of plastics. Reilly, Jordan, Cooke, and Ozeki all illustrate that plastic will be here long after we are not. Part of the horror in Jordan's images, for instance, is that the birds have rotted around plastics that look no different than if they had been thrown away yesterday. And of course, the transmutability of plastic means that even if it does change its shape and become unrecognizable, it will still be there in a less spectacular form. This is not to naturalize the global ecological depredations through capitalism, nor to make the immiseration of human and animal life more palatable, but is rather an attempt at articulating a radical interconnection between all forms of living and nonliving matter. Focusing on the grandiose and spectacular images of solid trash islands obfuscates a far more insidious point: plastic is everywhere. We need to recognize the materiality of not only the more spectacular bits but also the way opaque plastic beads spread through the ocean. In other words, rushing to describe the garbage patch as "the size of Texas" misses that it is much, much larger. Part of the change in this thinking is a movement away from the neoliberal privatized subject and toward something more collective. Or, as Timothy Morton might put it, a shift of emphasis from the subjective or intersubjective to the "interobjective," the "strange interconnectedness of things."[43] Perhaps this is a question of orientation to affect—thinking what directions affect traverses. By unmooring affect from epistemological claims reliant on the individual human subject as codifier, collector, sorter, and meaning maker, perhaps the vibrant, wondrous, and terrifying materiality of the world comes into sharper relief. Each of these authors attempt to represent something that is perhaps beyond representation, but is crucial to represent as ecological crisis drastically worsens. I am arguing that we need images that are able to organize affect toward transformational politics, but that do not, simultaneously, fall into a disingenuous, regressive, or cynical recoil away from action. In other words, how can we imagine interconnection in the slow time of things, in gyre time, in plastic temporalities, and what sorts of epistemologies, representations, and materialisms are up to that task? And, finally, what kind of mariner are we able to hear; and what kind of wedding guest might we be?

NOTES

1. Jason W. Moore's *Capitalism in the Web of Life: Ecology and the Accumulation of Capital* (London: Verso, 2015) is an essential text in describing the interconnection of capital accumulation and shifting global ecologies. For an excellent book on art, capitalism, and waste, see Amanda Boetzkes's *Plastic Capitalism: Contemporary Art and the Drive to Waste* (Cambridge, Mass.: MIT University Press, 2019).
2. Boetzkes, *Plastic Capitalism*, 185.
3. The Great Pacific Garbage Patch also gets much more attention than the other four, perhaps because of its size or perhaps because of the populations it affects.
4. Patricia Corcoran, Charles Moore, and Kelly Jazvac have referred to the conglomerate of plastic, rock, seashells, and other debris as the "plastiglomerate" in "An Anthropogenic Marker Horizon in the Future Rock Record," *Geological Society of America Today* 24, no. 6. (June 2014), https://www.geosociety.org//gsatoday/archive/24/6/article/i1052-5173-24-6-4.htm.
5. Jane Bennett, *Vibrant Matter: A Political Ecology of Things*. (Durham, N.C.: Duke University Press. 2010), ix.
6. Mel Y. Chen, *Animacies: Biopolitics, Racial Mattering, and Queer Affect* (Durham, N.C.: Duke University Press. 2012).
7. Chen, *Animacies*, 225.
8. Rob Nixon, *Slow Violence and the Environmentalism of the Poor* (Cambridge, Mass.: Harvard University Press, 2011), 13.
9. Nixon, *Slow Violence*, 264.
10. This is especially true if we take into consideration that the recycling plans of countries like the United States and United Kingdom have until recently been basically just to ship everything to China. However, now that China has placed restrictions on imports of certain recyclables, U.S. cities are now having to either pay higher fees or stop recycling. See, for instance Alana Semuels, "Is This the End of Recycling?" *The Atlantic*, March 5, 2019, https://www.theatlantic.com/technology/archive/2019/03/china-has-stopped-accepting-our-trash/584131/.
11. Charles Moore, "Choking the Oceans with Plastic," *New York Times*, August 25, 2014.
12. Timothy Morton, *Hyperobjects: Philosophy and Ecology after the End of the World* (Minneapolis: University of Minnesota, 2013).
13. Heather Houser, *Ecosickness in Contemporary U.S. Fiction: Environment and Affect* (New York: Columbia University Press, 2014), 223.
14. Kyle Bladow and Jennifer Ladino, "Toward an Affective Ecocriticism: Placing Feeling in the Anthropocene," in *Affective Ecocriticism: Emotion, Embodiment, Environment*, ed. Kyle Bladow and Jennifer Ladino (Lincoln: University of Nebraska Press. 2018), 17.

15. See, for instance Oliver Milman, "Full Scale of Plastic in the World's Oceans Revealed for the First Time," *The Guardian,* December 12, 2014; or John Metcalfe, "There Are at Least 5.25 Trillion Pieces of Plastic in the Ocean," *Citylab,* December 10, 2014, http://www.citylab.com/weather/2014/12/there-are-at-least-525-trillion-pieces-of-plastic-in-the-ocean/383600/. The research was originally published as Marcus Eriksen, Laurent C. M. Lebreton, Henry S. Carson, Martin Thiel, Charles J. Moore, Jose C. Borrero, François Galgani, Peter G. Ryan, and Julia Reisser, "Plastic Pollution in the World's Oceans: More than 5 Trillion Plastic Pieces Weighing Over 250,000 Tons Afloat at Sea," *PLoS ONE* 9, no.12 (2014): e111913. doi:10.1371/journal.pone.0111913.
16. Margaret Ronda, *Remainders: American Poetry at Nature's End* (Stanford, Calif.: Stanford University Press. 2018), 1.
17. Amitav Ghosh, *The Great Derangement: Climate Change and the Unthinkable* (Chicago: University of Chicago Press, 2016), 73. While I don't particularly agree with his take on genre fiction, Ghosh also notes that climate fiction is almost always taken unseriously and relegated to science fiction, or the margins of genre fiction more generally (7).
18. Evelyn Reilly, *Styrofoam* (New York: Roof, 2009).
19. Reilly, *Styrofoam,* 9–10.
20. Ronda, *Remainders,* 20.
21. Catherine Malabou, *Ontology of the Accident: An Essay on Destructive Plasticity* (London: Polity, 2012), 17.
22. Malabou, *Ontology of the Accident,* 11.
23. Mel Y. Chen, *Animacies: Biopolitics, Racial Mattering, and Queer Affect,* 3.
24. Reilly, *Styrofoam,* 51.
25. The final section of *Styrofoam* is a long list of the molecular makeup of different kinds of plastics. The long strains of alien-sounding syllables are disorienting in their specificity, but also speak directly to Ghosh's contention that ecological crises are too ugly for poetry to represent.
26. Houser, *Ecosickness,* 7.
27. Houser, *Ecosickness,* 7.
28. Jordan has also produced a film called *Albatross* (2017) covering the same locations as his photography project.
29. Chris Jordan, *Midway: Message from the Gyre,* http://www.chrisjordan.com/gallery/midway/#about.
30. Ted Mathys, "Wastepickers and the Seduction of the Ecopoetical Image," *Evening Will Come* 37 (January 2014).
31. Boetzkes, *Plastic Capitalism,* 234.
32. Moore, *Capitalism in the Web of Life.*
33. Boetzkes, *Plastic Capitalism,* 237.
34. Jennifer Cooke, "Second Hand," *The Other Room Anthology 4,* ed. James Davies and Tom Jenks (Manchester, UK: The Other Room, 2012), 36.
35. Cooke, "The Second Hand," 36.

36. Cooke, "The Second Hand," 37.
37. Ruth Ozeki, *A Tale for the Time Being* (New York: Penguin, 2013).
38. There is a potentially rich discussion of salvage economies here and the circulation of plastic waste as reusable in different ways that I do not have time to attend to in this piece.
39. Ozeki, *A Tale for the Time Being*, 112.
40. Ozeki, *A Tale for the Time Being*, 113.
41. Ozeki, *A Tale for the Time Being*, 114.
42. Houser, *Ecosickness*, 3.
43. Morton, *Hyperobjects*, 83.

◊♦◊ **PART IV** ◊♦◊

Postplastic Futures?

11

From Protoplastics to the Plastiglomerate

Science Fiction's Shifting Synthetic Sensibilities

Lisa Swanstrom

In the final moments of *The Blob* (1958),[1] a very young Steve McQueen succeeds in defeating the titular extraterrestrial antagonist by freezing it. Once the deed is done, the Air Force comes in to retrieve it, shoves it into a large Globemaster cargo plane, and parachutes it into the icy waters of the Arctic Ocean. As relieved as he is about the removal of the Blob from his small Pennsylvania town, McQueen suspects that it is not really dead. The movie concludes with an exchange between him and a police officer, who confirms this suspicion. The officer concedes that while he does not "think it can be killed . . . at least we've got it stopped." McQueen responds with a line that seems weirdly prescient now: "Yeah, as long as the Arctic stays cold, huh?"

The Blob has been read as a metaphor for Cold War aggression,[2] as a way of understanding Hannah Arendt's conception of the social,[3] and as a descendent of H. P. Lovecraft's "The Color Out of Space,"[4] among other critical interpretations. It is only recently, however, that it has taken on concrete, rather than metaphoric, significance in terms of the environmental history and toxicity of plastic. After all, although "alien," its appearance as an ever-expanding gelatinous menace oozing through town recalls the image of crude oil escaping up from a derrick, and hence suggests a shared heritage with other petroleum byproducts that are quite clearly earthly in origin. But the Blob now also serves as a handy way to name widescale ecological abnormalities in the Pacific Ocean. These include the "warmer-than-usual water off the Pacific coast that has persisted since fall 2013,"[5] the "Great Pacific Garbage Patch,"[6] which is itself largely composed of plastic, and the ever-expanding presence of the "plastiglomerate."

In their landmark study of the shorelines of Kamilo Beach on Hawai'i's big island in 2012, Patricia L. Corcoran, Charles J. Moore, and Kelly Jazvac identify and name this new form of pollution: "We use the term plastiglomerate to describe an indurated, multi-composite material made hard by agglutination of rock and molten plastic."[7] In the context of their study, the plastiglomerate refers to an alloy of plastic detritus that has melted and reconstituted itself as a part of the littoral landscape. Cross sections and photos of such specimens reveal intricate, warren-like structures comprising fishing nets, seashells, coral, and sand. This all-too-real manifestation of plastic as not merely a pollutant, but a pollutant with the potential to bind together disparate in/organic materials into convoluted assemblages, stands in stark contrast to the way that plastic has been understood both historically and within the popular imagination. Understanding how plastic manifests in its myriad guises in literary and artistic expression can aid our understanding of its cultural roles in ways that are more experiential than scientifically or technologically quantifiable. Science fiction (SF) is an especially instructive genre along these lines. As the wide variety of critical interpretations of *The Blob* suggests, imaginary synthetic substances—be they of man-made or extraterrestrial origin—prompt connections to important social, cultural, and political issues. These concerns are reciprocated in SF scholarship, which has been since its inception largely preoccupied with the genre's relation to capital, i.e., to political ideology,[8] with more recent scholarship attendant to the political and intersectional natures of subjectivity, gender, biopolitics, and the legacies of colonialism.[9]

While *The Blob* provides a useful and widely known example of a work of SF that suggests both plastic and its corroded plastiglomerate offspring, in this paper I use it as a springboard to dive into the genre in a more expansive, transhistoric manner. In particular, I analyze two texts that bookend the distinct ways SF has imagined plastic in its two-hundred-year-plus history: H. G. Wells's *First Men in the Moon* (1901) and Steven Barnes's "Woman in the Wall" (2000). This wide purview will provide, I hope, a complement to the other SF-centered essay in this collection, Phillip E. Wegner's superb reading of two contemporary texts in "Futures in Plastic: Science Fiction, Climate Change, and the New Normal." My argument is twofold: in the first place, I demonstrate that SF seems to have a peculiar blind spot about plastic. Even as very early SF begins to depict synthetic materials with some degree of satirical disdain, plastic per se largely avoids censure as a pollutant. That is to say, plastic remains fairly secure in its role of signifying futurity, technology, wealth, and prosperity, even in very contemporary science fiction.

Second, I argue that a latent "plastiglomerate" trope co-occurs with depictions of plastic in more contemporary works; this trope is characterized by descriptive images of agglutination, trash, penetration, disruption, and destruction. Often in such instances these discarded components are employed for strategic purposes, enabling unexpected, subversive, or unlawful narrative trajectories. Strangely enough, although such descriptions and plot sequences often *include* plastic in their depictions of trash, they do not single it out. Instead, plastic often works as it does in real life, as a largely invisible but powerful binding agent that collects together and cements a variety of unruly and "unnatural" assemblages.

SF's Proto-Plastics, or Plastic Curtains in Outer Space

Cavorite, Argine, Liquid Glass, Carobundum, and Siliconey: Even before plastic becomes known as such, writers of early SF imagine a variety of these and other synthetic substances that, like plastic, supersede the functionality of known materials. In the *First Men in the Moon* (1901), H. G. Wells imagines a fantastic but scientifically feasible substance that has some striking similarities with plastic. Existing scholarship on Wells is abundant, and the critical attention paid to *First Men on the Moon*, while perhaps not as robust as that paid to *The Time Machine* (1895) or *War of the Worlds* (1898), is also plentiful.[10] This is not surprising. Revered as one of the founders of the genre, Wells himself was also a scientist, trained by T. H. Huxley, with an expertise in Darwinian evolution and biology, and remains a fundamental figure for thinking through issues that are intrinsic to SF as well as to literary and cultural history more generally.

In this novel, a bankrupt financier named Bedford secludes himself in a small town in England to write a play, in hopes of recovering his fortune. He finds himself instead distracted daily by a peculiar man named Cavor, a physicist filled with a frenetic, almost electric, energy. Cavor is consumed with the ambition to create a material that will be "opaque to gravitation." The lucrative potential for Cavor's proposed substance ignites the narrator's imagination; he swiftly abandons his playwriting efforts and establishes himself as the physicist's business partner. This antigravitational substance—unsurprisingly called "Cavorite"—is "a complicated alloy of metals" and mixed with "something very gaseous and thin," which Bedford suspects is helium, a newly discovered and still-exotic element delivered to the physicist "from London in sealed stone jars."[11]

While the substance eventually allows the two men to travel to the moon, the first experiment with it proves nearly fatal. As Bedford recounts, "the premature birth" of Cavorite occurs as the physicist is taking an evening walk. Bedford spies the approaching silhouette of his friend against the "autumnal sunset" and comments upon the charming landscape that surrounds his domicile: "the chimneys of his house," he notes, are only slightly taller than the "gloriously tinted group of trees" that stand next to them. Vivid descriptions of a quaint pastoral setting cohere fleetingly before the subsequent lines destroy the narrator's moment of appreciative contemplation, when the Cavorite is prematurely unleashed: "And then! The chimneys jerked heavenward, smashing into a string of bricks as they rose, and the roof and a miscellany of furniture followed" (29). The ruin of domestic space is followed swiftly—both in narrative sequence and in measurable space—by a fiery fury: "overtaking [the furniture] came a huge white flame." The idyllic trees "swayed and whirled and tore themselves to pieces, then sprang towards the flare," launching like spikes into the air, and Cavor himself follows the same trajectory: he "was seized, whirled about, and flew through the screaming air." Bedford watches as his friend, "kicking and flapping, came down again, rolled over and over on the ground for a space, struggled up and was lifted and borne forward at an enormous velocity, vanishing at last among the labouring, lashing trees that writhed about his house." A sonic boom follows this spectacle, breaking all the windows and leaving the narrator "deaf on one side for life" (30).

When the dust has settled, Bedford laments the damage caused by the explosion. The physicist's retort is educational: "It was not an explosion," he corrects. On account of Cavorite's gravity-repelling properties, "It formed a sort of atmospheric fountain, a kind of chimney in the atmosphere." Fortunately for the two men, the real chimney has saved them from this more dangerous and metaphoric one: "If the Cavorite itself hadn't been loose and so got sucked up the chimney . . . the air would be rushing up and up over that infernal piece of stuff now" (35). Horrified by this close call, the two men work themselves into an apoplectic frenzy of exclamations: "Good heavens! Why, it would have squirted all the atmosphere of the earth away! . . . It would have whipped the air off the world as one peels a banana, and flung it thousands of miles . . . an asphyxiated world!" Yet in spite of the fact that the Cavorite very nearly results in "the death of all mankind!" they begin to refine its production in the next chapter (36).

Let us put aside the strange implication that it is the chimney—recently obliterated and reconstituted as a "string of bricks"—that somehow prevents this giant air funnel from forming. Rather, let us focus on two important features of this exchange. In the first place, the manner and content of the conversation is by contemporary standards so absurd as to function as a type of "naïve" camp.[12] Corny and cartoonish, it is the type of exchange that might be affectionately mocked in an episode of *Mystery Science Theater 3000*, yet its power to evoke laughter, while patently silly, is potent. The importance of camp to queer theory is well established, and the interconnections between SF and queer theory are becoming increasingly so.[13] And while not yet related directly to plastic—that shiny, cheap emblem of both the future and a camp aesthetic—this moment in *First Men in the Moon* functions as queerness in situ. I call attention to it now, as a placeholder, for when we return to the topic of "queer plastic" later on, in response to contemporary plastiglomerate tropes.

Second, Cavorite's synthetic properties, as well as the manner of its creation, align convincingly with the production of early synthetics. In the context of the history of plastic as both a real and imaginary substance, there are several things to unpack from this moment. In the first place, Cavor's creative innovation is swiftly channeled into a money-making scheme. Before the narrator declares his bald financial ambitions, Cavor himself seems content merely to speculate about the possibilities of its manufacture. Then, the fact that Cavorite is "opaque to gravity," in contrast to other substances that are "transparent" to it, makes it an ideal property for leaving behind the literal force of the Earth's pull. So far, then, Cavorite is light, airy, and potentially lucrative. That it leaves behind a wake of destroyed property in its celestial flight path, however, demonstrates that it is also a destructive one. Equally interesting for our purposes is how Cavorite also achieves a disruptive *aesthetic* intervention, in its nearly ridiculous obliteration of the pastoral.

In a hyperbolic moment that anticipates Leo Marx's description of the "machine in the garden," this pastoral serenity is utterly destroyed by the appearance of Cavorite.[14] While the moment is comedic, it achieves a serious consequence. Wells creates Cavorite as wholly opposed to a natural setting and, indeed, to natural physical laws. It quite literally repels the earth's gravitational pull and destroys anything unlucky enough to impede its antigravitational propulsion. As far-fetched as Cavorite seems, it provides an apt precursor for many of the properties that will come to be associated with plastic, including the risks involved in its production. As Jeffrey L. Meikle documents in *American Plastic: A Cultural History,* the production of celluloid plastic, which was the dominant form of plastic in Wells's time, was, on account of its highly flammable nature, fraught with risks, especially of fire hazards and the potential for explosions. Meikle notes that one factory alone, in Arlington, Virginia, "experienced a 'disastrous explosion' in 1888. . . . Only ten years later a major fire that began in a seasoning room destroyed several buildings and led the company to purchase additional land on which to construct unconnected seasoning sheds."[15]

Cavorite itself is a similarly volatile alloy, stretched into a "thin, wide sheet," which depends upon proper cooling techniques for successful deployment. In its next evolution, Cavorite retains its thin, sheet-like properties, now integrated into the structure of a spaceship: "Imagine a sphere," the physicist explains, "made of steel lined with thick glass," but coated entirely in Cavorite. Bedford is immediately skeptical, on account of the fact that Cavor's new vision seems to offer no way for the men to get inside of it. Cavor's solution to this problem depends upon the necessity of heating and cooling the substance: "while the Cavorite was warm," they would climb into the craft and seal themselves in. Once the shape was perfected and the men were safely ensconced inside, the substance would cool, and "As soon as it cooled it would become impervious to gravitation, and off [they] would fly." Here we see that heating is fundamental for the shaping of Cavorite, but that it is only through the cooling process that the substance sets and becomes fully functional.

This doubt allayed, Bedford raises another, more challenging obstacle: "What is to prevent the thing travelling in a straight line into space forever? . . . You're not safe to get anywhere, and if you do—how will you get back?" (43). Cavor responds with a simple but effective solution: he proposes to cut the Cavorite into, essentially, curtains:

> The Cavorite exterior of the sphere will consist of windows or blinds, whichever you like to call them. . . . When all these windows or blinds are shut, no light, no heat, no gravitation, no radiant energy of any sort will get at the inside of the sphere, it will fly on through space in a straight line. . . . But open a window, imagine one of the windows open. Then at once any heavy body that chances to be in that direction will attract us.

Cavor designs it to cover the windows of the sphere like drapes, but once they are operational they work additionally like the sails of a boat, with sheet lines (or blind tilts) used to attract or repel gravitational pull, allowing the characters to "tack about in space" (44).

It is fitting that the substance of Cavorite is described here as if it were a fabric—as a curtain, blind, or sail—given Wells's biography. At fourteen, he became a reluctant apprentice to a draper and learned enough about this detested profession to write a comical novel about it decades later (*The History of Mr. Polly,* 1910). But it is also fitting for another reason. Cavorite here—shaped as it is into something that is like a curtain, blind, or window—carries connotations of domestic space. This is significant in terms of plastic's history as something that is of vital importance to military warfare, as well as something that becomes an essential component of a well-run household. In the following two advertisements, for example, plastic's marketing boasts of its importance to military safety on the one hand (Figure 11.1) and to a clean and orderly kitchen on the other (Figure 11.2). In the first ad, in particular, which details an astonishing array of plastic's diverse applications, ranging from X-rays to gas masks to flower containers, the central image is a curved windshield of an airplane. "Cellulose plastics are CLEAR," the ad states, calling attention to the crystal-clear transparency of the window and suggesting safety for the men behind its clear surface. Although the curved transparent cowling of the airplane has something in common with the curved surfaces of Wells's space "sphere," I do not suggest an equivalence. These ads follow Wells's novel by 43 and 47 years, respectively—clearly one does not represent the other. Rather, what I wish to imply is this: Wells, himself an actively engaged and practicing scientist, was in his fiction in dialog with a variety of technological advancements that were developing in his time. Among these was the development of an exciting class of newly patented synthetic substances.

Cavorite is at once transparent and opaque. Its malleability depends upon high heat while its functionality only emerges after a period of cooling. It is composed of earthly properties, but when these components are combined, the resulting substance quickly seems to surpass them in terms of its potential malleability. And although its creation is consistent with laws of nature (i.e., physics), once created it seems entirely to rewrite or disrupt these same laws, destroying in its first iteration nearly everything it its path and disrupting gravity's status as a universal constant. Collectively, these features of Cavorite transpose easily upon the production of plastic, in terms of the way that early synthetics were developing during Wells's time.

Although Bakelite does not come onto the market until ten years after *First Men in the Moon,* celluloid had been in existence for

FIGURE 11.1. This advertisement for Cellulose highlights the transparent yet durable nature of plastic. The curved cowling of the aircraft, especially, resonates with Wells's description of the Cavorite-powered spacecraft. Advertisement by the Hercules Company (1944). Image courtesy of the author.

nearly fifty, and the newly developed Galalith—"milk stone"—was patented in 1899. The production and description of Galalith are in keeping with the fabric-like manufacture of Cavorite. An early manual, entitled *Casein: Its Preparation and Technical Utilisation,* details how this class of plastics is made. After batches of casein

FIGURE 11.2. Visqueen's transparent plastic film contributes to a well-appointed and sparkling clean kitchen in this advert. Advertisement by Visqueen, a subsidiary of the Visking Company (1948). *Good Housekeeping*, February 1948, 240. The Women's Magazines Archive I, Marriott Library, University of Utah. Accessed August 1, 2020. https://about.proquest.com/products-services/Womens-Magazine-Archive.html.

(cow's milk) have soaked for one to two days in a "borax solution," they are "afterwards rolled together for three to four hours between rollers, and thus furnish a transparent or translucent and perfectly homogeneous mass . . . drawn out into sheets 2 to 4 inches thick. These sheets are pressed together . . . the block being thereupon cut into plates of desired thickness."[16] In general, such substances were murky in appearance, and the patent for Galalith states its intention of improving upon caseins that were "only translucent, not transparent" by including an additional step of centrifugal separation. Starting with "55 gallons of milk," this process cleanses the casein of "all impurities" and results in a substance that is "colourless and transparent in thin sheets" (97).

Additionally, the destructive nature of Cavorite has many things in common with the risks involved in the production of early plastics, not just for damaged property but also damaged lives: "Stacks of celluloid sheets in a warehouse were only as homogeneous as a highly imprecise process could make them. The manufacturing process itself exuded uncertainty and risk. . . . In a single month in 1917, for example, more than a hundred injuries occurred" in a single work site.[17] These include "a hand crushed in a mixer, another caught and lacerated in a rolling machine, and three fingers cut off under a sheeting knife" (13). Such instances, Meikle notes, were "not that rare," even resulting in the death of workers. That same explosion in Arlington, Virginia, referenced earlier, for example, was caused by an insufficient cooling and finishing process: "Triggered in the drying room, it killed two workers and brought about an almost total destruction of the company's works" (14).

Consumers also had to worry about flammability, after "hearing reports of an Ohio congressman whose celluloid visor caught fire, engulfing his head in flames, as he tried to light a cigar" (22–23). Indeed, a rather darkly comedic moment occurs in Wells's novel that speaks to these types of risks. Once Cavor has recovered from his unexpected "flight" he concocts a story about a cyclone to explain the damage:

> My three assistants may or may not have perished. That is a detail. If they have, it is no great loss; they were more zealous than

> able, and this premature event must be largely due to their joint neglect of the furnace. If they have not perished, I doubt if they have the intelligence to explain the affair. They will accept the cyclone story. (37)

This moment speaks to the lack of agency that factory workers of every kind suffered in Wells's time. Wells's writing is largely socialist, and the rights of workers is a theme he returns to repeatedly in his work. But it also functions as a clear template for what will become an SF trope near and dear to conspiracy theorists of all stripes: the cover-up, as well as an all-too-familiar story in terms of the real-world lives of factory workers. And lest the reader give Cavor the benefit of the doubt—he has, after all, just experienced a humbling trauma and could be speaking prematurely—Cavor offers another zinger. After he has had some time to recover, the two men discuss next steps in Cavorite's production as they reconstruct the laboratory: "Of course we must make it again . . . If we can possibly avoid wrecking this little planet of ours, we will. But—there *must* be risks!" (39). Cavor's arrogance is astonishing, but this sort of hubris becomes par for the course in similar works of SF.

Finally, there is another science fictional template that *First Men in the Moon* helps to instantiate that connects to our discussion of Cavorite's role as a protoplastic. This is the motif of violent, extraterrestrial colonialism. As John Rieder notes in his introduction to *Colonialism and the Emergence of Science Fiction*, "early science fiction lives and breathes in the atmosphere of colonial history."[18] When the vessel nears landing, the narrator describes the terrain he espies from the open Cavorite blinds in menacing terms: "The whole area was moon, a stupendous scimitar of white dawn with its edge hacked out by notches of darkness, the crescent shore of an ebbing tide of darkness" (70). That the moon takes the shape of a "scimitar," a curved blade "used chiefly by Arabs and Turks," suggests both foreignness and danger, while the "hacked" light of its "white dawn" implies a thick, jungle-dense terrain. Upon landing on the moon, Bedford and Cavor are rude, obnoxious explorers. They view the Selenites and mooncalves they encounter as primitive insectoids, with Bedford describing them as one might describe ants tending to aphids. They lose track of their sphere, grow hysterical from lack of nourishment, and out of desperation eat lunar fungus, which intoxicates them. In his mushroom-induced state of inebriation, Bedford declares: "We must annex this moon. . . . There must be no shilly-shally. This is part of the White Man's Burthen." (129). Yet even after the mushroom's properties wear off, the two continue to follow the well-worn path forged by the genre of the colonial travel narrative. When they come upon a group of Selenites, Cavor views them with contempt. "'Insects,' murmured Cavor, 'insects! And they think I'm going to crawl about on my stomach—on my vertebrated stomach!'" (130). Enraged by a fantasy of insectoid insurrection entirely of his own invention, justified by what he perceives as his evolutionary superiority as a "vertebrate," he attacks the Selenites without provocation.

The depiction of the Selenites is Wells's own, but the book is in conversation with a variety of lunar narratives that offer the same treatment of the moon's native lifeforms, especially Jules Verne's *From Earth to the Moon* (1865), which precedes Wells's vision, and Georges Méliès's *Voyage dans la lune* (1902), a film that, coming only one year later, took great inspiration from it. But it is also in dialog with the larger problem of colonization. In terms of its content, the novel shares striking similarities with Joseph Conrad's *Heart of Darkness* (1899). And in terms of the description of Cavorite, it inaugurates the synthetic substance as a tool for colonization and commodification. At this point, it may seem unfair to associate Cavorite with the ugly manner of conquest that Cavor and Bedford exhibit—to confuse, as it were, the invention with the inventor. After all, although colonization and Cavor are causally linked, *Cavorite* and colonization are not. Yet even a cursory study of the marketing of early plastics reveals an eye toward conquest, warfare, and colonization, with much of plastic's military applications widely deployed and celebrated during World War I. The following ad for Bakelite, for example, which appears in the May 30, 1925, issue of the *Saturday Evening Post*, asserts confidently that "Bakelite resists heat" (Figure 11.3). The statement is fair enough. Bakelite becomes a successful insulator in the production of electricity, replacing the "highly flammable" celluloid.[19] But the ad's depiction of a dark-skinned man in

128 THE SATURDAY EVENING POST May 30, 1925

BAKELITE RESISTS HEAT

plus–

- ¶ electrical resistance
- ¶ strength
- ¶ resistance to oil and water
- ¶ permanent finish and color
- ¶ light weight
- ¶ hardness
- ¶ resistance to acid
- ¶ resistance to chemicals
- ¶ resistance to warping

–in one industry after another

Bakelite Pipes made by the leading pipe manufacturers

Bakelite Radiator Cap
THE NASH MOTORS CO.

Bakelite Percolator Handles
THE GORHAM CO

ONCE in a generation a new material is discovered. So it was with rubber, steel, aluminum and celluloid. Now comes this new material, Bakelite, known chemically as phenol resin.

In one industry after another, Bakelite has provided a combination of qualities which never before could be found in any one material.

Heat resistance, for example, is the most important of many essential properties in manufacturing certain products. Some of them are illustrated here.

But the important point to remember is that Bakelite is the *only* material in which you can find heat resistance combined with *all* the properties listed at the top of this page.

The uses for Bakelite are almost limitless. In its pure form, as a molding material, in sheets, rods and tubes: or as a varnish, lacquer, enamel or cement, our Engineering Department is continually perfecting new applications. Is there a place for Bakelite in your business?

Send for our illustrated booklet, "The Material of a Thousand Uses"

BAKELITE CORPORATION

247 Park Avenue, New York 636 West 22d St., Chicago

Electric Iron—Bakelite Handle
SIMPLEX ELECTRIC HEATING CO.

Bakelite Distributor Head
NORTH EAST ELECTRIC CO.

Bakelite Lamp Cement
THE NATIONAL LAMP WORKS

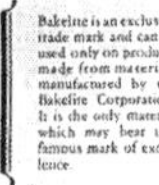

Bakelite is an exclusive trade mark and can be used only on products made from materials manufactured by the Bakelite Corporation. It is the only material which *may* bear this famous mark of excellence.

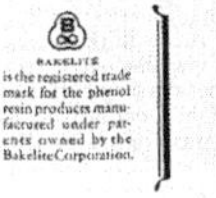

BAKELITE is the registered trade mark for the phenol resin products manufactured under patents owned by the Bakelite Corporation.

FIGURE 11.3. In this early advertisement for Bakelite, plastic is promoted directly as a cooling agent and indirectly as a civilizing agent. Advertisement by Bakelite (1925). *Saturday Evening Post,* May 30, 1925, 128. Image courtesy of Oregon State University Collections.

a fantastic Polynesian costume who is—presumably—dancing on or walking across hot coals, is highly problematic. If the "heat" that Bakelite resists is somehow embodied in this scene, then, linked as it is to non-Western people, it is a heat that is equivalent to a kind of cultural primitivism. And this, the ad suggests, is something else that Bakelite can allay. The features of Cavorite are of course specific to Wells's vision in the novel. But they are also fairly consistent with other imaginary substances in SF's early history. In such instances, regardless of cost or the danger to subordinate lives, the features of transparency, durability, and pliability are integrated with a material that allows mankind to leave the earth behind and explore—and colonize—the cosmos.

Queering Plastic, or Toward a Postcolonial Plastiglomerate Aesthetic

Now that H. G. Wells's text has provided us with an early origin story for synthetic polymers in science fiction, we shall travel, Tardis-like, through time, moving swiftly forward one hundred years, in order to consider a more contemporary text in which plastic loses its transparency, yields to something more complex, and resonates with contemporary discussions of queerness. As with the Tardis, which depends upon the compression of time and space to function, we must fly by some important moments and movements within the genre: the Golden Age's fascination with plastic personhood and plastic-as-progress; the New Wave's delight in experimental form, which is as malleable as the plastic it describes; cyberpunk's suspicion of and fascination with plastic as both treasure and trash; and—slowing down and circling back a bit now to 1977—to the first film in the *Star Wars* franchise (in keeping with time travel, it is now the fourth).[20] Luke, Leia, Han, and Chewie hide out in a trash compactor, wading through a soup of broken parts and threatened by a malevolent space creature. Just as it seems they will be squashed and flushed out into space with the rest of the Empire's flotsam,[21] the rebels climb out of the mess. Importantly, they are able to do so by using the very means of the surrounding structure that has very nearly just killed them: the walls, the detritus, and broken pipes have been reconfigured so they now serve the purpose of creating an inelegant means of escape. Next, moving forward in time but going slower still, we see the "rasquache" aesthetic of Alex Rivera's *Sleep Dealer* (2008), a film set in a future Mexico that looks eerily like the present.[22] The wall between Mexico and the United States has been built, and water is a privately controlled commodity. The main character, equipped with a book titled *Hacking por principiantes*, alters his body so he can plug into a global communication network—literally. With long, slender plastic tubing punched into his dermal "nodes," he works in an SF version of a *maquiladora*. Soon after comes Neil Blomkamp's *District 9*, with its abhorrent junk heaps that double as refugee sites for the stranded aliens that have landed in South Africa.[23] Such texts embody the plastiglomerate to greater and lesser degrees. In all cases, however, the presence of plastic both binds the protagonists to their environment and, at the same time, provides the means of resistance to it. In all these instances, as well, a campy, ludic impulse threads through the narrative. Such works take a playful delight in recognizing refuse as means of emancipation or resistance. In this they are in keeping with a playful politics of appropriation, using plastic as a motif to critique a larger system in which plastic is itself a sign of debasement.[24] But now, finally, we circle back again to the turn of the century to a short story that offers its fullest expression and whose expression of a distinct registry of queerness is perhaps most potent, even as it lacks the levity of its predecessors: Steven Barnes's "Woman in the Wall."[25]

This piece of prose fiction, which appears in the *Dark Matter* SF anthology (2000), illustrates the remarkable shift from plastic as a shining symbol of futurity in early SF (as it appears in Wells's novel) to its fragmented, discarded, yet potent status in more contemporary writing, especially from within or about the Global South. In this story, an African-American visual artist named Shawna is traveling with her husband and stepdaughter when their airplane is shot down over Africa. Her husband dies in the crash, and she and her stepdaughter, Lizzie, are imprisoned in "nearly a square kilometer of clustered ramshackle cabins, tents, and makeshift huts. The spaces between them were dotted with cook fires and outhouses, roving knots of starving refugees. . . . Concentric rings of concertina and razor wire walled the entire camp" (237). The environment itself, a refugee camp that turns out to be a quarantine zone, speaks to real-world spaces of this nature—in Africa, in Europe, in the United States—and plastic here serves a familiar function. Just as plastic zip ties are used as handcuffs in real-world arrests, and just as plastic is used as a component in court-ordered ankle-bracelet monitors, plastic here serves as a way to mark difference, criminalize disease, and ensure surveillance: "The black wraiths roaming the camp craned toward the gate. . . . They looked like refugees anywhere on this blighted continent, with one exception: Each wore a blue plastic collar. Within each collar was a radio device keyed to transceivers around the camp perimeter."

Shawna takes inventory: "Against nearly a kilometer of concertina wire, stood a makeshift wall of six feet high and almost two hundred meters long." Unlike the other walls of the camp, this wall is composed of "shells and rocks, rags and pieces of board, splashes of paint and twists of clay" (237). It serves a different purpose. Rather than confinement, this wall provides an outlet of expression—as well as a literal outlet from the camp, as we shall see. Shawna is fascinated by the wall: "The faces of Africa stared out from the wall. Kwanta faces carved of wood and Adansi images of bone. A hundred different animals . . . a thousand symbols. . . . Here were artistic styles and animals from every corner of Sub-Saharan Africa" (238–39). Shawna lingers at the space: "There were dozens of animals in the wall, but also tiny automobiles, and trees, and human faces by the hundreds." Her "fingers traced one especially striking image, a laughing man, an Ashanti-style mask rendered in what might have once been a plastic canopy. The planes and facial curves were burned in, so that the image was expressed in the concavity" (246–47). As an artist, "Shawna knew what the wall was. It was a tapestry of loss, a mosaic of human pain. Memories of freedoms and childhood wonders, a collage of dead dreams" (247).

Portraits of lost loved ones stretch out for nearly two hundred yards. These portraits and the wall they hang on are consistent with what I am calling the plastiglomerate aesthetic. Composed of scraps of refuse, the wall works as both a medium of expression and an invitation to contribute to its unruly and heartbreaking composite.

Shawna, an artist, accepts this invitation. Her bricolage self-portrait earns her approval from the other prisoners. By expressing her suffering in this shared space—itself composted of a diversity of castoff materials—and peoples—she inserts herself into the community: "Rendered in stick, in bits of wood and plastic and paper, was Shawna Littleton. The profile was hers, caught there in a curve of wire. Hair was suggested by a knot of string. Her arms were outstretched fragments of particle board. Shawna's plastic face was drawn, anguished. Her pottery-shard lips were frozen open, locked in an eternal scream for help" (253). Once she adds her portrait to this collective, she learns that the wall itself provides a means of escape. Her contact "met her in the shadows. He pointed toward the wall. 'Near end. Face of laughing woman. Take lip, pull up. Crawl through. Grab thread, and follow . . . Follow thread to other side. Pull up. You be safe'" (256). This moment in the story provides the fullest expression of the claim I am making about the potential of plastiglomerate aesthetic. This is artwork, but it is artwork that emerges from raw, human pain. Its materials of expression are scavenged, not selected. Additionally, it echoes the sharp, piecemeal edges that make up the surrounding camp. Here plastic, intentionally molded with other components, serves as a decorative element, yes, but also as something that disguises a means of escaping the site. In a locodescriptive manner, something that initially appears as detritus opens to a literal escape route. That the main character rejects it and chooses instead to return to her stepdaughter speaks to an ethics of family, community.

In "Toxic Progeny: The Plastisphere and Other Queer Futures," Heather Davis describes plastic as a signal of a "queer futurity" and discusses its potential in science fictional terms: "It is quite likely that these vibrant attached communities may develop complex bacterial societies, flourishing on their synthetic surfaces, eating each other and the vast sources of unlocked carbon energy, mutating and evolving."[26] This is not necessarily an optimistic reading in terms of a conventional, heteronormative narrative of futurity; nor is it in keeping with the more playful elements of a queer camp aesthetic. It is nevertheless instructive for thinking through alternatives. "Queerness," she writes, "does mean the end of the future, a non-teleological orientation to time that brings about a social disruption. . . . In this position there might be something to be learned for politics in our given moment" (240).

In keeping with science fiction's penchant for time travel, I have covered in this paper a sweeping lineage of SF history in a compressed and highly adumbrated fashion. While I do not have the space here to develop the evolution of plastic in SF in all of its peculiar phases, I hope I have nevertheless been able to point the discrepancy that exists between its use in its early years to how it is now more commonly (but not exclusively) occurring. The proto-plastics of Wells and early SF are fairly consistent with a variety of modernist trajectories that affirm heteronormativity, rationality, the subordination of nonhuman beings, and the superiority of the West. The plastiglomerate aesthetic that I am outlining does not. Rather, when plastic "trash" operates in the way it does in "The Woman in the Wall," it is the consequence of make-do accretion and is coextensive with the disenfranchised; it binds the disenfranchised to the place they inhabit with powerful but nearly invisible force. At the same time, because it is seen as junk, it manages to disguise avenues for escape.

As a geographic reality, the plastiglomerate emerges as an abomination, a clear sign of the Anthropocene, which is to say, as a human-made affront to naturally occurring ecologies. It is not recuperable. And yet the plastiglomerate is a consequence of the neoliberal capitalist system that dominates our planet. When it can re-form in such a way that it includes the most vulnerable entities—animals, aliens, refugees—who can make use of its disturbing architecture to resist capitalist hegemony, then it becomes an aesthetic worth fuller consideration. As Davis writes, "I want to think through what kinds of queer affordances might be possible that work to skew the social. How, in other words, to think about slow decline, a kind of gerontology, or crip theory for the current biosphere?"[27] A plastiglomerate aesthetic, which evolves from plastic's smooth, colonizing origins in order to resist the power structures that have created such inequity in the first place, offers one response to this question.

NOTES

1. Irvin S. Yeaworth, dir., *The Blob* (1958; Thrill Kill, 2003), DVD.
2. Susan Sontag, "The Imagination of Disaster," in *Against Interpretation* (New York: Farrar, Straus & Giroux, 1961), 209–25.
3. Hanna Fenichel Pitkin, *The Attack of the Blob: Hannah Arendt's Concept of the Social* (Chicago: University of Chicago Press, 2000).
4. Nicholas Diak. "Meteor Madness: Lovecraftian Horror and Consumerism in the Battle for Small Town USA," in *Horror in Space*, ed. Michele Brittany (Jefferson, N.C.: McFarland, 2017), 50–65.
5. Eli Kintisch, "The Blob Invades Pacific, Flummoxing Climate Experts," *Science* 348, no. 6230 (April 3, 2015): 17–18. doi: 10.1126/science.348.6230.17.
6. Susan L. Dautel, "Transoceanic Trash: International and United States Strategies for the Great Pacific Garbage Patch," *Golden Gate University Environmental Law Journal* 3, no. 1 (2009): 181–208.
7. Patricia L. Corcoran, Charles J. Moore, and Kelly Jazvac, "An Anthropogenic Marker Horizon in the Future Rock Record," *GSA Today* 26, 6 (2014): 5. doi: 10.1130/GSAT-G198A.1.
8. Darko Suvin, *Metamorphosis of Science Fiction* (New Haven, Conn.: Yale University Press, 1979).
9. See, for example, N. Katherine Hayles, *How We Became Posthuman* (Chicago: University of Chicago Press, 2001); Wendy Gay Pearson, Joan Gordon, and Veronica Hollinger, *Queer Universes* (Liverpool: University of Liverpool Press, 2008); Sherryl Vint, *Bodies of Tomorrow* (Toronto: University of Toronto Press, 2007); John Rieder. *Colonialism and the Emergence of Science Fiction* (Middletown, Conn.: Wesleyan University Press, 2008).
10. See, for example: Graham J. Murphy, "Archivization and the Archive-as-Utopia in H.G. Wells's *The First Men in the Moon* and 'The Empire of the Ants,'" *Science Fiction Studies* 42, no. 1 (March 2011): 1–19; Aaron Worth, "Imperial Transmissions: H. G. Wells, 1897–1901," *Victorian Studies* 53, no. 1 (Autumn 2010): 65–89; and Arthur B. Evans, "Jules Verne's Dream Machines," *Extrapolation* 54, no. 2 (2013): 129–46. Such texts use Wells's novel to think through knowledge organization in the age of empire (Murphy and Worth), or to consider Jules Verne's methodic, science-based fiction to Wells's more improvisational style (Evans). There is not to my knowledge any extant scholarship about its connection to the development of synthetics.
11. H. G. Wells, *The First Men in the Moon* (London: George Newnes, 1901), 21.
12. Susan Sontag, "Notes on Camp," in *Against Interpretation* (New York: Farrar, Straus & Giroux, 1961), 275–92.
13. See, for example, Alexis Lothian, *Old Futures: Speculative Fiction and Queer Possibility* (New York: New York University Press, 2018).
14. Leo Marx, *The Machine in the Garden: Technology and the Pastoral Ideal in America* (Oxford: Oxford University Press, 1960).

15. Jeffrey L. Meikle, *American Plastic: A Cultural History* (New Brunswick, N.J.: Rutgers University Press, 1997), 23.
16. Robert Scherer, *Casein: Its Preparation and Utilisation* (London; Scott Greenwood & Sons, 1906).
17. Meikle, *American Plastic*, 23.
18. Rieder, *Colonialism*, 3.
19. *Encyclopedia Brittanica*, "Plastic," https://www.britannica.com/science/Bakelite.
20. George Lucas, dir., *Star Wars* (Lucasfilm, 1977).
21. A similar technique occurs in *The Empire Strikes Back* (1980), when Han Solo hides his ship on the back of an Imperial star destroyer. Solo knows that the Empire ejects its trash into space before it makes the jump to light speed, so he cuts the power of the Millennium Falcon and waits until the trash starts flowing. When it does, he floats right out with it, unnoticed.
22. Alex Rivera, dir., *Sleep Dealer* (Maya Entertainment, 2008).
23. Neill Blomkamp, dir., *District 9* (QED, 2009).
24. See, for example, Marciano Christina Ferraira and Daiane Scaraboto, "My Plastic Dreams," *Journal of Business Research* 69 (2016): 191–207; Deirdre McKay and Padmapani L. Perez, "Plastic Masculinity: How Everyday Objects in Plastic Suggest Men Could Be Otherwise," *Journal of Material Culture* 23, no. 2 (2018): 169–86; Katie Schaag, "Pleasures of Teaching Plastic," *Edge Effects* (2018), https://edgeeffects.net/teaching-plastic/.
25. Steven Barnes, "Woman in the Wall," in *Dark Matter: A Century of Speculative Fiction from the African Diaspora*, ed. Sheree R. Thomas (New York: Warner, 2000), 235–59.
26. Heather Davis, "Toxic Progeny: The Plastisphere and Other Queer Futures," *philoSOPHIA* 5, no. 2 (2015): 235.
27. Davis, "Toxic Progeny," 244.

12

Futures in Plastic

Science Fiction, Climate Change, and the New North

Phillip E. Wegner

The question of plastic is always already deeply imbricated with that of futurity. At the same time, the nature of futurity is likewise plastic: open, malleable, and to be shaped by the choices we make (if not, usually, in conditions of our own choosing). In the pages that follow, I will look at two recent works of science fiction—Tobias S. Buckell's techno-thriller *Arctic Rising* (2012) and Emmi Itäranta's lyrical debut, written simultaneously in Finnish and English and published under the titles *Teemestarin kirja* (The tea master's book) (2012) and *Memory of Water* (2014)—that delve into the complex relationship between plastic and futurity in some especially interesting and valuable ways.

In a spring 2018 issue of *The Atlantic*, the astrophysicist Thomas Frank queries as to what traces might still exist, say 100 million years in the future, of the human geological era of the Anthropocene, and especially the post–World War II period referred to as the Great Acceleration. Frank ultimately and not unexpectedly concludes that "the most promising marker of humanity's presence as an advanced civilization" will be the massive amounts of carbon released into the atmosphere as a result of the burning of fossil fuels. However, Frank also surveys a number of other possible candidates—including the excessive nitrogen in the soil produced by chemical fertilizers, synthetic steroids, and "the rare-Earth elements used in electronic gizmos"—before singling out for special prominence the low-cost and easily synthesized petrochemical organic polymers popularly known as *plastic*: "Studies have shown increasing amounts of plastic 'marine litter' are being deposited on the seafloor everywhere from coastal areas to deep basins and even in the Arctic. Wind, sun, and waves grind down large-scale plastic artifacts, leaving the seas full of microscopic plastic particles that will eventually rain down on the ocean floor, creating a layer that could persist for geological timescales."[1]

For much of the last century there has been a deep association between imaginings of the future, both near and far, and the contemporary industrial material of plastic. One of the two lines of dialogue from Mike Nichols's *The Graduate* (1967), selected in 2005 by the American Film Institute for inclusion on its list of Top 100 Movie Quotes, is a single word: "Plastics."[2] The character who utters this line, Mr. McGuire (Walter Brooke), immediately follows it up with the proclamation, "There's a great future in plastics. Think about it. Will you think about it?" However, the "great future" being promoted by Mr. McGuire to the recent college graduate Benjamin Braddock (Dustin Hoffman) is nothing more than an indefinite extension of the present into any foreseeable future. That is, while the future seems anything but settled for Benjamin, Mr. McGuire and his contemporaries struggle to shape it for him, molding his plastic nature in their own image. As we shall see below, this is an early expression of what Catherine Malabou identifies as the neoliberal "ideological avatar of plasticity," *flexibility*.[3] By the film's conclusion, it is exactly such a closed future that Benjamin rejects: rather than be flexible in the ways his elders demand, Benjamin, like many of his real-world contemporaries, reaches for a very different kind of plastic future.

A quarter century earlier, the pioneering science fiction magazine *Amazing Stories* published in its April 1942 issue a single-page essay by editor Raymond A. Palmer, writing under the pseudonym of Henry Gade. Palmer's essay, entitled "Future City on Earth," was inspired by one of celebrated science fiction artist Frank R. Paul's most well-known images, printed for the first time on the issue's back cover (Figure 12.1). (The same image of the future city was again used in 1984 as the cover of the catalogue for the Smithsonian exhibition, *Yesterday's Tomorrows: Past Visions of the American Future*.) Palmer opens with the claim, "In the holocaust of today's war, with giant bombs smashing cities all over the earth, the picture of the future looks pretty grim. But in a scientific sense, all this destruction will lead toward a great quickening of progress toward the city of the future."[4] He further observes, "Already we realize that the future will be called the Plastic Age. Plastics are coming into their own with dramatic suddenness. . . . Everywhere in industry, plastic materials are springing up." Thus, Palmer determines that the future metropolis will not be "a city of steel and stone, of brick and mortar, of wood and nails." Rather,

> It is a city of seamless, cast and rolled plastic materials of brilliant and beautiful colors. . . . Here in this new city will be broad, plastic-paved walks, lined with garden areas, brilliantly sunlit, and uncrowded by towering buildings. . . . Up above the city, aerial traffic will be heavy. . . . Landing ramps will be vast circular platforms of solid plastics, amazingly light in weight, and tremendously strong, transparent, so as to cut off very little light.

Palmer concludes by proclaiming that such a future city will be "a miracle of architecture, a symphony of beauty and color and grace, a mecca of peace, quiet and contentment, and a wonder-house of science and industry and mechanical coordination. It is Man's Utopia at last." Plastic is presented here as the means to a veritable end of history, neutralizing conflict and change and ushering in a docile global community.

As Lisa Swanstrom affirms in her essay in this collection, concerns with the nature and potential of plastic have been an important aspect of science fiction since its founding in the work of H. G. Wells.[5] And while it is true that in the past plastic very often, as in *The Graduate* and Palmer's essay, signified a hollow progress, a colonization of the future by the status quo, it has come to take on other connotations in more recent and far darker science fiction presentations of imaginary futures. This is the case in both the Steven Barnes story discussed by Swanstrom and in the two more recent novels of interest here, *Arctic Rising* and *Memory of Water*. Rather than prognostications, the images of a future in plastic presented in all these works have the estranging effect of "transforming our own present

FIGURE 12.1. Frank R. Paul, artist, "City of the Future"; back cover of *Amazing Stories* (April 1942). Image courtesy of the personal collection of Phillip E. Wegner.

into the determinate past of something yet to come. . . . The present is in fact no less a past if its destination prove to be the technological marvels of [Jules] Verne or, on the contrary, the shabby and maimed automata of P[hilip] K. Dick's near future."[6] What we do with such a new understanding of our present is up to us.

The Persistence of the Plastic Present

While quite distinct in tone and approach, Buckell's and Itäranta's novels share a number of similarities. First, both authors hail from the margins of the contemporary world political and literary systems: Itäranta comes from Finland, and Buckell was born in Grenada and has lived extensively in the Virgin Islands. Moreover, Caribbean settings and characters feature prominently in many of his novels—indeed, the action of *Arctic Rising*'s sequel, *Hurricane Fever* (2014), is located exclusively in the Caribbean. Both novels also imagine worlds shaped by violent national and corporate struggles over access to natural resources, especially oil, and both share a setting in the region that the geographer Laurence C. Smith names the "New North": "all land and oceans lying 45° N latitude or higher currently held by the United States, Canada, Iceland, Greenland (Denmark), Norway, Sweden, Finland, and Russia."[7] Finally, both novels take part in the tradition of what Tom Moylan terms the "critical dystopia"—texts that at once "resist both hegemonic and oppositional orthodoxies" and "inscribe a space for a new form of political opposition."[8] Finally, in addition to mapping the ways our plastic present might shape things to come, they open up onto what Malabou names the potential plasticity of any actual future, "the possibility of a closed system to welcome new phenomena, all the while transforming itself."[9]

The near-future setting of Buckell's *Arctic Rising* parallels in a number of ways the world of 2050 forecast in Smith's exercise in futurology (a very different genre than science fiction): a world shaped by the fourfold dynamics of "demography," "the growing demand that human desires place upon natural resources, services, and gene pool of our planet," "globalization," and "climate change."[10] In

Buckell's novel, these combined forces have wrought a thoroughgoing reorientation of the geopolitical landscape toward the far north. Early on, the reader is introduced to the contemporary Canadian city of Resolute (whose 2016 population is reported to be 198, down from 2011's 214 people):[11]

> Another port deep in the Arctic Circle. Another island detached from the mainland of Canada, like Baffin. Just farther west. Most of these places were barely presences at the turn of the century. Forty years later, they were bursting with prefabs and activity. When the ice left, the Canadian North opened up. Once-tiny towns exploded, particularly once shipping traffic began to stream through the Northwest Passage, and ports rapidly built themselves up. Places that were actually on the Canadian mainland, like Bernard Harbour, Coppermine, Gjoa, and Taloyok, had become powerful economic and demographic engines that made Canada the lead of the so-called "Arctic Tiger" nations that benefitted from the warm polar oceans. The megalopolis Anchorage turned into had made Alaska one of the more powerful states in the U.S.A.[12]

The influence of the United States as a whole, however, has diminished in this new world order—"The Americans lost tremendous public credibility at the turn of the century, just as the Soviets did in the middle of the last century" (131)—while new powers have emerged. Buckell introduces his readers to the now-independent nation of Greenland:

> The Greenlanders were mostly First Nations people, with some Danish background. They'd encouraged First Nations peoples to emigrate from Northern Canada, Alaska, and Russia. But as the glaciers receded and Greenland's interior released a bounty of natural resources, there was more work than people in Greenland. Companies had to reach out to find workers, and they trickled in from Africa, the United States, and Northern Europe.
>
> There had been protests and some strikes by international workers who ran out of their three-month stays, demanding to

> be treated fairly and given a chance to apply to become Greenlanders, but the Greenlanders didn't want to become minorities in their own country. And they were First Nations peoples. They'd seen the rush to Northern Canada's newly opened and ice-free land displace enough Inuit there. They knew history. (95–96)

However, the advantageous consequences of this reordering of the globe are not shared equally. One of the novel's main characters, Prudence "Roo" Jones—a former member of the Caribbean intelligence agency who will become the central protagonist of *Hurricane Fever*—responds to the question "Who was Anegada?" with, "What, not who. It used to be home, . . . Before the sea levels rose" (119). Later the person who posed this question—Anika Duncan, a Nigerian-born airship pilot employed by the United Nations Polar Guard—reflects, "For her, the rants about global changes seemed far off. To Roo, it was personal. This hit his family, his people. Everything" (233). In this new world then, as much as in our own, "Westerners get all the benefits" (167).

As Smith also underscores, one of the key factors driving any future economic boom in the New North will be the desire for untapped reserves of limited natural resources, especially oil. Buckell characterizes his near-future world as one "with oil reserves the world over at uncertain levels, geologists claiming a limited supply anywhere outside of the booming Arctic, and oil at increasingly higher prices" (101). However, Buckell also indicates that in such a world the demand for oil is no longer primarily driven by energy or transportation—indeed, most of the vessels we encounter are wind or solar powered—but rather for the production of plastic: "Global oil production was mostly focused on making plastics, not burning it" (178). Roo concisely characterizes the situation in this way: "Plastic has to be made. It covers the modern world" (149–50). Even the radical corporate environmental activist Paige Greer argues, "We hammer the idea that the best use of oil isn't to vaporize it through combustion and then never have access to it again, but to use it in plastics, which are recyclable. Our civilization can't exist without that. Save the plastic, burn something else" (229). It is plastic,

Buckell teaches his readers, that forms the real foundation of the contemporary global order.

The main action of the narrative follows Anika's gradual discovery of a conspiracy undertaken by the heads of the powerful Gaia Corporation, Ivan Cohen and Greer, to reverse the effects of global climate change. They become determined to use their corporation's immense resources to "terraform Earth to stop it from turning into Venus" (167), by releasing millions of programmable mirrors into the atmosphere that will deflect the heat of the sun away from the earth. Anika reflects on the consequences of such a plan:

> If Gaia was effective in its attempt to "terraform" Earth, the gold rush to the Arctic Circle would slow down as the oil and other resources were buried back under the ice.
>
> The economies of the Arctic Tigers would slow down. Denmark, Finland, Norway, Greenland, Iceland, Russia, Canada. Alaska would fall back into pre-warming levels of expansion. (178)

While our protagonists do successfully thwart this undertaking—an issue I will return to in the next section of this essay—Greer raises a significant concern for the new world presented in the narrative:

> We keep punting the question of what that is doing to the atmosphere to the next generation. We're doing it again. It's warmed up enough that we're experiencing all the benefits of global warming: increased land for northern countries, the release of the Arctic's resources, and a whole new shipping lane and ocean to exploit. But now there's a precipice we're perched on. Who goes over it? Not our problem, right? (229)

Greer makes evident that the world in *Arctic Rising*—and the same could be said for that in Smith's futurology—whatever its other differences, is one where the fundamental institutional structures of neoliberal capitalism remain solidly in place. In this regard then, Buckell's narrative seems to reconfirm Fredric Jameson's often-repeated observation from the early 1990s, "It seems to be easier for us today to imagine the thoroughgoing deterioration of the earth and of nature than the breakdown of late capitalism."[13]

One version of the world that might result from the refusal to address the longer-range consequences of contemporary trends can be found in Itäranta's *Memory of Water.* The action of the novel is set in a much more distant future, in which both our contemporary moment and the near future imagined in *Arctic Rising* have become part of the period that the narrator and central protagonist Noria Kaitio names the "past-world":

> Near the end of the past-world era the globe had warmed and seas had risen faster than anyone could have anticipated. Tempests tore the continents and people fled their homes to where there was still space and dry land. During the final oil wars a large accident contaminated most of the fresh-water reserves of former Norway and Sweden, leaving the areas uninhabitable.
>
> The following century was known as the Twilight Century, during which the world, or what remained of it, ran out of oil. With this a major part of the past-world technology was gradually lost. Staying alive became the most important thing. All that wasn't considered necessary for everyday survival faded away.[14]

These cataclysmic changes have led to the rise of a military oligarchy centered in China that dominates contemporary life in the occupied territory of the Scandinavian Union. This reflects very real contemporary Finnish anxieties about the loss of national autonomy at the hands of other, and especially Russian, powers.[15] (Interestingly, in more recent years, some young people in China have begun to claim that they are "jingfen, or 'spiritually Finnish.'"[16])

Since almost all remaining print books from this past have been confiscated by the state and military (67), the primary traces of the past-world are to be found in former waste dumps, renamed by Noria the "plastic grave":

> The plastic grave was a large, craggy, pulpy landscape where sharp corners and coarse surfaces, straight edges and jagged

> splinters rose steep and unpredictable. Its strange, angular valleys of waves and mountain lines kept shifting their shape. People moved piles of rubbish from one place to the next, stomped the plains even more tightly packed, dug big holes and elevated hills next to them in search of serviceable plastic and wood that wasn't too bent out of shape under layers of garbage. (23–24)

At the opening of the novel, teenager Noria resides in the rural countryside of northeastern Finland where she is being trained by her father to become a tea master. Conflict arises when an ambitious young military officer, Commander Taro, seeks to find the hidden spring that has for centuries been under the care of the Kaitio tea masters. After her mother's departure for a university posting in Xinjing and her father's sudden and unexpected death, sole care of the spring devolves to Noria. Moreover, in coincidence with her father's death, an uprising erupts in the near-by city of Kuusamo (in our world, a major tourist center for winter sports), which results in a military crackdown and dramatic restrictions on water rations. Everyday life in her village is quickly reduced to the barest minimum. When the infant sister of her closest companion Sanja becomes dangerously ill, Noria first shares her water with Sanja's family and then reveals the spring to the young woman. These actions result in other villagers discovering the long-held secret, and Noria is forced to share more and more water. Eventually, the military learns the truth and they place Noria under house arrest. After she refuses to become a spy in their service, she is executed as a "water criminal."

Although the production of new plastic, along with oil, largely has disappeared from the world of *Memory of Water*, plastic still plays a crucial role in the village's economy, especially in the waterskins that are vital to the community's survival. Early on, Noria observes, "My father tossed the waterskin on the grass where a couple of others were already waiting. Mending the skins didn't always work out, but they were expensive, like anything made of durable plastic, and it was usually worth a try" (7). The scarcity of plastic has even given rise to the new profession of "plasticsmith" (15).

The powerful estranging irony at play in the novel is that plastic itself has become a kind of "natural" resource, literally mined from the landscape:

> I kept an eye on anything worth scavenging, but passed only uninteresting items: crumbled, dirty-white plastic sheets, uncomfortable-looking shoes with broken tall heels, a faded doll's head. . . . We wandered on the plastic grave for a while longer, but we only found the usual rubbish—broken toys, unrecognisable shards, useless dishes and the endless mouldy shreds of plastic bags. (24–25)

A little earlier, Noria notes, "Junk plastic, on the other hand, never seemed to run out, because past-world plastic took centuries to degrade, unlike ours" (21). Plastic thus serves as an emblem in the novel—as in *The Graduate*, Frank's and Palmer's essays, and *Arctic Rising*—of the ways our contemporary practices will persist far into the future, seemingly determining its fate as much as our own.

Plasticity and Possible Worlds

In her analysis of the homologies between dominant models of the human brain and ideologies of neoliberalism, Catherine Malabou draws a distinction between two forms of change: "*continuous change*, without limits, without adventure, without negativity, and a *formative change* that tells an effective story and proceeds by rupture, conflicts, and dilemmas."[17] The latter she relates to the central concept in her project, that of dialectical *plasticity*: "the relation that an individual entertains with what, on the one hand, attaches him originally to himself, to his proper form, and with what, on the other hand, allows him to launch himself into the void of all identity, to abandon all rigid and fixed determination."[18] Malabou contrasts such plasticity with "its mistaken cognate," and not coincidently the dominant category for thinking neoliberal globalization, *flexibility*:

> Flexibility is the ideological avatar of plasticity—at once its mask, its diversion, and its confiscation. . . . To be flexible is to receive a form or impression, to be able to fold oneself, to take

> the fold, not to give it. To be docile, to not explode. Indeed, what flexibility lacks is the resource of giving form, the power to create, to invent or even to erase an impression, the power to style.[19]

This is exactly what is demanded of Benjamin Braddock from his elders: to be docile, to not explode. Similarly, Palmer champions plastic in his 1940s essay as a means of transforming the explosive conflicts that had produced "the holocaust of today's war" into a docile "mecca of peace, quiet and contentment." Plasticity on the other hand, Malabou maintains, "far from producing a mirror image of the world, is the form of another possible world."[20]

Up to this point, my discussion has focused on the ways *Arctic Rising* and *Memory of Water* model docile human flexibility in the face of what both novels show to be futures dominated by "continuous change," or what Walter Benjamin famously terms the "homogenous, empty-time" of capitalist modernity.[21] However, the deeper interest of these two novels lies in their intimations of more radical "formative change," of possible explosive ruptures with the deadening continuity of our present. Both novels, in good critical dystopian fashion, strive to educate their reader's desires to create another possible world and thereby displace a repetitive future in plastic with an open-ended future plasticity.

Buckell develops a number of figures of other possible worlds emerging in the interstices of the dominant one. During the course of the latter part of the narrative, Anika comes to function like the detective in the noir fiction of Raymond Chandler, the critical investigation serving as an excuse, the motivation of the device, for introducing the reader to some of these other possible worlds.[22] For example, Anika's inquiries take her to Pleasure Island—an entertainment district of "bars, casinos, and other venues" that had "accreted around the remains of a shut down offshore platform" on the western edge of the Northwest Passage (175)—and in particular to a strip club named Pussy Galore. When Anika suggests that the club's labor organization might be "communist," she is corrected by a middle-aged employee named Kerrie:

> It's a worker-owned small business. We all have shares. Don't let serf-acquiring corporations bullshit you into their feudalistic mind-sets. The harder we work, the more fucking money we make because we're each part owners of the company, and part of the profit-making mechanism. We're not working *our* asses off to profit some distant fucking middle manager or stockholder. . . . People living in a democratic world go all floosy for corporations run like the most asshat evil empires ever seen. Get all wet when some corporate ruler shits all over the environment, cuts costs by laying people off, but handed over a nice quarter according to the nerds in accounting. The sort of shit they'd scream about if it were dressed up as politics, they just shrug when it happens under a corporate byline. Fuck that, we got democracy, baby, and its profitable. (181–82)

On an even larger scale, Buckell introduces the reader to the new collective social formations that develop in the independent nation of Thule, located around the North Pole's last remaining ice: "Someone, somewhere, once realized that the Arctic Circle needed its very own Hong Kong, its very own Singapore. A replication of relatively unfettered laissez-faire mercantilism run amok. A free-trade harbor. Low-tax haven. A place for the edges of Arctic society to experiment and innovate" (211). A little further on, Buckell writes, "Oil might have fueled the rush to the North, but Thule's constituents had a radical commitment to power independence that was visible right from the air" (213). While Thule claims national sovereignty in the framework of the global order, it functions internally in a way very different than the older nation-states: "The various entities that made up Thule were called demesnes, each allowed to create its own legal and political system. Last count, Anika recalled there being some forty mini-countries within Thule, each an experiment in whatever its founders considered the most optimal way to thrive" (214). Later Anika encounters one such experiment:

> Peary's modeled after Brazilian participatory budget and radical municipal democracy, with a few variants. People

> committee-vote on all municipal budget matters and draw up the budgets and where tax money goes; municipal employees serve as expert consultants, but have no say in the budget or projects list, they are contractors that execute what the voters decide every quarter needs done. Stops backscratching and corruption. These guys take it a step further: there are no municipal employees, municipal spots are volunteer positions. If you can't find the time, then you can pay to have a subcontractor do your duty. (241)

Thule thus becomes a scale model—in a way similar to some of the great recent global utopias, including Kim Stanley Robinson's Mars Trilogy (1992–96) and its "sequel," *2312* (2012), Ken MacLeod's "The Fall Revolution" Quartet (1995–99), and Karen Lord's *The Best of All Possible Worlds* (2013)[23]—of what Jameson theorizes as the form of utopia appropriate to our planetary system: "a Utopian archipelago, islands in the net, a constellation of discontinuous centers, themselves internally decentered . . . federalism would be an excellent name for the political dimensions of this Utopian figure, until we have a better one."[24]

The challenge taken up in the novel arises from the fact that these emergent possible worlds remain local experiments within a global order that in its totality differs very little from the one we currently inhabit. These possible worlds are, to use Raymond Williams's terms, "merely alternative" formations, which "may be tolerated as a deviation" as long as they are not perceived as a threat to the dominant and effective status quo.[25] The nature of such a situation is indicated in Kerrie's diatribe against corporations I cited above. This is also the reason that Anika and those aligned with her oppose the terraforming project of the Gaia Corporation. Near the novel's climax, Cohen asserts, "Man is sinful, dark. We are capable of great evils. Just ask the fucking whales. The Earth needs a protector, not more arguing, not more markets, not more products. It needs a solution. It needs Gaia" (248). Later when Mr. Gabriel, a security agent from the United States, challenges Anika with the question, "You would just let Ivan Cohen dominate you all, then?," she responds, "Your people and him, they are the same. They dictate from on high.

They are convinced that they, and only they, have all the answers. They have to force the issue. The ends justify the means" (289–90).

It is her realization of the continuity of the older world into the present that spurs Anika to action: "We're all just statistics, in the long run. That is true. But in this modern world, I am not some anonymous creature, like a serf in the middle ages. I bow to no man. This is a flat world, Mr. Gabriel. One of information, and democracy, and access. I am your equal" (134–35). Later, in explaining her opposition to Cohen's plan, Anika proclaims, "I fucking prefer democracy to one person with a vision. Because sometimes you're safe in that person's vision, and sometimes you're an acceptable casualty" (262). (A far darker representation of the consequences of corporate elites taking upon themselves the power to change the world is central to the plot of *Hurricane Fever.*) In these declarations, and even more importantly in her actions that follow from them, Anika transforms herself from an individual-in-a-multiplicity into that far rarer thing Alain Badiou names the *subject,* one who is compelled "to *invent* a new way of being and acting,"[26] or, in the terms I have been developing in this essay, she shifts from a flexible to a truly plastic subjectivity, taking to herself "the resource of giving form, the power to create, to invent or even to erase an impression, the power to style."[27] After the group thwarts Cohen's plot, Roo also indicates his own newly achieved status as a plastic subject: "I think we did the right thing. You were right; we'll do it better the next time around. We can reverse engineer these things, given time. It'll happen" (297–98). He then announces his plan to go "from floating demesne to demesne to convince them to get towed down south" to the archipelago of the Caribbean, to which Anika responds, "It sounds good. Messy, democratic, and good" (298).

Memory of Water takes the form of a classic dystopia: as in the tradition established by Yevgeny Zamyatin's *Мы* (*We*) (1921), the narrative perspective is limited, with one important exception I will touch on in the essay's conclusion, to Noria's first-person point of view.[28] As a result, the glimpses of utopian alternatives already within the world of the novel are more fleeting. One small-scale pocket utopia invoked by Noria is the tea ceremony: "I reminded myself of the idea built within the heart of the tea ceremony: before tea, everyone is equal, even if their lives never cross outside the walls of the teahouse" (190). However, the evidences of other similar possible worlds are few and far between.

In such a situation of seeming repetitive closure—of what Malabou calls "continuous change"—hope becomes a precious resource. At one point, Noria expresses the motivation to action she finds in "perhaps a near-vain hope, that there had to be more than this to life, that outside the village, somewhere under the sky, there must be a reason to believe that the world wasn't dry and scorched and dying beyond all repair" (137). A little later, Noria reads the following exchange in the diary of one her tea master ancestors:

> *"You do realise none of us will probably see the time when water runs free again?" she said.*
>
> *"I do, but that's not enough of a reason to give up hope that it might happen one day."* (153; italics in original)

Even during her imprisonment, Noria still asserts, "There is nothing more persistent than hope" (233).

Of far more significance, however, is the story of Noria's self-transformation from a passive flexible into an active plastic subject who acts in fidelity with the promise of formative change. The trigger for Noria's self-transformation is ironically enough an old piece of plastic. During their forays into the landfill, Anika uncovers a single compact disc—made, as all CDs, of thin polycarbonate plastic. When Sanja is able to restore an old player, the two young women hear on the disc a voice speaking of a Twilight Century journey into what they had heretofore been led to believe are the uninhabitable regions of northern Norway: "This is the log of the Jansson expedition, day four. Southern Trøndelag, near the area previously known as the city of Trondheim" (56).

This electrifying contact with the past leads Noria to undertake a quest to find the grail of the story of the undertaking. One important clue occurs in her predecessor's diary, where the author tells of his decision to hide in the secret spring the survivors of the expedition (148–53). Later while exploring the cave, Sanja stumbles across a sealed box containing six more discs recording the expedition's discoveries. What the two women hear has the effect on them of what Badiou theorizes as an encounter with an *event*, something that happens "that cannot be reduced to its ordinary inscription in 'what there is'":[29]

> Outside clouds were covering the sky, and behind them the sky was the colour of deep summer, even if we did not see it. Grass grew, people breathed, the world turned. But inside, in this workshop, in these words everything changed: changed what we knew, changed what we felt, changed like a sea that rises and swallows all streets and houses, will not withdraw, will not give back what it has claimed. . . . She switched the past-machine off. The disc slowed down and eventually stopped. Of all silences I had encountered this was the gravest and most inevitable: not the silence of secrets, but of knowing. (194–95)

Near the end of her life, Noria recognizes that such a truth was something "those holding power in New Qian had sought to destroy, just like they had destroyed almost everything else about the past-world. And yet I was holding it in my hands: not the whole truth, because the whole truth never survives, but something that was not entirely lost" (253).

It is her deep fidelity to this truth—that we make the world and it can be made otherwise—that provides Noria with the plasticity to refuse Commander Taro's offer. At the conclusion of their final conversation, Taro asks Noria, "Do you believe that there is some reward waiting for you, in another life or afterlife, if you do what you imagine is the right thing?" (246). She replies in a way that recalls the response of Sonmi-451 to her interrogator in David Mitchell's *Cloud Atlas* (2004):[30]

> "No," I said. "I believe that we must make hard choices every day despite knowing that there is no reward."
>
> "Why?" he repeated.
>
> "Because if this is all there is, it's the only way to leave a mark of your life that makes any difference." (246)

In this moment, she comes to embody the plasticity articulated in the tea master's oath: "I am a watcher of water. I am a servant of tea. I am a nurturer of change. I shall not chain what grows. I shall not cling to what must crumble. The way of tea is my way" (102). This ethos stands in contrast to the nihilism expressed by the infinitely flexible and hence absolutely immobile Taro: "'Because if this is all there is,' he finally said, 'I might as well enjoy it while it lasts'" (247).

While Noria does not survive, she hopes that her mark, her transformative impression, will be sustained beyond the existence of her body. This is why Noria spends her last hours writing her own story in the back of the old tea master's diary: "The words were slow to come at first, faint and wan in the darkness where they'd been stowed away for a long time. But as I reached for them, they began to flicker and flash and float towards me, and their shapes grew clearer. When they finally burst to the surface, bright and bold, I caught what I could and let them pour out of me" (254). She then hides the book under the floorboards of the teahouse in the hope that this letter to futurity will arrive at its destination.

At first it seems that *Memory of Water* follows the pattern of too many dystopias before it, as Noria's execution and the silencing of her oppositional voice appear to have quashed the dim hopes represented by her final acts. However, immediately following the close of her narration, the novel concludes with a brief third-person epilogue—the first and only time in the book we get outside Noria's point of view. The epilogue signals that Noria has in fact already succeeded, leaving her impression on the once only flexible but now plastic Sanja. In the epilogue, the reader learns that Sanja has traveled across the continent to deliver a mysterious package to Noria's mother. The novel closes with these words:

> "I don't know what you want to do, Mrs Kaitio," Sanja says at length. "But I know what I need to do." She goes quiet for a moment. "I brought you something." She takes a threadbare roll of fabric from her bag and places it on the desk. She unfolds the knot.
>
> Seven silver-coloured discs are glistening on top of the worn cloth.

> This morning the world is dust and ashes, but not devoid of hope. (263)

This extraordinary final image also speaks more generally to the power of *Arctic Rising, Memory of Water,* and other critical dystopias like them. Both novels pass on the message, helping keep hope present in our own world, which too often seems to be nothing but dust and ashes. Brushing against the grain of the false promise of a future in plastic, these novels celebrate the open-ended possibilities of plasticity, of the shared project of struggling, together, to produce the form of another possible world.

NOTES

1. Adam Frank, "Was There a Civilization on Earth Before Humans?" *The Atlantic,* April 13, 2018, https://www.theatlantic.com/science/archive/2018/04/are-we-earths-only-civilization/557180/.
2. "AFI's 100 Years . . . 100 Movie Quotes," *American Film Institute,* https://www.afi.com/afis-100-years-100-movie-quotes/.
3. Catherine Malabou, *What Should We Do with Our Brain?,* trans. Sebastian Rand (New York: Fordham University Press, 2008), 12.
4. Henry Gade (Raymond A. Palmer), "Future City on Earth," *Amazing Stories* 16, no. 4 (April 1942): 240.
5. I discuss the place of Wells's work in the development of science fiction in *Shockwaves of Possibility: Essays on Science Fiction, Globalization, and Utopia* (London: Peter Lang, 2014), Ch. 1.
6. Fredric Jameson, *Archaeologies of the Future: The Desire Called Utopia and Other Science Fictions* (New York: Verso, 2005), 288.
7. Laurence C. Smith, *The New North: World in 2050* (London: Profile, 2012), 6–7. Published in the United States under the title *The World in 2050: Four Forces Shaping Civilization's Northern Future* (New York: Dutton, 2010).
8. Tom Moylan, *Scraps of the Untainted Sky: Science Fiction, Utopia, Dystopia* (Boulder, Colo.: Westview, 2001), 190.
9. Catherine Malabou, *The Future of Hegel: Plasticity, Temporality and Dialectic,* trans. Lisabeth During (London: Routledge, 2005), 193.
10. Smith, *The New North,* 9, 13, 17, and 21.
11. "Census Profile, 2016 Census," *Statistics Canada/Canada Statistique,* https://www12.statcan.gc.ca/census-recensement/2016/dp-pd/prof/details/page.cfm?Lang=E&Geo1=CSD&Code1=6204022&Geo2=CD&Code2=6204&Data=Count&SearchText=Resolute&SearchType=Begins&SearchPR=01&B1=All&GeoLevel=PR&GeoCode=6204022&TABID=11.

12. Tobias S. Buckell, *Arctic Rising* (New York: Tor, 2012), 39. Hereafter cited in the text.
13. Fredric Jameson, *The Seeds of Time* (New York: Columbia University Press, 1994), xii.
14. Emmi Itäranta, *Memory of Water* (New York: Harper, 2014), 65. Hereafter cited in the text.
15. Anna Nemtsova, "Trump and Putin Are Welcome in Helsinki—Not," *The Daily Beast*, July 15, 2018, https://www.thedailybeast.com/trump-and-putin-are-welcome-in-helsinki-not.
16. "Why Do Millions of Chinese People Want to Be 'Spiritually Finnish'?" *The Guardian*, August 5, 2018, https://www.theguardian.com/world/shortcuts/2018/aug/05/why-do-millions-of-chinese-people-want-to-be-spiritually-finnish.
17. Malabou, *What Should We Do with Our Brain?*, 79; emphasis added.
18. Malabou, *What Should We Do with Our Brain?*, 80.
19. Malabou, *What Should We Do with Our Brain?*, 12.
20. Malabou, *What Should We Do with Our Brain?*, 80.
21. Walter Benjamin, "On the Concept of History," in *Selected Writing, Volume 4, 1938–1940*, trans. Edmund Jephcott and others (Cambridge, Mass.: Harvard University Press, 2003), 395.
22. See Fredric Jameson, *Raymond Chandler: The Detections of Totality* (New York: Verso, 2016).
23. I discuss MacLeod's quartet in *Shockwaves of Possibility*, Ch. 8; and Robinson's *2312* and Lord's *The Best of All Possible Worlds* in *Invoking Hope: Theory and Utopia in Dark Times* (Minneapolis: University of Minnesota Press, 2020), Ch. 7.
24. Jameson, *Archaeologies of the Future*, 221 and 224.
25. Raymond Williams, *Problems in Materialism and Culture* (London: Verso, 1980), 42.
26. Alain Badiou, *Ethics: Toward an Understanding of Radical Evil*, trans. Peter Hallward (New York: Verso, 2001), 41–42. I further unpack the value of Badiou's insights for developing new practices of reading in *Invoking Hope*, Ch. 1.
27. Malabou, *What Should We Do with Our Brain?*, 12.
28. I discuss *We* in some detail in *Imaginary Communities: Utopia, the Nation, and the Spatial Histories of Modernity* (Berkeley: University of California Press, 2002), Ch. 5.
29. Badiou, *Ethics*, 41.
30. I discuss this aspect of *Cloud Atlas* in the Conclusion to *Invoking Hope*.

13

Plastic's "Untiring Solicitation"

Geographies of Myth, Corporate Alibis, and the Plaesthetics of the Matacão

Jennifer A. Wagner-Lawlor

> If it's true that plastic is not degradable, well, the planet will simply incorporate plastic into a new paradigm: The Earth plus Plastic. The Earth doesn't share our prejudice towards plastic. Plastic came out of the Earth! The Earth probably sees plastic as just another one of its children. Could be the only reason the Earth allowed us to be spawned from it in the first place. It wanted plastic for itself. Didn't know how to make it; needed us. Could be the answer to the age-old question, "Why are we here?" PLASTIC!!! ASSHOLES!!!
>
> —George Carlin, *Jammin' in New York*

The connection between plastic and capitalism has never been mysterious.[1] Plastic was featured at the 1939 World's Fair in New York City, where nylon stockings were introduced, and "the potential of newly evolving plastics [was] fully exploited,"[2] particularly in the sale of souvenirs. From 1957 to 1967, Disneyland visitors toured Monsanto's House of the Future made entirely of plastic, based on a French architectural design, including molded furniture, carpeting, tableware, tables, and every stitch of the synthetic clothing hanging in the closets. This was the future, now.[3] This was a new phase of humanity, unburdened from labor by a "convenience" culture of disposable products. The cultural imperative of convenience was simple: want it, buy it, use it, throw it away. And repeat. The more the better. This is Utopia, a dream made real, a seemingly self-generative principle of invention and freedom, made possible by technology. American, of course. Print and television advertisements filled out this vision: Monsanto Chemicals' 1944 print ad (Figure 13.1) presents a bright, "wide-eyed" schoolgirl named Julia, clear plastic 3-D glasses in hand, leaning eagerly into a molded-polymer plastic desk and bench described as a "Front row seat . . . *to history in the making*" (emphasis in the original).

"History in the making"—this rhetorical stroke of genius resonates with meaning. Monsanto Chemicals "make history" through manufacturing. The once "commonplace" things of today are proleptically historicized as relics in an imagined future into which eager "Julia" leans from her desk. Already, she stands ready to witness to "new wonders . . . [only] dreamed of today in the laboratories and designing rooms," that she in turn will "take for granted." The rupture of the present *by the future* defines "history" not as a record of pastness but of futurity, in the generation of products "*entirely new to man*" (original emphasis). "*Hard to believe?*" the ad asks. If yes, you are looking in the wrong place; notice Julia's streamlined desk. It is an open book, literally; one side the flat desk she leans on, the other hanging open toward the TV screen she purportedly focuses on. Belief is not grounded in the past, but in a creative evolution "made" real through the complex dimensionalities of plastic. Note: Julia herself is not "making history"; she is a spectator to it, a consumer of its images. Which brings me to plastic narratives, and myth.

I have commented elsewhere on the relationship of narrative plasticity, futurity, myth, and utopia, by reading Roland Barthes's essay on plastic in his famous 1957 collection *Mythologies* against Catherine Malabou's extensive work on plastic subjectivities and/as neuroplasticity.[4] This essay pulls together my ten-year critical engagement with plastic (the stuff) as an activist with Plastic Pollution Coalition (www.plasticpollutioncoalition.org); as a literary scholar (specializing in utopian literature and theory); and as proposer and cocurator, with Heather Davis (The New School) and Joyce Robinson (Palmer Museum of Art), of a major international art exhibition called *Plastic Entanglements: Ecology, Aesthetics, Materials,* which showed at four universities (starting at Penn State) from February

FIGURE 13.1. This May 1944 advertisement from Monsanto Chemical Company brilliantly exemplifies the plastics industry's wartime rhetoric of American exceptionalism and technological superiority. The ad appeared, aptly enough, in *Fortune* magazine as plastics manufacturers boasted of their role in revolutionizing military equipment from protective gear to airplanes, and began setting their sights on the enormous potential of a postwar consumer market.

2018 to January 2020.[5] Barthes and Malabou have accompanied me all this way, and in turning from "the plasticity of narrative" to "narratives of/about plastic," Barthes in particular remains essential. In the lengthy essay, "Myth Today," which concludes *Mythologies*, the critic analyzes not only capitalist myth, but the nature of Myth itself as (only apparently) depoliticized speech. Barthes is "[impatient] with the 'naturalness' . . . [invoked] to dress up reality" (xi), and wants to expose the semiotic duplicity of mythical invention and investments: the "what-goes-without-saying" of "ideological abuse hidden there" (xi).[6] Thus his accumulation of essayistic critiques of "our bourgeois world" (xi) in which myth-agents (media, politicians, scientists, artists, etc.) act to "*sublimate the true limits* of their situation" (xii, emphasis added). The ontology of limits is, this essay avows, at the heart of the matter of/with plastic.

Emphasizing the historic specificity of versions of myth, Barthes proposes a "study of the social geography of myths" (263). The *social geography of myth* is an apt figuration for contemporary plastic fiction's[7] own project, as each individual text wraps us in a myth of plastic clearly molded by capitalism. These novels, I argue, serve as case studies to Heather Davis's concise definition of plastic as "the substrate of advanced capitalism."[8] The texts find ways of complicating and resisting formations of myth within narrative, but also as narrative. As the reader inhabits the literary landscapes and plastic topographies of accumulation, Barthes's enumeration of the "tools" of myth exposes capitalism's false "alibi" (his word) as a disinterested political economy—simply the way of the world. Barthes's deconstruction of mythical language, however, eschews any such universalization, which in narrative terms means resisting *any* ideological manipulation of narrative closure.

Focusing on Karen Tei Yamashita's *Through the Arc of the Rain Forest* (1990)[9] I argue that the plastic nature of myth undoes the mythical nature of plastic in the novel.[10] This deconstruction is not unique to Yamashita's novel but is characteristic of any novel I can think of that takes up the objective (material) and subjective (agential, mythical) "nature" of plastic. The ambivalence of each one of these novels reduces to a single proposition: *that the material we call plastic is itself a betrayal of the quality of plasticity.* These narratives often leave us at the brink of environmental and social catastrophe, if not fully involved in it; yet that fact provides an opening for a prefigurative politics guided by a generative structuralization I call *plaesthetics*: an aesthetics of formal indeterminacy belonging to the form(alization) of *plasticity*, or metamorphosis. At an aporetic crux, where the meaning(s) of myth lie, emerges what Uri Gordon calls a "prefigurative politics of hope."[11] Yamashita's posthuman narrator—itself a "little world" of animate plastic—denies the possibility of hope up to its final word; but the narrative itself offers another possibility.

Poesis and/as the Myth of Plastic and the Novel

Until the invention of the material itself that goes by that name, the word *plastic* was never a noun, but an adjective. It was not a substance or a thing, but a *quality* defined by its capacity to be formed and transformed by some agent or pressure. Change, metamorphosis: plasticity's ends and means are inseparable, in the sense that if plasticity has some essential telos, it is to resist teleological finality.[12] Critical thinkers and artists as early as the mid-1950s are already suspicious of the conflation of the substantial and insubstantial, of history and myth, that was accreting around the stuff, and the idea, of plastic. Roland Barthes's once-overlooked 1957 essay "Plastic" is an astonishing critique of the nascent myth of plastic as a modern *mythopoetic*, that is, a myth of "making-modernity."[13] Its inclusion in the *Mythologies* collection frames the essay as one facet of his critique of capitalism and its agency in "molding" the world—people, systems, "nature," the planet itself—to conform to the shape of myths it tells about itself. The (ultimately cruel) optimism of myth under the sign of Capitalism is captured in its narratives of rationalistic and material progress, mastery of Nature, "history in the making." Yet the function of ideological myth-/mystification is to "immobilize the world":

> [Myths] must suggest and mimic a universal order which
> has fixated, once and for all the hierarchy of possessions. . . .
> Myths are nothing but this ceaseless, untiring solicitation,

> this insidious and inflexible demand that all men recognize themselves in this image, eternal yet bearing a date, which built of them one day as if for all time. For Nature, in which they are locked up under the pretext of being eternalized, is nothing but a Usage [that myths] must take in hand and transform.[14]

Thus those chemical industry ads boast of "making history," while creating and then exploiting the myth that "deprives the object of which it speaks of all History. In [myth], history evaporates" (264–65). With that evaporation, "determinism and freedom" too are sublimated: "Nothing is produced, nothing chosen: all one has to do is possess these new objects from which all soiling trace of origin . . . has been removed" (265).[15] Barthes explicitly resents the "confusions" of "Nature and History (with capital N and H) in the description of our reality . . . I wanted to expose in the decorative display of what-goes-without-saying the ideological abuse I believed was hidden there" (xi). That confused display *is* "Myth."

In a retrospective preface to a 1970 edition of *Mythologies,* Barthes describes his work of thirteen years earlier as an effort to "account in detail for the mystification which transforms petit bourgeois culture into a universal culture" (ix). The function of "myth today," however, is to "empty reality" (255): "[Myth today] has turned reality inside out, it has emptied it of history and has filled it with nature," he writes, understanding "nature" here as an "Idea," a constructed and naturalized form of capitalist ideology. In "Plastic," therefore, Barthes refers to the material plastic as a "quick-change talent" (194) in its capacity to take on appearances, change its surfaces, its forms, possessing no identity or essence of its own. Barthes brilliantly asserts that myth is an *alibi*—literally, an "other-where," which in its common legal context typically implies innocence or nonresponsibility. Myth is a "conjuring trick" (151)—but Barthes gives us numerous memorable tropes for the semiotic operation he sees "realized" in the invention and proliferation of plastic: "the trace of a movement" (193); "the itinerary of a secret" (193), a "sudden conversion" (193). Just as myth empties out meaning in order to impose another, plastic devalues nature by *naturalizing* plastic's substantial artifice. Plastic partakes of its mythic identity precisely by re-forming "the relations between the man and the world" (252)—in *its* image. The investment of modern plastics with this godlike capacity, however, is a false narrative.

There is a certain logic, therefore, in plastic's increasingly common role, and increasingly complex figuration, in contemporary fiction that takes up the possibility of environmental apocalypse. When the myth of plastic narrative betrays itself, the defensive posture is to threaten an ending; thus the aptness of Fredric Jameson's reminder that "it is easier to image the end of the world than the end of capitalism."[16] As a corollary: It is easier to imagine the end of the world than a world free of plastic. Anticipating his later notion of "social geographies of myth," Barthes characterizes the narrative space generated by myth as an alibi conforming to capitalist designs. The mythic image, however, imposes a "relation of negative identity ('I am not where you think I am, I am where you think I am not')," and activates a spatiotemporal gap: "The meaning [of myth] is always there to *present* the form; the form is always there to *outdistance* the meaning. . . . They are never at the same place. . . . Yet, under the sign of Myth, there is no contradiction" (233). Therein lies the aporia of myth's indeterminacy, which belies myth's performative, ideological role as "the decorative display of what-goes-without-saying" (xi).

In the essay "Plastic," the material's takeover of the natural world's geography is troped as a "resurfacing" of nature with polymer, "a sudden transformation of nature," the scope of which gives man pleasure, even amazement, as "the measure of his power . . . since the very itinerary of plastic gives him the euphoria of prestigious free-wheeling through Nature" (194). But this gesture toward a technological sublime is undermined by the assertion that plastic "figures as a disgraced material, lost between the effusiveness of rubber and the flat hardness of metal; it embodies none of the genuine produce of the mineral world: foam, fibres, strata. It is a 'shaped' substance: whatever its final state, plastic keeps a flocculent appearance, something opaque, creamy and curdled, an impotence ever to attain the triumphant sleekness of Nature" (194). Characteristic of its disgrace, the story of plastic obscures its blatant imitation of a much older myth that places life in "the plastic hand of God,"[17] whose manufacture makes visible the "ubiquity" of His own, complete and finished, divine forms.

Barthes's essay traces plastic's "diminishing" of "nature's ancestral function": "[nature] is no longer the Idea, the pure Substance which is to be regained or imitated; an artificial substance, more fecund than all of the world's deposits, will replace it, will command the very invention of shapes" (195). The ultimate substitution is made: "the whole of the world, even life itself, *can* be plasticized, since, I am told, plastic aortas are beginning to be manufactured" (195).[18]

Barthes's disquiet in seeing the "ubiquity" of plastic as a replacement material for Nature itself presages a future imaginary populated by citizens unconscious of their conformity to regulatory ideological formations. This, he implies, is the prefigurative politics of advanced capitalism, its apocalyptic end—the universal plasticization of life—a real possibility. In a parallel way, Barthes finds "sickening" in myth "its resort to a false nature," which is "motivated" to push away any other possible form or meaning, eliminating wonder or surprise—or even an argument (266). This new material, plastic, is already becoming the basis for an aesthetics rooted in bad faith. Plastic's "quick-change talent" of taking on appearances produces its artificial feel, its lack of warmth, the absence of any "human touch": plastic is literally *anaesthetic.*[19] Barthes is offended by the surfaces of plastic; but he singles out the "hollow sound" of plastic, an empty voice even more indicative of its essential absence of meaning.[20] As a material that can take any shape, plastic is at once anything and nothing—like myth itself.

To a remarkable extent "Plastic" crystallizes the argument of the *Mythologies* volume: that *plastic betrays plasticity* in the way that myth betrays futurity. The word *betray* comprises a crux: to betray is "to be evidence of" or "to unintentionally reveal," but also to maliciously reveal hidden information, to "deliver to an enemy."[21] This ambiguity deeply informs many literary fictions that concern themselves with the "story" of modern plastic and its myth. These fictional figurations of plastic betray an interest not only in the becoming-object of plastic materiality—but also in a peculiar subjectivity that seems to get invested in plastic, and even speaks to/as its status as "alibi."

Enter the Orb.

Sacred Ground: The Plastic Geography of the Matacão

Karen Tei Yamashita's *Through the Arc of the Rain Forest* (1990) is an uncannily precise fictional worlding of Barthes's attribution of mythic, even "miraculous"[22] status to plastic. Plastic's "prestigious slide through Nature" is engendered by a "fashion for plastic [that] highlights *an evolution in the myth of the simili*":[23] its manufactured "likeness" to the rarest natural substances invests the material with a powerful, enigmatic "magic"[24] that seems to elevate it from substance to idea: "ubiquity made visible."[25] Equally striking is the novel's literalization of Davis's definition, cited above, of plastic as the "substrate of advanced capitalism," in the "plastic geography" of the novel's central setting within the heart of the Amazon Basin. The so-called Matacão region is accidentally discovered to sit atop a five-foot thick layer of impenetrably hard material eventually identified as plastic—a particular type of polyurethane, in fact. The "mythic" quality imparted to this plastic infiltrates the figures and forms of the text in ways that affirm Barthes's perception of plastic's paradoxical influences on aesthetic, sociopolitical, and indeed ecological realities.

The modest but rich body of criticism on *Through the Arc* variously describes the novel as an example of magic-realist petrofiction[26] and as "an allegory of the dispossession of peasant communities by multinational capitalism";[27] as an analysis of how "reflections on regional identity translate into scenarios of global connectivity and ecological alienation";[28] and as a narrative that brings together "a myriad of environmental, social, economic, and political forces that destabilize a series of conventionally accepted binaries."[29] Closest to my topic here is Aimee Bahng's assertion that the novel is a critique of "the historical amnesia that often accompanies progress narratives," and that "within the speculative space of the novel's ravaged rainforest are all sorts of discarded, forgotten, and disavowed histories."[30] Imperialist fantasies fuel "the complex movements of capital and empire [that] prove difficult to trace through time and space,"[31] Bahng argues; and right there we see one figuration of Barthes's "itinerary of a secret." My reading of the novel in no way displaces any of these previous readings, but places them within the novel's mythological structuring.

The plastic geography of the Matacão, a lush, jungle region located in the primeval Amazon Basin, has been stripped by the Brazilian government of whatever natural resources were there (manioc crops, fish, trees that supply rubber and nuts); rendered infertile and valueless, the land is given to a poor subsistence farmer, Mané Pena, to garden. Torrential rain wipes the area of whatever topsoil is left, leaving an extensive, million-acres expanse of "some unknown solid substance" with a "slick, shiny surface, hard surface" that, as Mané already knew, "always blocked well-diggers." The area "seemed to glow in the dark on moonlit nights" (17), and to be invested with a mysterious attractive power that remained in any object manufactured from the material. Eventually "billed as one of the wonders of the world" the Matacão inspires a devotee, Chico Paco, to raise an altar to its "possible spiritual magnetism." The altar "magically" adheres to the material, as if it had always been an integral part of it. The Catholic Church determines that the Matacão is "without doubt the natural base for the world's greatest church" (50), and claims it as Church lands. Indigenous and global religious institutions alike find inspiration in supposed "miracles" of healing or fortune: "this was the magic of the God-given mind, greater than TV" (83), the narrator explains, following the logically challenged theory of Mané Pena regarding the Matacão's influence: "Look at TV—they say the pictures are sent through the air by invisible waves. . . . Principle's the same here—invisible waves, a force you can't see" (79).

The Matacão becomes sacred ground for capitalist enterprise as well.[32] The American GGG Corporation provides a huge influx of capital to its Brazilian counterpart in order to raise a new office building that becomes "the creative center of this brainstorm" of sensational Matacão products. The plastic fuels a fetish economy that starts with *feathers* believed by locals to partake of the area's "force"; that fashion for Amazonian plastic "euphorically" glides, as Barthes put it, over the surface of the globe in a wave of hyper-consumerism. Scientific computation eventually reveals that the five-foot-thick plastic "mantle" consists of "NHCOO [molecular] linkages indicat[ing] rigid, tightly bound polymer. Polyurethane family commonly known as plastic. The material appears to be indestructible, undrillable, uncuttable" (96–97). But when GGG "cracked the code in drilling and extracting the stuff" and is able to "control it" (142) the Matacão displays the "infinite" possibilities of its material capacities: it can "assume a wide range of forms . . . moulded into forms more durable and impenetrable than steel"; it can form sheets "as thin as tissue paper with the consistency of silk"; it possesses an "incredible ability to imitate anything" (142). So "true to reality" are its manufactured products that even by "palpating" the surface one is unable to distinguish the real from the fabricated except "in reverse": e.g., the real flowers begin to wilt, while "the plastic lily remained the very perfection of nature itself. Matacão plastic managed to recreate the natural glow, moisture freshness—*the very sensation of life*" (142; emphasis added).

The gas-permeable plastic revolutionizes plastic surgery, civil engineering, housing, architecture: every thing, no matter how prosaic (Barthes's term), could suddenly "take on miraculous forms" (143) and a new aesthetic (anticipated by Gaudí, it is noted) infiltrates, along with the plastic itself, "every crevice [we might say the topography] of modern life" in "the Plastics Age" (143). Moreover, the "magical" nature of the plastic also makes it edible: and food manufacturers experiment with artificial food ("healthy, nonfattening and noncholestric"; also, it "of course, could not spoil"). "After all," the narrator opines, "Matacão plastic had been molded into everything imaginable, both life-size and life-like. An entire world could be created from it" (167). Later, the narrator must describe to us the sad deterioration of "once healthy plastic flesh" (207).

As if channeling Barthes's figurations, these passages associate the meaning and/as "value" of Matacão plastic with alchemy: GGG had "accomplished what no one before had been able to achieve: it had turned plastic into gold," prompting speculation that a "nationalized MCC [MasterCard Corporation]" system might replace cold currency (142). Northern Brazil is "a gold mine in plastic" (144), overrun with modern prospectors who weep at "the dull reflection of their happiness" in the shiny surface, though they lack the technology even to chip it. GGG's "prestigious glide through nature"[33] is literalized in a relentless, "ruthless" (144), corporate ravaging of indigenous homelands and virgin forests. GGG director J. B. Tweep regards the Matacão as a "national monument"—or rather, he quickly corrects himself, an "international monument," in deference to the company's colonialist takeover of the area as well as its global aspirations. Of course NASA is interested as well, "anxious to find new materials for their space vehicles" (97)—adding to the space junk that already, in the novel's universe as in our own, orbits the globe.[34]

Barthes's theorization of myth's capacity to empty a form of meaning and then refill it with its own authorized meanings and nuances creates in this novel a kind of general (false) equivalency of value. The complex plotting of the *Through the Arc of the Rain Forest* revolves around shifting sites and systems of exchange, such as: the "growing system of favors and outright graft" (96) that grants access to the Matacão; the recycling of capital (the Matacão, like GGG, had a "a way of recycling everything" [75]). The material itself is described as infinitely moldable—but also as a rock substance "harder than stainless steel—or diamonds for that matter" (97). Souvenir plastic jewels are sold next to pencil sharpeners. Fake food is as good as real food; a completely plastic car retains the exterior shine of a custom paint job, the softness of its interior plush, and the toughness of the engine, all without signs of wear. Visitors participate in a catholic set of activities: "to gasp, grovel, get a tan, pray, relax, study, wonder, hang out, make love, worship, meditate, or pay homage to its existence" (95). The "universal" meaning of life in the Plastics Age begins and ends—is authorized by—GGGs control of Matacão plastic, toward which everyone and every *thing* gravitates or is "attracted" as if under a magic spell. Even incinerated trash at Chico's altar (not placed there, but attracted there like filings to a magnet) is inexplicably converted into the composition of the Matacão plastic itself. Speculation on "what enormous power could possibly have been present in the Amazon Forest, other than decay, to mold such a perfect block of plastic" (98), prompts "wonder and outright fear": what is the possible impact of this magnetic source to "the Earth's gravitational pull in the solar system . . . to human civilization? to extraterrestrial life in the universe? to the apocalypse?" (98).

Ultimately, the "power source" is never discovered—or, rather, not revealed. GGG either authorizes or withholds authorization to every aspect of the plastic's productive life as long as the Matacão generates wealth; only when its plastic power fails to be profitable does the reader learn the "true nature" of the material. Up to that point origin stories had abounded: theories included CIA activity, extraterrestrial beings, divine intervention (Christian or indigenous); geothermic action from below the surface, and more. The truth or falseness of these stories makes no difference to the GGG monopoly. Whatever "mystique" surrounds the material is advantageous to sales. Occasionally the company floats its own fabricated stories, just to whip up the prospecting craze. These stories highlight myth's role as alibi, deflecting attention from the "the key to this incredible source of wealth" and from the "I" who apparently narrates the story. This narrator is not human, but in fact a piece of flying Matacão debris (from a sudden explosive event off the coast of Japan.[35]) The object strikes a child named Kazumasa, who "felt the Divine Wind ripple through his hair and scatter with the clouds over the ocean's mercuric mangle" in the days before his "accident." This spherical bit of plastic floats, "a tiny impudent planet" that follows Kazumasa throughout his life. We learn "the true nature of the Matacão" at the same time (only in chapter 30 out of 32) that we also surmise the true nature of the little planet. Both are made from the same stuff: nonbiodegradable garbage from the twentieth century that metamorphoses into the unnatural, plastiglomerate substratum of the earth's surface:

> The Matacão . . . had been formed for the most part within the last century, paralleling the development of the more common forms of plastic, polyurethane and Styrofoam. Enormous landfills of nonbiodegradable material buried under virtually every populated part of the Earth had undergone tremendous pressure, pushed ever farther into the lower layers of the

> Earth's mantle. The liquid deposits of the molten mass had been squeezed through underground veins to virgin areas of the Earth. The Amazon Forest, being one of the last virgin areas on Earth, got plenty. (202)

The reader inevitably thinks of the creation of oil deposits created from plant and animal remains transformed by billions of years of heat and pressure. This "mantle" of plastic functions "mythically" as the naturalization of humanity's own attraction to the "false nature" of fetishized commodities produced from it. In a final scene of "recycling," the architecture of Matacão amusement park, made entirely of the stuff, becomes "horribly disfigured, shot full of tiny ominous holes, the mechanical entrails of everything exposed beneath once healthy plastic flesh" (206–7). The figural embodiment of plastic capitalism is literalized here as "healthy plastic flesh," being consumed from within. Frantic efforts to preserve "this contemporary geological and, many insisted, spiritual miracle" (207) fail. The plastic ball and everything made from the miraculous plastic are drained of life. GGG withdraws and is "beset" with lawsuits; consequently, the global stock market collapses. Even the GGG leader's "golden parachute" fails: he jumps from a 23rd-floor window—but the parachute, too, was made of Matacão plastic, and disintegrates. On the novel's final page, we learn that "the old forest has returned once again" to recycling in its own way, by composting: "secreting its digestive juices, slowly breaking everything into edible absorbent components, pursuing the lost perfection of an organism in which digestion and excretion were once one and the same. But it will never be the same again" (212). To an ecologically anxious reader, this sounds like a statement of failure and regret: we've lost the battle. And yet . . .

Whose voice is this? And what is this "it" that will never be the same? Is "it" the whole sad history of the Matacão, the one being narrated by the floating satellite, which has already recounted its own death, but somehow keeps on talking? Is "it" the returning forest, re-covering the "whole world" of Matacão plastic geography, and seeking its "lost perfection" as a complex, self-sustaining organism? Or, is that sense of failure implied in the words "But it will never be the same again" an indication of capitalism's failure to contain its own essential contradictions? An unwitting betrayal of capitalism's inevitable self-destruction by its own self-contradictions? Why does the orb claim clairvoyance, its memory "complete," only to coyly close with this provocation: "Whose memory you are asking? Whose indeed" (212). In fact, the narrative *opens* with the as-yet-unidentified, nonhuman narrator explaining that he is "*brought back* by a memory," reborn, "like any other dead spirit" among local devotees of the Candomblé religion (3). The orb therefore "[has] become a memory, and as such, [I] am commissioned to become for you a memory" (3). "Commissioned?" By whom, and for what? A "dead spirit's" voice that disclaims identity, yet would "become" *our* memory, and claims the controlling consciousness of the novel's narrative voice? What coy "god-trick"[36] is this?

In Barthesian terms, this joining of beginning and end makes perfect sense. In Yamashita's opening pages, the narrator-satellite spins into play myth's "untiring solicitation"—Barthes's characterization of the seductive quality of mythical figuration that, like the satellite itself, "demands that all men recognize themselves in this image, eternal yet bearing a date, which built of them one day as if for all time" (270). Barthes notes that myth creates a "relation of negative identity": nothing in itself, but invested with a shape at different times and places. The orb, a self-universalized figuration of plastic priority, claims to haunt not just the text, but the world beyond the text—a gesture of appropriation that Barthes names as one of seven principle rhetorical figures of bourgeois myth (264): the "privation of History." Being "of" the plastic geography of the Matacão myth, the satellite re-presents itself as at once past, present, and future, the perfect legacy of the Matacão as "the whole world." Now formless and immaterial, the nonentity vacates itself from the responsibility of agency: it simply will become whatsoever it is *commissioned* to be. Its negative identity slides into whatever form it is commissioned to be. In so stating the orb fulfills its mythic status, according to Barthes: "The meaning is always there to *present* the form; the form is always there to *outdistance* the meaning. . . . They are never at the same place" (233), and never at the same time.

The perfect alibi. Almost.

The temporal-spatial sleight of hand in the orb's rhetoric belies the "emergent entailments"[37] of nature's own creative evolution, or plasticity. To return to a concept introduced at the opening of the essay, however, the plaesthetic nature of myth—akin in ways to Plato's notion in the Timaeus of the *khora*—must finally undermine "the external figurings"[38] of ideology. Which is to say, plaesthetics foregrounds plasticity's ontology of limits in the indeterminacy of a generative structuralization of forms. Plaesthetics eventually pokes holes in human fantasy, as surely as the sun melts the hardened wax of Daedalus's feathered wings; just as surely as, centuries later, a colony of plastophage bacteria called Mutant 59—in the sci-fi novel of that title (see note 7)—finds an endless food source in every last molecule of plastic polymer holding together the inventions of modern world. Like our own hybrid plastispheres of bacteria and virus, these little sparks of natural life just want to eat and reproduce, regardless of what humans have to say about it. While Icarus's fall to the earth resonates with tragedy, what reader of *Mutant 59* cannot help but laugh when a full passenger jet begins disintegrating from the inside out, one plastic-coated wire and molded-plastic seat-frame, one luggage bin, pilot-control-stick, and polymeric joint at a time, until whole metallic sections (and the hapless passengers) drop from the sky? Myth is capable of any mode or form, the tragic as easily the farcical.[39]

As a materialization of advanced capitalism's aspirational seizure of the entire surface of our planet (and indeed below it, to comprise what artist Pam Longobardi calls "the archive of the future"),[40] plastic products nonetheless betray plasticity's "generative disposition towards the future."[41] The paradoxical nature of plastic and of myth are entangled to form a space of deconstruction and critique: *plaesthetics*. As Gordon's notion of prefigurative politics proposes, we might consider, even as we acknowledge the possibility (if not likelihood) of environmental catastrophe, a contemporary, "anxious [form] of hope" that resists the universalizing designs of advanced capitalism. This hope lies within the "germ" of becoming-plastic, recovering the essential restlessness of plasticity itself.

There Is No "Away"

In the mathematical language of numbers and ratios, the raw data tell the "real" story of unchecked flows of plastic waste circulating in expanding gyres of trash within what Captain Charles Moore describes as the largest human garbage dump, "downhill of everything": the ocean.[42] "Just throw it away!" is the by-word of our "convenience" culture: convenience itself is (etymologically) a "coming together": an accumulation, if you will, of consent to a practice that is wholly inconvenient to ecological sustainability on a global scale. Like much involving the nature of plastic and its use in our contemporary world, however, there is a productive, if more difficult, paradox at work. When the environmentalist slogan "There is no 'Away'" challenged our culture of disposability, the words immediately hit home. The conveniently thrown-away object is not present in either a spatial or temporal sense: its short life is long ago, far away, and utterly unmemorable, since its sole purpose for existence is to be used. Once used, it is valueless, trash to be tossed away. We "get" the slogan, "There is no 'Away,'" but also go on believing, or at least acting as if, a place called Away actually exists. We believe in plastic's dematerialization—even as it "materializes" somewhere else, in some form. The consumer population worldwide continues to purchase, and throw away, all manner of products packaged in or made with plastic, a material that, quite literally, *never* goes "away": ultimately, plastic loses its plasticity entirely, when it can no longer be recycled, downcycled, or upcycled to "be" anything other than an array of microplastic. "There is no 'Away'" has, still, excellent staying power.

The irony of modernity's iconic industrial achievement—the invention of plastic—is the recognition (too late?) that plastic has no "past" nor has it ever "gone away." It is ever present, and ubiquitous because it can never be "naturally" digested, but simply breaks down into smaller, eventually microscopic, bits. Beyond that, the sheer scale of the global consumption of plastic means that in ways we perhaps did not quite anticipate, Barthes's famous characterization of plastic as "ubiquity made visible" is more right than he could have known. The world is literally colonized by plastic, as Yamashita's text allegorizes with great clarity. "There are virtually no places left which have not been incorporated into [waste's] production process," observes Jody Baker. "The problem is compounded because if the entire world becomes colonized then there is no outside, no geographical other, no place left to put wastes. This is becoming the meta-crisis of late modernity."[43]

Could Barthes have imagined the ubiquitousness of plastic now? Not in the sense he originally meant. The secret itinerary of plastic is no secret any more: it ends up in landfills, waterways, gyres; it is in that sense that plastic is "ubiquity made visible," as it circulates first as consumer products and then as detritus across the globe and back. Barthes's sensibility was not particularly "ecological"; he was hardly thinking about the chemical toxicity of plastic, what that might do to our bodies, or to a planet that has no natural system for getting rid of such a substance—as the Matacão orb points out. Plastic is immortality made visible, insofar as dead plastic "lives," or at least exists, indefinitely. "Away" is our new wild imaginary, a powerfully mythical space wherein the reality of the West's economic complicity is obscured. Where is it located? At the plaesthetic fold between reality and myth that sits at the dystopian horizon of a social geography of the modern myth we call plastic.

NOTES

1. Carlin's skit was part of his *Jammin' in New York* sessions, performed in Manhattan in April 1992. Playing with just the contradictions explored throughout this essay collection, Carlin ironically observes that the invention of plastic might be the whole reason that humanity exists at all. *New Yorker* published a full transcript online on August 22, 2019.
2. Carolyn Clark, "The World of Tomorrow: 1939 New York World's Fair," *plastiquarian.com*.
3. World's Fairs were prominent showcases for new products and technology, including plastics of many kinds; see Folke Kihlstedt, "Utopia Realized: The World's Fairs of the 1930s," in *Imagining Tomorrow: History, Technology, and the American Future*, ed. Joseph J. Corn (Cambridge, Mass.: MIT Press, 1986), 97–118; and Philip Ball, "The Myth and Magic of Plastic," *Nature Materials* 3, no. 11 (2004): 757, https://doi.org/10.1038/nmat1250. Important general histories of plastic include Stephen Fenichell, *Plastic: The Making of a Syn-*

thetic Century (New York: Harper-Collins, 1996); Jeffrey Meikle, *American Plastic: A Cultural History* (New Brunswick, N.J.: Rutgers University Press, 1997); and Susan Freinkel, *Plastic: A Toxic Love Story* (New York: Houghton Mifflin Harcourt, 2011). See also Heather Davis, "Life & Death in the Anthropocene: A Short History of Plastic," in *Art in the Anthropocene: Encounters Among Aesthetics, Politics, Environments and Epistemologies*, ed. Heather Davis and Etienne Turpin (London: Open Humanities, 2015), 347–58.

4. Roland Barthes, *Mythologies* (1957; Hill and Wang, 2011). Among Malabou's central texts are *The Heidegger Change* (Albany: State University of New York Press, 2011); *What Should We Do with Our Brain?* (New York: Fordham University Press, 2008); *The Ontology of the Accident: An Essay on Destructive Plasticity* (Boston: Polity, 2012); *Changing Difference* (Boston: Polity, 2011); and *Plasticity at the Dusk of Writing: Dialectic, Destruction, Deconstruction* (New York: Columbia University Press, 2010). Important scholarly assessments of Malabou's concept of plasticity include two edited collections: *Plastic Materialities: Politics, Legality, and Metamorphosis in the Work of Catherine Malabou*, edited by Brenna Bhandar and Jonathan Goldberg-Hiller (Durham, N.C.: Duke University Press, 2015); and *Thinking Catherine Malabou: Passionate Detachments*, edited by Thomas Wormald and Isabell Dahms (London: Rowman & Littlefield, 2018).
5. *Plastic Entanglements* included sixty works from nearly thirty artists representing six continents. After its opening at Penn State's Palmer Museum of Art (www.palmermuseum.psu.edu), the exhibition travelled to the University of Oregon, Smith College, and the University of Wisconsin–Madison.
6. Also see Barthes's "Myth Today" on the duplicity of myth as "motivated form" (236).
7. These texts include, most notably, J. G. Ballard, *The Drought* (New York: Liveright / W. W. Norton, 2012); Kit Pedler and Gerry Davis, *Mutant 59: The Plastic Eaters* (New York: Viking, 1972); Karen Tei Yamashita, *Through the Arc of the Rainforest* (Minneapolis: Coffee House, 1990); Ruth Ozeki, *A Tale for the Time Being* (New York: Viking, 2013); Amrita Ghosh, *The Hungry Tide* (Boston: Houghton Mifflin, 2005); Jeanette Winterson. *The Stone Gods* (Boston: Houghton Mifflin, 2007); William Gibson, *The Peripheral* (New York: G. P. Putnam's Sons, 2014); and Emmi Itäranta, *The Memory of Water* (London: Harper Voyager, 2014). Don DeLillo's *Underworld* (New York: Scribner's, 1997) and even China Miéville's fantastical *Perdido Street Station* (New York: Del Ray, 2001) have a place in this history, as does Ernest Callenbach's more pedestrian and pedantic *Ecotopia* and *Ecotopia Emerging* (Berkeley: Banyan Tree Books, 1975).
8. Davis, "Life & Death in the Anthropocene," 349.
9. In a longer version of this essay I would add the texts mentioned above (note 7), each embedding scenes of shape-shifting assemblages of plastic represented

alternately as "plastic graves" (as in Itäranta), or as circulating gyres of plastic drift and granular detritus (Ozeki; Gibson), or as landfills forming ironical archives of cultural disposability (DeLillo; Miéville; Winterson).

10. By focusing on "the distortion which the one [meaning] imposes on the other [form], I undo the signification of the myth, and I receive the latter as an imposture" (Barthes, *Mythologies*, 239).
11. Uri Gordon, "Prefigurative Politics between Ethical Practice and Absent Promise," *Political Studies* 66 (2018): 521–37.
12. Ovid's invocation to the gods at the opening of *The Metamorphoses* acknowledges the poet's incapacity as creator: he must, perforce, describe something essentially uncontainable by containing it within language, through stories that wonder at the metamorphic vitality of a world, and that also warn those who would "stay" the vitality of the world's evolving, by containing it with some idea, some expressed form, of perfect completion.
13. See also the contemporaneous productions of Alain Resnais, who directed the phantasmagoric documentary *La Chant du Styréne,* produced with industry support from Pechiney, a French manufacturer. (Paris: Les Films de la Pléiade, commissioned by Pechiney Plastic Packaging); and of French singer-songwriter Léo Ferré's ironical "Le Temps du Plastique" (Ferré 1956). Song-writers have a notable role in plastic's very recent cultural history, from Ferré's quirky ode to plastic to Jackson Browne's politically infused "If I Could Be Anywhere" (from *Standing in the Breach,* Inside Recordings, 2014) and "Downhill from Everwhere" (from *Downhill from Everywhere,* Inside Recordings, 2021), to Keb' Mo's jaunty "Don't Throw It Away" (featuring Taj Mahal, Concord Records, 2019).
14. Barthes, *Mythologies*, 270–71.
15. As I have described elsewhere, this privation of determinism and freedom is the source of Barthes's wholesale objection to plastic toys, which make a young child simply a user of things that "*literally* prefigure the universe of adult functions . . . constituting for him even before he can think about it the alibi of a Nature which has created for all time soldiers, postmen, and Vespas" ("Toys," in *Mythologies*, 58, emphasis in original).
16. Fredric Jameson, "Future City," *New Literary Review* 21 (2003): 64–79.
17. Thank you to fellow contributor Crystal Bartolovich for reminding me, on the MLA panel (2018) preceding this volume, of the rich association of the word *plastic* with the creative power of God in seventeenth-century texts and beyond.
18. According to Julie Sanders, myth "is a form in which the reader is asked to be aware of the constructing author, of the artifice of the piece. . . . The process of universalization remains, then, for Barthes a deeply political and politicized activity" (*Adaptation and Appropriation*, 2nd ed. [New York, Routledge, 2016], 64, 71). Catherine Malabou anticipates Sanders in recog-

nizing that "Roland Barthes alone has devoted to [plastic] a short chapter of *Mythologies*. . . . Barthes warns . . . that plastic's ability to become anything at all may reduce anything to nothing by dissolving all differences. . . . Because plastic never presents itself without form, plastic is always thought as a factor of identification, standardisation, globalisation, and never as a possible welcome of the other" ("The living room: Hospitality and plasticity," *springerin* 2/2013 [*Unrest of Form*], n.p.).

19. In "Toys" Barthes decries plastic's elimination of "the pleasure, the gentleness, the humanity of touch" (60).
20. See William Gibson's description of the "song of the plastic island" in *The Peripheral* (2014): the island's "polymeric" aesthetic (based on its previous status as the Great Pacific Garbage Patch) includes the construction of plastic tube-like pipes that function like an Aeolian harp to produce a "low moaning, the island's hallmark soundscape" (18). U.K. artist Steve McPherson (featured in the *Plastic Entanglements* exhibition) has experimented with plastic soundscapes as well, an example of which can be found on his webpage, https://www.stevemcpherson.co.uk/.
21. "Betray, n." Merriam-Webster Dictionary, 2019, www.merriamwebster.com.
22. Barthes, *Mythologies*, 193.
23. Barthes, *Mythologies*, 194.
24. Yamashita, *Through the Arc of the Rain Forest*, 195.
25. Barthes, *Mythologies*, 293.
26. See Treasa De Loughry, "Petromodernity, Petro-finance and Plastic in Karen Tei Yamashita's *Through the Arc of the Rainforest*," *Journal of Postcolonial Writing* 53 (2017): 329–41; Jennifer Wenzel, "Petro-Magic-Realism: Toward a Political Ecology of Nigerian Literature," *Postcolonial Studies* 9 (2006): 449–64.
27. De Loughry, "Petromodernity," 329.
28. Ursula K. Heise, "Local Rock and Global Plastic: World Ecology and the Experience of Place," *Comparative Literatures Studies* 41 (2004): 127.
29. Andrew Rose, "Insurgency and Distributed Agency in Karen Tei Yamashita's *Through the Arc of the Rainforest*," *ISLE: Interdisciplinary Studies in Literature and Environment* 26 (2019): 125.
30. Aimee Bahng, "Extrapolating Transnational Arcs, Excavating Imperial Legacies: The Speculative Acts of Karen Tei Yamashita's *Through the Arc of the Rain Forest*," MELUS (2008): 124.
31. Bahng, "Extrapolating Transnational Arcs," 125.
32. Yamashita anticipates DeLillo by over a decade on this. Still, his *Underworld* (New York: Scribners, 1997) contains such memorable passage as "The more dangerous the waste, the more heroic it will become. Irradiated ground. The way the Indians venerate this terrain now, we'll come to see it as sacred in the next century" (289).

33. Barthes, *Mythologies*, 194.
34. See Martin Coleman, "Debris: The Plastic of the Sky," *Via Satellite / Satellite Today*, April 15, 2019.
35. By the time Ruth Ozeki composes her magnificent *A Tale for the Time Being* (2013), the tsunami becomes the power-source for a new myth of plastic, this time one that can imagine the structuralization of difference, in the entanglements of space, time, and the gyre.
36. Donna Haraway, "Situated Knowledges: The Science Question in Feminism and the Privilege of Partial Perspective," *Feminist Studies* 14, no. 3 (Autumn 1988): 575–99.
37. See Jane Guyer, "Prophecy and the Near Future: Thoughts on Macroeconomic, Evangelical, and Punctuated Time," *American Ethnologist* 34 (2007): 409–21.
38. Jeanette Winterson, *Art Objects: Essays on Ecstasy and Effrontery* (New York: Vintage, 1997), 60. Obviously there is little space here to consider the relevance of the *Timaeus* and its theorization of the *khora*. Often called a "receptacle (*hupodochê*) of all becoming" (49a5–6), the *khora* can, according to Donald Zehl, "be thought of as matter, or as space . . . [I]t is possible to think of it coherently as having both of those roles. . . . Chora receives everything, without ever taking the form of the objects that enter her. She is made as a model for all things, which moves and takes the shape of everything she receives; and this is why it seems to be different each time" (Donald Zeyl and Barbara Sattler, "Plato's *Timaeus*," *Stanford Encyclopedia of Philosophy* [Summer 2019 Edition], ed. Edward N. Zalta, https://plato.stanford.edu/archives/sum2019/entries/plato-timaeus/).
39. See chapter 4 ("'It's a Very Old Story': Myth and Metamorphosis") in Sanders, *Adaptation and Appropriation*. Barthes plays an important part of her analysis of mythic structure, which "lends itself to this dual plane of exploitation" (Sanders, *Adaptation and Appropriation*, 80).
40. See Pamela Longobardi: "Plastic objects are the cultural archeology of our time. These objects I see as a portrait of global late-capitalist consumer society, mirroring our desires, wishes, hubris and ingenuity . . . with unintended consequences that become transformed as they leave the quotidian world and collide with nature to be transformed, transported and regurgitated out of the shifting oceans" (driftersproject.net/about).
41. Uri Gordon, "Prefigurative Politics between Ethical Practice and Absent Promise," *Political Studies* 66 (2018): 532.
42. "The ocean is downhill from everywhere—the principal repository for vagrant plastic waste." Captain Charles Moore, www.captain-charles-moore.org.
43. Jody Baker, "Modeling Industrial Thresholds: Waste at the Confluence of Social and Ecological Turbulence," *Cultronix* 1 (August 14, 1994).

Contributors

Crystal Bartolovich is an associate professor of English at Syracuse University and coeditor of *Marxism, Modernity, and Postcolonial Studies.*

Maurizia Boscagli is a professor of English and comparative literature at the University of California, Santa Barbara. She is the author of *Stuff Theory: Everyday Objects, Radical Materialism* and *Eye on the Flesh: Fashions of Masculinity in the Early Twentieth Century* and translator of *Insurgencies* by Antonio Negri (Minnesota, 1999).

Christopher Breu is a professor of English at Illinois State University. He is author of *Insistence of the Material: Literature in the Age of Biopolitics* (Minnesota, 2014) and *Hard-Boiled Masculinities* (Minnesota, 2005), and coeditor of the forthcoming *Noir Affect.*

Loren Glass is a professor of English at the University of Iowa and author of *Authors Inc.: Literary Celebrity in the Modern United States* and *Counterculture Colophon: Grove Press, the Evergreen Review, and the Incorporation of the Avant-Garde.*

Sean Grattan is a lecturer of American literature at the University of Kent and the author of *Hope Isn't Stupid: Utopian Affects in Contemporary American Literature.*

Caren Irr is a professor of English at Brandeis University and the author of *Toward the Geopolitical Novel: U.S. Fiction in the Twenty-First Century, Pink Pirates: Contemporary American Women Writers and Copyright,* and *The Suburb of Dissent: Cultural Politics in the United States and Canada during the 1930s.*

Nayoung Kim is a PhD student in English at Brandeis University.

Jane Kuenz is a professor of English at the University of Southern Maine and the coauthor of *Inside the Mouse: Work and Play at Disney World* and *Strip Cultures: Finding America in Las Vegas.*

Paul Morrison is a professor of English at Brandeis University and author of *The Explanation for Everything: Essays on Sexual Subjectivity* and *The Poetics of Fascism: Ezra Pound, T. S. Eliot, and Paul de Man.*

W. Dana Phillips is a professor of English at Towson University in Maryland and research associate at Rhodes University in Grahamstown, South Africa. He is author of *The Truth of Ecology: Nature, Culture, and Literature in America.*

Margaret Ronda is an associate professor of English at University of California, Davis and the author of *Remainders: American Poetry at Nature's End.*

Lisa Swanstrom is an associate professor of English at the University of Utah, coeditor of *Science Fiction Studies*, and the author of *Animal, Vegetable, Digital: Experiments in New Media Aesthetics and Environmental Poetics.*

Jennifer A. Wagner-Lawlor is a professor of English and women's, gender, and sexuality studies at Pennsylvania State University. She is the author of *Postmodern Utopias and Feminist Fictions* and cocurator of *Plastic Entanglements: Ecology, Aesthetics, Materials*, an exhibition at four university museums from 2018 to 2020.

Phillip E. Wegner is the Marston-Milbauer Eminent Scholar at the University of Florida. His books include *Periodizing Jameson: Dialectics, the University, and the Desire for Narrative*; *Shockwaves of Possibility: Essays on Science Fiction, Globalization, and Utopia*; and *Invoking Hope: Reading Theory and Utopia in Dark Times* (Minnesota, 2020).

Daniel Worden is an associate professor of interdisciplinary humanities at the Rochester Institute of Technology and author of *Masculine Style: The American West and Literary Modernism*, editor of *The Comics of Joe Sacco: Journalism in a Visual World*, and coeditor of *Oil Culture* (Minnesota, 2014) and *Postmodern/Postwar—and After.*

Index

Abbing, Micheil, 20–23, 29n19, 29n23, 29n25, 29n27, 30n34
Adorno, Theodor, 34, 38, 54n8, 55n20, 166, 168, 177, 178n4, 178n8
advertisement, 54n17, 112n16, 192, 224–26, 230, 260–61
aesthetic/s, 6, 11, 35, 43–44, 46–48, 49, 56n37, 63, 65–66, 68, 70, 75, 80, 85, 88, 98–99, 110, 118, 121–22, 137–38, 144, 147–49, 151–52, 154, 184, 193–95, 201, 222, 232, 235, 263, 266, 268–69, 279n20; aesthetic challenge, 4; aesthetic concern/problem, 6–7; aesthetic consumption, 47; aesthetic failure, 141; aesthetic life, 33; aesthetic mapping, 195; aesthetic mode, 106, 123, 199; aesthetic production, 33, 37; aesthetic response, 2; aesthetic sensibilities, 61, 66; aesthetic value, 46–47, 138; camp aesthetic, 221; compromise aesthetics, 188; of excess, 13; plaesthetics, 263, 274, 276; plastiglomerate aesthetic, 233–35; queer aesthetic, 67, 234; of understatement, 13
affect, 14, 47, 72, 149, 199, 203, 205, 207, 209–11; affective, 76, 147, 149, 155, 194, 199–209; affective engagement, 144; affective impact, 154; affectively charged, 75, 144; affective mapping, 199; affect theory, 203
Ai, Weiwei, 137, 144–45, 149, 151–53, 155–56, 160n30, 161n33; *Human Flow*, 151; *Laundromat*, 151; *Reframe*, 152; *Safe Passage*, 152; *Soleil Levant*, 152
Ammons, A. R., 25, 30n36
anthropocene, 6, 20–21, 98, 146–49, 160n27, 182–83, 235
Armerio, Marco, 148, 160n27
assemblage, 5, 179n21, 179n26, 218–19, 277n9

Badiou, Alain, 253, 255, 258n26, 258n29
Bahng, Aimee, 267, 279nn30–31
Bakelite, 35, 43, 99, 165–67, 177, 224, 229–31
Baker, Jody, 276, 280n43
Baker, Kyle, 106, 113n26
Barnes, Steven, 219, 232, 237n25, 241
Barthes, Roland, 5, 7n7, 34, 54n11, 54n18, 55n37, 119–20, 123, 127, 134n10, 137, 146, 158n1, 159n15, 165–68, 178n1, 178n5, 260, 262–70, 273, 275–76, 277n4, 277n6, 278n10, 278n14, 278n15, 278–79nn18–19, 279nn22–23, 279n25, 280n33, 280n39
Bartmanski, Dominick, 61, 76n1
Bazin, Alfred, 34, 54n10
Beatles, The, 64–67, 70, 74; *Sgt. Pepper's Lonely Hearts Club Band*, 65–66, 72–73, 75

Beaty, Bart, 112n7
Beautiful and the Damned, The, 34
Benjamin, Walter, 33, 54n3, 144, 154, 161n38, 250, 258n21
Bennett, Jane, 147, 160n25, 166, 178n3, 179n26, 201, 212n5
Berger, John, 31, 53n2, 85, 92n22
Berlant, Lauren, 186, 196n19
Bladow, Kyle, 203, 212n14
Blob, The, 217–18, 236n1
BODY WORLDS, 77, 79, 88, 89n4, 91n17; black-market organ traffic and, 79
Boetzkes, Amanda, 5, 7n9, 20, 29n21, 34, 54n5, 54n11, 54n17, 99, 106, 110, 112n8, 113n27, 114n36, 160n30, 182–83, 195nn5–7, 200, 207, 212nn1–2, 213n31, 213n33; with Andrew Pendakis, 8, 99, 112
Bonneuill, Christophe: *The Shock of the Anthropocene: The Earth, History, and Us*, 98, 111n3
Bonomo, Joe, 72
Bordo, Susan, 43, 55n31
Boscagli, Maurizia, 81
Boyle, Robert, 168, 171–72, 174–76, 178n17
Brave New World, 34
Brinkema, Eugenie, 49, 56n46
Brown, Wendy, 197n25
Büchel, Christoph, 138, 142–44; Barca Nostra, 138, 141–42, 152, 154–55, 159n11
Buckell, Tobias S., 239, 243–46, 250–51, 258n12
Bukatman, Scott, 98, 100, 112n6, 112n12
Burn, Stephen J., 184, 196n15

CAConrad, 122, 135n19
capitalism, 6, 97, 148, 160n27, 167–68, 172–74, 177, 182–84, 191–92, 195, 211, 212n1, 259, 262–63, 265, 273; advanced capitalism, 37, 262, 266–67, 274; consumer capitalism, 37, 49, 108, 113n30, 119, 183; contemporary capitalism, 193; emergent capitalism, 177, 178n12; free market capitalism, 129; global capitalism, 195, 199–200; industrialized capitalism, 122; late capitalism, 20, 137, 247; multinational capitalism, 267; neoliberal capitalism, 246; petrocapitalism, 2, 5, 183; racial capitalism, 131, 179n26
capitalocene, 183
Carlin, George, 259, 276n1
celluloid, 1, 33, 99, 222, 224, 227, 229
Chang, Jeff, 74, 76n8
Chen, Mel Y., 136n34, 201, 205, 212nn6–7, 213n23
circulation, 4, 45, 201–2, 206, 208
Clare, Ralph, 186, 189, 196n20, 196n24
climate: climate change, 2, 24–25, 27, 115, 122, 181–83, 193–94, 199, 201–4, 243, 246; climate crisis, 2, 137, 183; climate emergency, 184; climate fiction, 213n17; climate instability, 109; climate refugees, 137
Cobb, Allison, 118, 123–25, 128, 135n21
cognitive mapping, 177, 199
Cold War, 121, 217
Cole, Jack, 101–2, 104, 106, 112n13, 112n17, 112n18, 112n22, 113nn22–23
Coleridge, Samuel Taylor, 122, 128, 135n17, 136n29, 206, 209
colonialism, 131, 146, 152, 175, 218
Columbia Records, 62, 70n2
consumer, 16–17, 23, 26, 43, 113n30, 127, 148, 157, 227, 260–61, 275–76; consumer capitalism, 37, 49, 108, 113n30, 119, 183; consumer choice, 79, 89; consumer culture, 28n12, 128; consumer goods, 23, 97, 100, 130, 182; consumer

identity, 120; consumerism, 2, 160n27, 206, 269; consumerist, 3, 102, 107, 110, 121, 187; consumer markets, 120; consumer society, 111, 280n40
consumption, 3, 23, 67, 107, 109, 147, 182, 187, 200, 202; aesthetic consumption, 47; capitalist consumption, 4; history of consumption, 81, 148; leisure consumption, 82; plastic consumption, 202, 275
contamination, 3, 147, 149
contemporary, 20, 28n12, 83, 97, 115, 137, 144, 154–55, 192, 207, 219, 221, 231, 243–44, 247, 249, 272, 274; Adult Contemporary, 74; contemporary aesthetics, 2; contemporary art, 106, 138, 144, 155; contemporary capitalism, 193; contemporary commodities, 2; contemporary ecopoetics, 118, 122, 135n18; contemporary fiction, 273; contemporary global order, 246; contemporary life, 182–83, 247; contemporary lifestyle, 82; contemporary migration, 154; contemporary narrative, 27; contemporary petrocapitalism, 2; contemporary plastic fiction, 262; contemporary poetics, 122–23; contemporary poets, 115, 122; contemporary science fiction, 219
Cooke, Jennifer, 208–10, 213nn34–35, 214n36
Cudworth, Ralph, 171, 179n20

Darwin, Charles, 38, 54n19; Darwinian, 220
Dauvergne, Peter, 23–24, 30n30, 30n32
Davis, Erik, 72
Davis, Heather, 111, 114n38, 118, 134nn6–7, 146, 159n17, 160n21, 234–35, 237nn26–27, 260, 262, 267, 277n3, 277nn7–8
Day, Ikyo, 176–77, 180n41
de Angelis, Massimo, 148, 160n27
DeLanda, Manuel, 179n21
DeLillo, Don, 277n7, 278n9, 279n32
Dempsey, Peter, 184, 196n15
Derrida, Jacques, 134n4
Dettmar, Kevin, 72
Dewey, Joseph, 184, 196n16
Dickinson, Adam, 118, 125–28, 134n8, 135nn24–25
di Trapani, Maria Chiara, 142
Divine, 31, 33, 37, 39–41, 43–44, 50–51, 53
Dougan, John, 72
Douglas, Mary, 6, 8n10, 23, 29n28
Dylan, Bob, 64–66, 68–69
dystopian, 4, 253, 256, 276; critical dystopia, 243, 250; dystopic, 34

ecology, 21, 195, 201; of disease, 25; of the Garbage Patch, 210; global ecology, 209; media ecology, 61; of plastic, 21; theoretical ecology, 28n12; world ecology, 181–83, 193–94
economy, 1–2, 110, 201, 248; Greek economy, 150; oil economy, 2, 183; petrochemical economy, 182; political economy, 190, 262; sexual economy, 40; world economy, 193–94
ecosystem, 22–24, 107, 190; aquatic ecosystems, 125; degradation, 123; flourishing, 131; human-generated, 24; infrastructure, 192; of Lesbos, 149; marine, 136n33; ocean, 129
Eisenstein, Sergei, 5, 7n6, 97, 111, 111n1, 111n2, 114nn39–40
Ellermann, Greg, 122, 134n5, 135n16
Ellis, Erle C., 29n22

Ellis, Havelock, 53, 57n56
Elongated Man, 107–8, 110–11, 113n28
environment, 3, 21–23, 25, 27, 29n17, 98–99, 110, 122–23, 205, 232–33, 251, 267; aquatic, 24; built, 23; degradation of, 1; environmental affects, 203; environmental catastrophe, 184, 203, 263, 274; environmental contamination, 147; environmental crisis, 98; environmental critics, 6; environmental discourse, 149; environmental fears, 2; environmental history, 23, 217; environmental imbalance, 121; environmental impact, 123, 127, 147; environmental injustices, 6; environmental literature, 19; environmental plastics, 26; environmental problem, 149; environmental transformation, 119; listening, 75; manufactured, 4; marine, 23–24; plastic, 5
extinction, 184, 195, 204
extraction, 131, 146; capitalist, 130; colonial, 108
Eyman, Scott, 56n43

Fenichell, Stephen, 54n12, 54n14, 54n16, 55n32, 55n34, 159n14, 276n3
fetish, 18, 44, 145, 154; fetishistic, 17, 28n11, 40, 148; fetishists, 17; fetishized, 60, 272
Findlay, Heather, 55n25
flexibility, 4, 98–99, 101, 106–11, 120, 126–27, 185, 240, 249–50
Foote, Stephanie, 185, 198n18
fossil fuels, 1, 100, 127, 204, 239
fossil of the future, 146–47
Foucault, Michel, 41, 43, 55n26, 55n29
Frank, Adam, 239, 249, 257n1
Freinkel, Susan, 3, 7n3, 19–20, 29n18, 120, 134n11, 135, 159n14, 277n3
Fressoz, Jean-Baptiste: *The Shock of the Anthropocene: The Earth, History, and Us*, 98, 111n3
Freud, Sigmund, 38–41, 44, 48–50, 53–54, 55n19, 55n23, 55n24, 56n45, 57n49; *Interpretation of Dreams*, 40; *Three Essays on the Theory of Sexuality*, 48

Gabo, Naum: *Constructions in Space*, 35–36
Gabrys, Jennifer, 29n20, 119, 130, 134n3, 134n9, 136n35
Gelatt, Roland, 65, 76n4
Genette, Gerard, 70–71, 76n5
Ghosh, Amitav, 204, 213n17, 213n25, 277n7
Gibbons, Sarah, 109, 114n35
Gibson, William, 277n7, 278n9, 279n20
globalization, 192, 243, 249
Gómez-Barris, Macarena, 131, 136n39
Gordon, Uri, 263, 274, 278n11, 280n41
Great Pacific Garbage Patch, 131, 145, 199–204, 208–10, 212n3, 218, 279n20. *See also* Pacific Gyre
Guben Plastinarium, 79, 82, 84, 87, 91n12, 92n23

Hale, Mathew, 171, 178n19
Hamid, Mohsin, 156–57, 161n39
Harman, Graham, 180n43
Harrington, James, 178n10
Hawkins, Gay, 6, 8n11, 17, 19, 26, 29n13, 29n15, 29n20, 119, 134n3, 134n9, 136n35
Hayles, N. Katherine, 183, 236n11
Hegel, G. W. F., 4, 7n4, 33, 45, 54n6
Heinrich, Ari Larissa, 81, 91n17
Heise, Ursula K., 5, 7n9, 98, 112n4, 112n5, 193, 197n28, 279n28
Heller, Dana, 55n33
Herman, David, 183, 196n10

heteronormativity, 17, 235
Hillyard, Daniel: *ICE,* 11, 28n1; *Plastic,* 11–19, 26–28, 28n5; *The Ride: Burning Desire,* 11, 28n1, 28n2
Hirschaur, Stefan, 81, 91n16, 93n30
Hirst, Damien, 138–41, 143–44, 152; *Treasures from the Shipwreck of the Unbelievable,* 138
Hobbes, Thomas, 168–69, 173
Hooke, Robert, 169, 178n14
Horace, 41, 55n27
Horkheimer, Max, 34, 38, 54n8, 55n20, 168, 177, 178n8
Houser, Heather, 203, 205, 210, 212n13, 213nn26–27, 214n42
hyperobject, 5, 203, 210

indigenous, 91n11, 131, 270
individual, 38, 63, 78, 81, 103, 144, 148, 154, 161n35, 172, 176, 189–90, 194, 199–200, 202–3, 208–11, 249; individual-in-a-multiplicity, 253; preference, 80; responsibility, 149, 189, 202; self-fashioning, 43
Itäranta, Emmi, 239, 243, 247, 258n14, 277n7, 278n9

Jameson, Fredric, 173–74, 176, 180n28, 183, 196nn8–9, 246, 252, 257n6, 258n13, 258n22, 258n24, 278n16
Jazvac, Kelly, 8n13, 81, 137, 145–49, 159n12, 159n13, 212n4, 218, 236n7
Jordan, Chris, 206–7, 210–11, 213n28, 213n29
Joyce, James, 56n47

Kamilo Beach, 6, 20, 137, 145–46, 148–49, 218
Kant, Immanuel, 33, 47, 54n6
Keller, Lynn, 123, 135n20, 135n23
Kendi, Ibram X., 180n26
King, Carole, 66, 72–73; *Tapestry,* 72–74
Kracauer, Siegried, 34, 54n9
Kubrick, Stanley: *Spartacus,* 50, 56n48
Kuppers, Petra, 91n16

Lacan, Jacques, 53
Ladino, Jennifer, 203, 212n14
landfills, 1, 3, 19, 127, 185, 271, 276, 278n9
Latour, Bruno, 166, 168, 172–77, 178n8, 179n21, 179nn24–25, 180n27, 180nn29–34, 180nn37–40; *Leviathan and the Air Pump,* 173; *We Have Never Been Modern,* 168, 175
Le Berge, Leigh Clare, 194, 197n29
LeMenager, Stephanie, 184, 196n12
Lerner, Sharon, 135n26
Lesbos, 149–51, 156
Letham, Jonathan, 72
Levertov, Denise, 121–22, 130, 134n13, 135n15
Levine, Caroline, 184, 196n14
Liboiron, Max, 24–25, 29, 30n35, 30n37
Litvak, Joseph, 47, 56n41
Lizama, Natalia, 92n24
Longobardi, Pam, 274, 280n41
Lothian, Alexis, 236n13

Malabou, Catherine, 4, 7n5, 137, 156, 158n2, 181, 195n1, 204–5, 213nn21–22, 240, 243, 249–50, 257n3, 257n9, 258nn17–20, 260, 262, 277n4, 278n18
Maliszewski, Paul, 189, 197n26
Marcus, Greil, 186, 196n21
Marks, Laura, 51, 57n51
Marston, John, 178n9
Marx, Karl, 54n3, 166–67, 172, 178n2, 182, 191, 197n27
Marx, Leo, 222, 236n14
Marxist, 168, 171–77, 179n24
Mathys, Ted, 207, 213n30

Mazzolini, Elizabeth, 185, 196n18
Meikle, Jeffrey L., 55n30, 99, 112n9, 159n14, 222, 227, 237n15, 237n17, 277n3
Miah, Andy, 92n21
microplastics, 21–23, 77
Middleton, Peter, 124, 135n22
Middleton, Susan, 128
migrants, 137, 142–45, 149–52, 155–56
Miller, William Ian, 55n28
Milne, Heather, 135n23
modernity, 20, 35, 137, 146, 168, 175–76, 275; capitalist modernity, 250; late modernity, 154, 276; making-modernity, 263
Mon Oncle, 146
Monsanto, 174–75, 259–61
Moon, Michael, 39, 55n22
Moore, Charles, 8n13, 137, 145–46, 156, 159nn12–13, 199, 202, 208, 213n15, 218, 236n7, 275, 280n42
Moore, Jason, 178n12, 180n40, 182–183, 195n3, 196n7, 207, 212n1
Morales, Rags, 110, 114n37
Morton, Timothy, 5, 7n8, 203, 211, 212n12, 214n83
Moylan, Tom, 243, 257n8

nanoplastics, 22, 24
narrative, 1, 3, 6, 12, 14, 16, 18–19, 27, 99, 101, 102, 109–10, 148, 149, 160n27, 168, 184–86, 189–92, 210, 219–20, 229, 232, 246, 250, 253, 260, 262–63, 265, 268, 273; contemporary, 27; developmental, 33, 37, 44; heteronormative, 234; macronarrative, 181, 186, 190; master; 168, micronarrative, 190; plastic, 260, 265; superhero, 99, 109, 111
Nelson, Sean, 72
neoliberalism, 93n29, 137, 149, 188, 249
network, 89n3, 171–77; communication, 232; heterogenous, 176; of relations, 166; transportation, 115
Newman, Barnett, 101–2, 112n14
new materialism, 26, 30n37, 178n12
Ngai, Sianne, 106, 113n25, 184, 196n13
Nichols, Mike: *The Graduate*, 1, 240
Nichols, Robert, 172, 179n23, 180n42
Nietzsche, Friedrich, 52, 57n54
Nixon, Rob, 160n21, 201–2, 212nn8–9
nonhuman, 4, 6, 78, 98, 101, 111, 123, 132, 145, 166–69, 172, 174, 177, 183, 201, 210, 235; actors, 184, 201, 203, 210; narrator, 273; resources, 175
Nordau, Max, 33, 52, 54n4, 57n55
nurdles, 22, 130, 208–9

oil, 105, 146, 201, 204, 217, 243; economy, 2, 182–83; industry, 5; painting, 85; Peak Oil, 27. *See also* petrochemical
Oldenburg, Claes: *False Food Selection*, 36
Olson, Charles, 121, 135n13
Orwell, George, 52, 57n53
Osborne, Richard, 63, 65, 76n3
Ovid, 31, 278
Ozeki, Ruth, 209–10, 214n37, 214nn39–41, 277n7, 278n9, 280n35

Pacific Gyre, 21, 200. *See also* Great Pacific Garbage Patch
Palmer, Raymond A., 240–41, 250, 257n4
Perez, Craig Santos, 115–19, 128, 130–33, 133n2, 136n38, 136n40
petrochemical, 100, 102, 105, 107–8, 118, 125, 126, 181–83, 187, 239; fantasy, 111; industry, 127; plastics, 100, 108; unconscious, 183–85, 189–90, 193–94; waste, 183. *See also* oil
petroleum jelly, 12–13, 16

Pierce, Charles, 41, 51
plasticity, 4, 6, 19, 28n12, 103, 107, 109, 118, 122, 134n5, 137, 156, 181–82, 185–86, 188, 190, 205, 240, 243, 250, 255–57, 263, 266, 274–75, 277n4; of the border, 157; of colonialism, 131; destructive, 187, 190, 192, 204; dialectical, 249; as form, 118, 129; narrative, 260, 262; productive, 190, 192; as threat, 103, 105
plastick, 169–71, 173, 178n9
plastiglomerate, 6, 20–21, 81, 137–38, 144–49, 142, 155–56, 160n19, 160n20, 160n26, 160n28, 212n4, 218–19, 232–33, 235, 271
plastisphere, 24, 111, 200, 208, 234, 274
poeisis, 118, 125, 132, 135n23
pollution, 23–24, 108, 117–18, 122, 147, 210, 218; plastic, 21–22, 130–31, 145, 149–50, 199, 202, 205–6
posthuman, 35, 37, 103, 194–95, 263
Powers, Devon, 71, 76n6
Powers, Richard, 181, 184–87, 190–94, 196n22; *Gain*, 181, 184–87, 190, 192–94; *The Gold Bug Variations*, 185, 194, *The Overstory*, 184; *The Time of Our Singing*, 194
prosthetic, 50–51, 53, 86–87, 118
Public Enemy, 75; *It Takes a Nation of Millions to Hold Us Back*, 66, 75
PVC (polyvinyl chloride), 16–17, 26, 37

queer: aesthetic, 67, 234; affordances, 235; futurity, 234; plastic, 221; queerness, 221, 231–32, 235; theory, 221

race, 52, 67, 81; racism, 172, 179n26, 180n26
rap, 74–75
realism, 34, 184–87, 190, 194, 195; literary, 29n16, 195; macrorealism, 192–93; magical, 157; micro-realism, 190, 193; scientific, 29n16
recycling, 150, 155, 202, 212n10, 270, 272; recycled, 20, 128, 160n30, 275; unrecycled, 2
Reddy, Helen, 73–74
Reilly, Evelyn, 135n23, 204–5, 206, 210, 213nn18–19, 213n24
representation, 35, 47–48, 80, 83–85, 91n12, 91n16, 92n17, 111, 183–84, 195, 199–200, 202–3, 208, 211, 253
Richards, M. C., 121–22, 135n17
Rieder, John, 228, 236n9, 237n18
Riskin, Jessica, 178n18
Robbins, Bruce, 186, 196n20
Roberts, Jody, 134n3
Robertson, Kirsty, 147–48, 160n19, 160n26, 160n28
Rockefeller, John D., 36–37
Rolling Stone, 63–67
Rolling Stones, 64, 66–67, 69, 74
Ronda, Margaret, 204, 213n16
rubber, 17, 34, 40, 77, 102–3, 108, 112n16, 113n30, 144–45, 149, 152, 156, 265

Sanders, Julie, 278n18
Scent of Mystery, 33
Schopenhauer, Arthur, 47, 56n40
science, 20, 82, 109, 149, 168, 241; "Big Science," 175; museums, 79–80, 88
science fiction, 7, 213n17, 218–19, 228, 231, 234–35, 239–41, 243
Sedgwick, Eve Kosofsky, 39, 55n22
sensory, 6, 37, 52, 67; appeal, 17; experience, 51; multisensory, 59; perception, 33, 54n3
sex dolls, 13–14, 16–18, 26, 28nn7–8, 29n17
sex toys, 17; dildo, 40, 55n25
Shonkwiler, Alison, 194, 197n29
Sinatra, Frank, 62, 64

Skinner, Jonathan, 121, 135n14
smell, 31–34, 37–39, 41, 51–53, 54n19, 57n52, 105, 204; Smell-O-Vision, 33, 51
Smith, Laurence C., 243, 245–46, 257n7, 257n10
Smith, Rachel Greenwald, 188, 196n23
somatic, 33–34, 37, 47, 52–53, 119, 121–22, 124, 126
Sontag, Susan, 236n12
Spiegelman, Art, 101–2, 112n13, 112n15
Star Wars, 231; *The Empire Strikes Back*, 237n21
Steingraber, Sandra, 181, 195n2
Steinweiss, Alex, 62, 64
subjectivity, 5, 43, 83, 155, 218
Superman, 100
survival, 118, 247–48
survivance, 131, 136n36
sustainability, 80, 150, 275
Suvin, Darko, 236n8

Taffel, Sy, 128, 136n27
Taylor, Jeremy, 178n11
temporal, 38, 59, 62, 67, 70, 210, 275; atemporal, 106; spatiotemporal, 183, 265; temporality, 209–11; temporal-spatial, 274
thermoplastic, 16, 20, 99
thermoset plastics, 20
Thing, The, 205
Tierney, Orchid, 118, 129, 136nn32–33
Todd, Zoe, 147, 160n21
totality, 171, 173–76, 179nn21–22, 183, 252
touch, 124, 130, 266, 279n19
toxic, 19, 27, 117, 119, 122, 131, 133, 192, 204, 206–7; history, 131; relationship, 16; toxicity, 6, 122, 181, 201, 205, 207, 217, 276
trash, 1, 6, 45, 127–29, 150, 206–7, 211, 219, 231, 235, 237n21, 270, 275; The Pope of Trash (John Waters), 46–47. *See also* waste
Tsamparli, Fereniki, 145, 150–51

utopia, 102, 252–53, 259–60; utopian, 2, 4, 7, 137, 146, 252–53, 260; utopianism, 2, 5

van Dijck, Jos, 86, 92n25
Venice Biennale, 138, 141–43, 159n11
Victor, Divya, 118, 131–33, 136n40, 136n41
vinyl, 6, 40, 60, 74–75; catsuit, 12; as records, 61, 67, 70, 74–76; Vinylite, 62
Vizenor, Gerald, 136n36
von Hagens, Gunther, 77–85, 87, 89, 90n4, 90n5, 90n6, 90n7, 90n9, 90n10, 91n14, 91n16, 92n18, 92n19, 92n20, 93n27, 93n28, 93n32, 93n33

Wagner, Doug: *ICE*, 11, 28n1; *Plastic*, 11–19, 26–28, 28n5; *The Ride: Burning Desire*, 11, 28n1, 28n2
Wark, McKenzie, 169n24
waste, 1, 3, 5, 6–7, 26, 36–37, 45, 54n17, 79, 106, 118, 130–32, 149, 156, 160n30, 182, 199–200, 202, 206, 212n1, 247, 276, 279n32, 280n42; hazardous, 26; petrochemical, 183; plastic, 1–3, 6, 21, 50, 129, 138, 146, 149, 202, 207–8, 214n38, 275. *See also* trash
wasteocene, 6, 77, 148, 160n27
Waters, John, 31–32, 39–51, 53, 55n33, 56n37, 56nn38–39, 56n42, 56n44; *Hairspray*, 46; *Pink Flamingos*, 31, 38–39, 45–46, 50; *Polyester*, 31–33, 37, 39, 41–42, 44–45, 47, 49–51; *Serial Mom*, 40, 45
Welles, Orson, 34

Wells, H. G., 218–19, 222–25, 227–29, 231–32, 235, 236nn10–11, 241, 257n5
Whitehead, Alfred North, 121
Williams, Raymond, 252, 258n25
Winterson, Jeanette, 280n38
wonder, 7, 18, 77, 117, 120, 205, 209–10, 233, 241, 260, 266, 271
Woods, Derek, 196n17
Woodward, Ian, 61, 76n1

Yaeger, Patricia, 129, 136nn30–31
Yamashita, Karen Tei, 262–63, 267, 273, 275, 277n7, 279n24, 279n26, 279n32
Yeats, William Butler, 35, 54n13, 208

Zamyatin, Yevgeny, 253
Žižek, Slavoj, 51, 57n50